The

Mocha

MANUAL

to MILITARY LIFE

Also by Kimberly Seals-Allers

**The Mocha Manual
to a Fabulous Pregnancy**

**The Mocha Manual
to Turning Your
Passion into Profit**

The

Mocha
MANUAL
to MILITARY LIFE

A Savvy Guide for Wives, Girlfriends,
and Female Service Members

Kimberly Seals-Allers

with Pamela M. McBride

Amistad

An Imprint of HarperCollinsPublishers

To James and Alma Seals; and to my greatest loves, Kayla and Michael,
who always shine brilliantly.

With all my love to the mocha military family that is closest to me:
Doug, Tré, and Taylor.

Contents

Acknowledgments

As the Mocha Manual™ series of books continues to expand, the list of thank yous and my running debt of gratitude could fill its own book. So, due to limited space I will simply thank all those who continue to support me, help me realize my dream, and encourage me when I lose sight of the mark.

I'm eternally grateful to my parents, James and Alma Seals, my brother, Jeffrey, and my sister, Katrina, for helping me become who I am. I am thankful to my grandmother, Helen Nurse, who teaches me the true meaning of courage and character and my uncle, James Billy, whose own life story inspires me. Thanks to my girlfriends, old friends (I didn't forget you this time, Will Dawson), rediscovered friends, partners in crime, and my #1 partner in possibilities.

Thank you to Dawn Davis and Amistad for believing in my vision and to Pamela McBride for sharing her journey and insights with me in this incredible book.

Lastly, I am increasingly indebted to my children, Kayla and Michael Jaden, who constantly inspire me to soar into stratosphere but laugh more along the way. Thank you. You are loved beyond words.

—*Kimberly Seals-Allers*

Thank God for bringing people and situations into my life at the right time; once again, timing was everything! Your blessings and guidance made this book come to life.

Doug, for all your love and support, I thank you a million times over. You are the reason I have this story and mentorship to share. *We* have kept our family *the* priority and been a twenty-year "dynamic duo" of unwavering support to Army soldiers and families. Hooah! Tré and Taylor, you have much to offer the world. Stay focused on God and family; they will both be with you forever. I love you dearly!

Dad, you are a godsend! Thanks for helping take care of the children, house, cars, dogs, yard, and anything else that came up when one or both of us were away. Sis, you are like no other. Much love and gratitude for being there for me and for my family no matter what! You are simply, the best. I'll always be there for you and your family, too.

Mom, thanks for being *the* cheerleader of the century. Love you much! Mom-in-law, much appreciation for always being only a phone call away. To my late father-in-law, we love you more today than ever.

Regina Galvin, my writing mentor and friend, and *the* reason I was offered this opportunity. Thanks for your tough love as an editor, and lots of opportunities, especially my current gig: homefrontonline.com.

Col. (Ret.) and Mrs. Paige, we *still* brag about you and share your advice. To President and Mrs. Obama, thank you for the impact you've made on families all over the world.

Kimberly, on behalf of military families, thanks for your vision of this book as the third in your Mocha Manual™ series. I have learned a great deal from my partnership with you. Thanks to the Amistad/HarperCollins family, especially Dawn Davis, Christina Morgan, and Maya Ziv.

Fellow mocha military families, may this bring you encouragement, tools, and lots of laughs. Remember, if we all take care of military families, we *will* remain the strongest military in the world. Hooah!

—*Pamela McBride*

The

Mocha
MANUAL
to MILITARY LIFE

Yes, You Can!

Living Your Best Military Life

Growing up, I had very little military experience in my life. I remember my cousin Benjamin always showed up to family reunions in a crisp green uniform with lots of medals, but, to be honest, I never bothered to ask why. More recently, my cousin Jamis attended West Point, and she is now a helicopter pilot for the army. And although I felt great pride knowing that West Point is a prestigious military institution, I know very little else of her life as a service member. For those of us on the outside, the military world seems like a strange club governed by lots of rules and protocol, requiring a level of discipline beyond what most of us could muster.

Lately, world events have made us all a lot more familiar with our armed forces. The "war on terror" has brought us countless images of wounded soldiers, monthly death counts, and a new and unwanted familiarity with IEDs (improvised explosive devices). We see news reports of soldiers leaving spouses and children for yearlong deployments, and images of sweet homecomings of flag-bearing kids waiting for returning dads. As a New Yorker living in post-9/11 America, I've seen more soldiers in our streets, train stations, and airports than ever before. But even now, despite a renewed awareness of our armed forces, we know very little about the people who love and support them, the people who kiss them good-bye. We often see these men and women as soldiers, not necessarily as everyday men and women with doting wives and husbands and bright-eyed children left behind.

That is why I feel very honored to team up with Pamela McBride, an army wife of more than twenty years and an accomplished journalist in her own right, to bring you this *Mocha Manual* for military spouses. This may sound like a bumper sticker, but after spending several months interviewing, spending time with, and learning about this unique group, I am thoroughly convinced that they are truly the heroes at home. But they are often overlooked. What's been missing from our wartime and peacetime coverage is an honest look at the toll the war takes at home for military families, particularly wives. Nobody is talking about how these women can cope, how they can be supported, how they can connect and keep their marriages strong. Nobody is talking candidly about the other woman in military marriages—the military.

That's where *The Mocha Manual* comes in. If you are, or about to become, married to the military, welcome to the world of military spouses—your new club. Consider this book your guide to managing every aspect of your new life: from all the crazy acronyms, rules, and bureaucracy to keeping your sanity during relocation and deployment. And while other guidebooks may only tell you the official story, *The Mocha Manual* tells you about the unwritten rules, guides you on how to work the system, and speaks to the special situations you may face as a woman of color.

Many bases are located in remote locations where there isn't much "mocha," making it harder to connect to an external community, find a church that feels like home, or establish a comfort level outside the base. And of course, we don't have to tell you the stories of spouses who can't find their favorite hair products or soul food items in their locale. We need those things!

And since the military community is a microcosm of the greater world, we know that racism exists among the military ranks as it does in the civilian world. That puts extra pressure on our African American service members, and even more pressure on the wives who support them. This book is particularly necessary since research proves that we do not typically access resources and services to address emotional and mental scars—two common by-products of military life.

To begin, let's just be clear that African Americans have a deep connection to the military. Our presence in the army still exceeds our presence in the general population. African Americans make up 25 percent of all enlisted army soldiers, while making up only 13 percent of the U.S. population. We are the largest ethnic group serving in both active duty and reserve personnel across all branches and units; therefore, we play a large part in the defense of this nation. What's more, the armed forces have long been seen as a key driver for the growth of the black middle class, giving many of our families a solid career, with good benefits and pay.

Recently though, African American enlistments have declined 40 percent. Still, the security and stability of military life remains attractive to many. In fact, your man may have joined the military as a way to get into college or to access more career options. And don't forget the perks like free medical care, free housing, free utilities, free marital counseling, free drug and alcohol counseling, free financial advice, subsidized child care, food and other necessities sold at cost, tuition assistance, free gym and pool membership, and free swimming lessons for the kids. Movie tickets at the base theater can cost as little as $2.50.

Yet those perks come at a high cost. Every day military spouses live in fear that their beloved service member may be injured or killed. They live with the constant risk of becoming widows. Beyond the physical effects of war, there are the emotional and mental effects of combat, which can be equally devastating. Meanwhile, military spouses cope with unpredictable deployments and struggle to raise children alone, often on small paychecks in a community both tight-knit and somewhat judgmental. Not even to mention the frequent relocation, which makes it difficult to have deeply rooted friendships and even harder to have a fulfilling career.

A growing cadre of military wives are educated professionals, who now have to fit into a unique ranking system that is very different from anything ever experienced in civilian life. For all of its modern advances, the military is still a hierarchical male-dominated subculture that puts considerable burden on its backbone of bystanders—military spouses.

And although the army has attempted to beef up its services and resources to save families, the general consensus among spouses is that the government as an institution, is, at worse, pretty ambivalent, and at best, pretty darn slow, about helping families. As the old saying goes, if Uncle Sam wanted you to have a wife, he would have issued you one.

Of course, while military life has some hardships, it also offers wonderful opportunities for spouses and children. This includes the chance to experience other cultures firsthand. Many military children learn to speak different languages, and living overseas gives them a broader worldview than the typical

American child has—and well beyond that of a typical black child. While researching this book, we've met sisters, both spouses and service members, doing their thang in Korea, Germany, and beyond, and loving it!

That's the beauty of *The Mocha Manual to Military Life;* you'll hear from scores of women who have been there, done that, and benefit from Pamela's extensive on-the-job training. The combination of my research insight and Pamela's real-life MS (military spouse) experience make this book the perfect companion for new as well as experienced military spouses and female service members. It's the girlfriend you will need as you navigate the spoken and unspoken maxims of military life and provides straight talk on everything in between, from your sex life and raising your children (a beautiful by-product of your sex life!) to building your career and keeping your marriage strong. As you read you will see a provocative portrait of today's military spouses as prideful, whole women with very unique needs and challenges. You will learn about strategies other spouses used to keep the flames alive in their marriage and keep their sanity during deployment. You'll learn the meanings of common military jargon, and tips on surviving frequent moves.

This book is mostly geared to military wives, but it's likewise a great resource for female service members who are also married to the military and often deal with similar issues of child care, finding friends, and fitting in. Since a change in federal legislation in 1990 when women could do any job in the military service except active combat, more than 180,000 women have served in Iraq, Afghanistan, and other countries, according to the Pentagon, with more than 8,000 African American women deployed in those areas. The ranks of sister soldiers are indeed growing. Plus, we have a special chapter for a growing group—dual military couples, who face their own set of unique challenges and concerns.

It is our hope that you will use this book to feel completely empowered in your life as a military spouse. Armed with knowledge and some real-deal sisterly love, you can be better prepared for the adventure of military wifey-ness, better able to support your man in his mission, and more prepared to have a strong, thriving marriage and fulfilling work. It is our goal that with this book, you, too, can be all that you can be!

CHAPTER ONE

Before You Say "I Do"

Everything You Need to Know About Dating or Marrying a Military Man

Warning: If you're reading this book, you may be suffering from "acute uniform syndrome." You may not have even been aware that you were afflicted with this debilitating, infectious malady, until a man in uniform walked in the door. You see a uniform; you think clean-cut, disciplined, steady job; and you're hooked! We probably don't have to spell it out for you, but the rest of the typical military love story usually goes something like this: first, you notice the uniform, then you fall head over heels in love with a military man. Then come the long-distance love letters and limited visits. The next thing you know, he proposes marriage and now you are dizzy with excitement, uncertainty, and insecurity.

If this sounds at all familiar, let us tell you now, we've got your back. We've spoken to hundreds of similar sufferers and created the prescription for success. But first, the sobering news: there is no prenuptial boot camp for soon-to-be military spouses. No nine-week basic training program, no special introduction for new recruits or mentorship program for entrée into military life. Nope, for military wives, the backbone of our armed forces, much of what you will learn is mostly on-the-job and from the school of Hard Knocks, Hard Times, and Hard Decisions. In the military, everyone has a role to play, discipline is demanded, perfection is rewarded, and the perception of an adventurous life often clashes with the realities of love, family, relationships, and day-to-day living in the armed forces.

With no preparation for the hierarchical culture of conformity, little training for life in a community that is both tight-knit and sometimes judgmental, and no experience with the minute-by-minute uncertainty that pervades every day of military life, wives often struggle with the feelings of anger, frustration, and heartache that come with prolonged separation, single parenthood, and emotional exhaustion.

It's a reality that I've come to understand after interviewing scores of military wives and armed forces experts for this book. Pamela lives it every day. Twenty years ago an ROTC cadet who looked "too fine" in his uniform caught her eye in the grocery store. Pamela, too, was unknowingly struck with acute uniform syndrome. On the very first night of training for a new job, she stepped into the doorway and he offered her a seat right next to him. He later said that the minute he saw Pamela, he knew there was something about her that intrigued him. After a few conversations, he appeared at her workplace one day in his uniform and she just couldn't keep her eyes off him! (I told you it's infectious and debilitating!) Between his completely engaging personality, his incredible level of confidence and commitment, and that uniform . . . she was hooked.

Two years later, her induction into the military life came rather unexpectedly. During his special weekend of college graduation and being commissioned into the army, he proposed. They married five months later. Like so many of the wives I've spoken to, Pamela had no inkling what military life was like. She will tell you how much she admired the dedication of her ROTC boyfriend who always rose at an ungodly hour for PT (physical training) regardless of how late they stayed out the night before. "I had no idea what awaited me, but thank God my husband-to-be sought to prepare me as much as possible. He arranged for us to talk with a black military couple who had been together many years. They shared the real deal about military life as they saw it. They were open and honest about the good, the bad, and the ugly. They answered every question we threw at them and sent us away with a multitude of things to discuss and basic decisions we would have to make in the long and short term. They also gave us plenty of encouragement. We thank God that they set us off on the right track. However, there was no way I could have ever been fully prepared for what came next," Pamela says.

For one, there was the frequent separation. For the first six months of their marriage they lived apart, in two different states, Massachusetts and Texas. When Pamela finally moved to be with her new husband, he left two weeks later to attend training for thirty days in California. Then, less than three months after his return, he was sent to war in Saudi Arabia for seven months. Rather than continue to list all the separations they had, we will sum it up this way: for the first six years of their marriage, they lived apart more than they lived together, almost two years of which were in separate countries, TWICE! Fast-forward to almost twenty years into their military marriage, and Pamela's husband continues on and off foreign deployments, often as long as fifteen months each.

Yes, military life is full of never-ending challenges, stressful expectations, and unspoken maxims. And with the turn of the century, they became more profound than ever before in recent history. There is simply no way to prepare you for the challenges without laying it all out on the line so you know what to expect. In this chapter, we'll give you a broad overview of some of the common challenges of military life, describe some basic personality traits that will help you succeed, walk you through the ins and outs of dating, and help you lay a solid foundation for your upcoming marriage. Ready? Let's get started.

The Real Deal: Deployment

One of the most potentially stressful aspects of your new life will be deployments and separations. Unfortunately, these are becoming more frequent. Since September 11, 2001, there has been a major increase in what the military calls the operational tempo (OPTEMPO), and therefore military families are faced with even more frequent separations and deployments, which are of longer durations and often at unpredictable times. Furthermore, the close-knit groups that lived on or near military installations years ago served as a support network, but now, with about 70 to 75 percent of military families *not* living on installations, and often moving "back home" when service members deploy, these military spouse networks, and the level of support they can provide to help families cope, may be dwindling.

Whether your spouse is away often because of attending military schools, being assigned unaccompanied tours of duty or extended work hours, or being deployed, wives experience a variety of emotions. They feel anger, fear, worry, depression, and loneliness before, during, and after the separations. These emotions, as well as the uncertainty of how you will cope, can wreak havoc on your relationship. And still, as a military spouse, what complicates matters even more is the intense feeling of pride you have. And rightly so. Doing what you do allows your soldier partner to do what he does. As much as you might try to "get along" during the stressful times surrounding separation, you, your spouse, and even your children are likely to lash out at one another over things that you might not otherwise have.

Coupling the military code of stoicism with how most black males are socialized to not express fear or sadness creates a unique challenge for African American couples, psychologists say. Women need to understand how these issues can affect your relationship and your spouse. Divorce rates among army officers skyrocketed 78 percent between 2003 and 2005, according to a recent *USA Today* article. Divorce rates among enlisted personnel rose 28 percent during the same period, and 53 percent since 2000. Dennis Orthner, a professor at the University of North Carolina at Chapel Hill who has studied military families for twenty-eight years, says he isn't surprised by the rise in divorces. "If the numbers are right, then we have more to worry about than just fighting a war," he says. "We're trying to fight a war with families that are struggling, and that's a real challenge."

Now military officials across the board are taking note of the need to equip military couples with the tools to communicate more effectively with each other about what they are experiencing to lessen the impact of the strain. We've got great advice on relationships in Chapters 2 and 10. For now, suffice it to say that military marriages do have unique challenges, but you can overcome them. We'll show you how.

Another grueling aspect of military life that you will get to know all too well is frequent relocation. Some sources note that about one-third of military families move each year; Pamela's son lived in six different states by the time he was seven years old. As a result of the frequent relocation, military spouses can suffer, too. They struggle to maintain friendships and build fulfilling careers. In a 2005 report by the RAND Corporation, *Working Around the Military: Challenges to Spouse Employment and Education,* researchers found that the majority of the eleven hundred military spouses interviewed indicated that they believed military life negatively affected their employment prospects. Opportunities for promotions, pensions, and other benefits that come with long-term employment don't happen for many wives. In addition, deployments, work-related travel, and extended work hours often leave the nonmilitary spouse to carry much of the parental responsibilities. If you decide to have children, know that you will often feel like a single parent.

And although black women are notoriously fond of their sister circles, it's often difficult for military wives to nurture meaningful friendships in the on-post or off-post communities. At times bases are located in areas where there may be few "sisters" (or sister-friendly products and services) around. Other times, just knowing they may not be in the area for long means they don't bother trying to make friends. Read more about the folly of this kind of thinking in Chapter 10.

Then there's the bureaucratic state of the government to contend with. Although the military is steeped in tradition and rigidly structured, those very things that in some ways create consistency for the military members may be the same things that create difficulties in getting things done. Spouses have long commented that getting anything done in the military takes an act of Congress. Whether it is filing the paperwork to reunite you with your household goods during yet another relocation, trying to get car registration stickers when they expire and your spouse is away, or navigating the murky waters of TRICARE medical benefits, some days it's easy to get frustrated and even angry about the madness.

"I have children with special needs but all the different offices we have to go to and things we have to do just to get our orders so we can leave is daunting," says Michelle Schofield, an air force wife based in Germany. "Offices get moved around. . . . Numbers for the offices are not always correct in the handbook and I have to call several numbers before I get the right one. When my husband is TDY (away from home on temporary duty) or deployed, it can be very frustrating and I feel like I am not doing anything right as a military spouse," Michelle says.

So if you're about to jump into the world of military life, you definitely need some support, and picking up this book is a great start. But we wouldn't be keeping it real with you if we didn't say that a big part of your success as a military wife is more about who you are and not what you do. After extensively studying and working with military wives, it's clear to us that certain qualities help military spouses be more successful in their journeys. I see those qualities in Pamela, and she attests to their "survivability factor"—that is, you are more likely to weather the storm and thrive as a military spouse if you can master a few key life strategies.

1. Commitment to yourself: Don't let your dreams go by the wayside just because you marry a military man. A successful military wife has professional, educational, recreational, spiritual, and other interests that make her who she is as an individual. That individual is who he was attracted to initially, and it will be that individual who makes the whole family unit successful.

2. Determination: Sometimes things will feel unmanageable. Those who get through the tough stuff are those who don't give up in finding a way to make it work.

3. Adaptability: So many aspects of your life can change at a moment's notice, and most often they will be outside of your control or your partner's. Resist the urge to fight the things that upset your groove and just go with the flow whenever possible. Having a good sense of humor also helps.

4. Confidence to be independent: There are going to be a lot of times when you and your loved one will be apart for days, weeks, months, or maybe more than a year. You have to be confident in your ability to independently hold down the home front and keep it running as smoothly as possible. That doesn't mean you have to do everything; you might just need to figure out *how* to get it done and what's most important. Successful strategies include eliminating unnecessary activities, delegating tasks, putting systems in place (like auto-paying the bills), and paying for some help (a local teenager or landscaper to mow the lawn) or exchanging "services" (like babysitting and carpooling) with another spouse.

5. Positive attitude: The right outlook makes a world of difference when dealing with your own stuff or someone else's. No, life isn't all greens and gravy, but things can be more bearable when you don't waste valuable time and energy complaining about things that you cannot change or listening to others complain too.

6. Willingness to be a friend: "The military has taught me to be an amazing friend. I try to maintain an open mind and an open heart

because you never know when you will need someone to be that for you," said one wife. "There may be a time when the pay is messed up, the bills need to be paid, and your usual friend has bailed on you. Then you really need to hold it together."

These are just a few of the real-deal ways to handle life matters that you will encounter on this journey into military wifedom. But don't worry, by reading *The Mocha Manual* you will learn not only how to "be," but also what to "do." Not only will we walk you through what resources are available to help you get through it all, but Pamela will share her personal experiences; and military experts, military spouses, and women in uniform who have been there, done that, and would do it all over again will share their best tips and advice. Despite some of the difficulties, there are many aspects of the life that military spouses wouldn't trade for the world. Some of them include lifelong friends, living all over the globe, excellent medical and dental benefits, being able to provide a good life for your family, the diversity of all the people you meet, and of course, that wonderful man they married!

But let's go back to the beginning, because before marriage comes. . . .

Dating a Military Man

Are you dating a military man? Then expect that your courtship might be a little different from the ones you have had in the past. "Many times you will end up having a long-distance relationship at some point in your dating because the military will send him away. When that happens, you won't be able to hang out doing things together and getting to know each other," said LaTanya, a ten-year air force wife.

Instead, phone calls and e-mail will replace face-to-face interaction. That doesn't have to be a bad thing, though. Pamela is pretty sure that her extended telephone calls with Doug during their courtship allowed them to have more in-depth conversations about such a variety of things that they got to know each other extremely well. They shared their thoughts, feelings, fears, and goals—even working out their disagreements over the telephone. "Looking back, I would definitely consider it as part of our 'training' for what eventually evolved into a normal part of our life together," Pamela says.

For LaTanya, the telephone was also the gateway to her military life. "My husband was in Texas attending tech school and I was back home in New York going to college when he called me and proposed over the phone," she said. Even though she told him yes on the phone, her hubby-to-be still got down on one knee and proposed when she went to visit him at school.

Another way your military courtship may differ from traditional dating is that because of separation, you, your honey, or other people in your life might push for a quick wedding because of the impending separation. "When Greg was scheduled to leave New York to attend AIT (Advanced Individual Training), all of our friends and family kept asking if we were going to get married before he leaves. As far as I was concerned, we had been together for four years and had such a good relationship that marriage wasn't going to change anything but our taxes," recalls Nicole, a twelve-year army wife.

Greg decided that the right time for him to propose was when he was nearly finished with AIT and was home visiting during the Christmas holidays. "I was wrapping gifts on the bed. He came in and pushed them aside and said, 'Nicole, I need to know before you lay your head down tonight if you will give me the gift of being my wife.'" They were married in July.

Obviously, every courtship with a military man won't land you at the altar, but just like with traditional dating, the courtship needs optimal conditions under which to flourish if it is going to do so. If you are dating a military man, here are some things that military spouses advise will get you to "the good part."

DATING DOS AND DON'TS

1. Get to know him and the military customs. Determine whether military life is for you. Get to know as much as you can as early as you can. Picking up this book is a great first step, if you're still in the dating phase. Familiarizing yourself with certain military protocols and asking him to explain certain things to you shows you have a genuine interest in his life. It also gives you a taste of what's in store and helps you figure out if you're up to the challenge—if not, move on to another man.

2. Be friends first. It is not realistic to expect to fall in love too soon. Resist the urge or pressure from others to get married quickly or before an upcoming deployment. By forcing a romantic or physical relationship immediately, you may jeopardize your ability to build a

solid foundation. Share your short-term and long-term goals, but don't start planning the rest of your life with a military man right off the bat.

3. Join an online military girlfriend community or forum. Shop around before joining, because each group has its own personality and flavor. Try to find a good match.

4. Develop honest and open communication. That includes being patient and understanding when your man can't tell you something because it's private and work related or because it's too disturbing to discuss at the time. Either way, you'll have to trust his decision.

5. Understand his commitment to the military. Whether he intends to be in the military for a few years or for his whole career, it is his livelihood for the time being. Don't make him feel guilty when he must fulfill the requirements of his job. He may not want to work late, go away, or miss a special occasion, but in many cases he won't have a choice. Be supportive and understanding by accepting the situation and planning a way to make up for it later, if you can.

6. Develop patience. This will be extremely handy. For example, when you visit the base without your boyfriend, you will usually need your driver's license, car registration, and proof of car insurance, and they may have you call your boyfriend to prove you have reason to enter the base. You may also have to present your documentation to the gate guard where they may inspect your vehicle. Then they can give you a visitor's pass. There can often be long lines for these, so bring something to read. And, like we said, a big bag of patience.

7. No CP time. Sorry, ladies, it doesn't exist in the military world. In fact, soldiers are penalized for being late. So practice arriving at functions fifteen minutes early as a general rule of thumb. And learn military time (the twenty-four-hour clock); it's not 7:00 P.M., it's 1900 hours.

8. No guilt trips. Never make him feel guilty while on deployment. Trust us, it's not easy.

9. Be civil about "civilian." Don't be easily offended if you are called a civilian or a "civvy" for short. This happens a lot. And since there are so many differences between the military world and the civilian world, members of the military often call all of those on the outside

"civilians." Sometimes, though, it can be used as an insult, and don't be afraid to defend yourself in those instances.

If you've been on the dating scene for some time now and are moving toward becoming a married couple, there are five surefire strategies to get you off to a strong start to learning the ropes, planning for your future, preparing to move, and making a strong commitment to your new love and your new life. The strategies are (1) consult the experts, (2) marry for the right reasons, (3) make life decisions a team effort, (4) master communication while together and when separated, (5) understand the rank and structure, (6) accept the military for what it is, and (7) communicate openly. We'll go through these one by one.

1. CONSULT THE EXPERTS.

    As a military family you will need to learn how to build support systems around you, no matter where you live or what stage you are in in your military life. There are many civilian and military resources available to prepare future and current military spouses for the road ahead, and you should take advantage of every one of them. Chapter 2 will discuss many of these in detail, but for now, let's focus on getting help before you tie the knot.

    Military chaplains help future couples prepare for married life much like civilian clergy do. Both offer private marriage preparation counseling and group counseling. In addition to performing religious ceremonies and services, they are also trained to conduct premarital counseling. They can help you take a close look at yourself, your relationship, and your expectations as well as set a foundation of skills that will help you manage the hard work of building and maintaining a strong marriage. Chaplains are very easy to find on base. Start with your fiancé's unit. The chaplain there is assigned to help the commander, the service members, and the families and is trained to respond to the needs of persons of all denominations and those who don't identify with any particular faith.

    There was a time when junior soldiers had to get counseled and approval to get married. Currently, there is no such rule.

However, *all* soldiers are highly encouraged to seek counsel from their respective chains of command if they plan to get married. More important, they are encouraged to get marriage counseling from the unit ministry team. Suffice it to say that getting "married to the military" is a little different from getting married to a local businessperson. The army is not just a job. It is a way of life. And it is very important to the overall success of the marriage that each partner understands what the union will bring and the potential challenges or obstacles that may lie ahead.

Chaplains and their assistants conduct seminars and retreats for premarital preparation and marriage enrichment once they tie the knot. They also are required to be knowledgeable about other available resources to which they can refer you. To find chaplaincy programs, you can visit your Airman and Family Readiness Center, Army Community Service Center, Fleet and Family Support Center, Marine Corps Community Services, or a chapel on post to explore the many resources they have available to you. If you don't live on or near a military post, just call the one that is nearest to you and ask for help. Or use the Local Community Resource Finder on the National Guard Family Program website at www .guardfamily.org.

Your current place of worship is also a great place to seek premarital assistance. It may even have a ministry that serves military families and be able to hook you up with couples who are willing to discuss "the life" as well as local resources. Pamela says, "I was completely surprised at the level of support I found in my most recent church home. Since we do not live near a military installation I thought I would really miss interacting with other military families. But fortunately, the veterans' ministry at my church is large, active, diverse, and close-knit. And during a time when my husband was deployed, it was nice to know that there were other people around me who really knew what we were going through and were there to help if we ever needed it. With military families, you just know in your heart that it is okay to trust them and that they will have your back."

With the consultation of all these experts, much of what you encounter along the way will be manageable if you marry for the right reasons.

2. MARRY FOR THE RIGHT REASONS.

The best reason we can think of for getting married is because you love someone unconditionally and want to be with them for the rest of your life, no matter what happens. To us, it's just that simple. Marrying for any other reason brings all kinds of complications into the mix and jeopardizes the permanence of the relationship. However, we all know that some people entertain the thought of marriage for many other reasons. Spouses we spoke with offer these dos and don'ts when it comes to making the decision to wed.

Don't marry because you are lonely, tired of being without your man, and want steady sex. Even when you get married, you will still experience loneliness and be without sex during frequent separation, deployment, and plain old long workdays. Instead, *do* learn how to cope with loneliness in positive and constructive ways. For example, spend your time involved in interests and hobbies to help you maintain your own identity rather than living through his.

Don't marry for the money. There is a real myth out there about military pay. Yes, it is no secret that your honey will bring in more dough just because he got married. In fact, over the course of his career, there will be many instances when he will receive "extra" pay, such as during deployment, upon the birth of a child, when serving in a hazardous location, and when living overseas, just to name a few. However, getting this extra pay helps the two of you live more comfortably as a family and should in no way be the reason you get married in the first place. A whole set of expenses go along with being married, too, so you are not likely to be much better off financially just because you tied the knot.

Do discuss how you will handle paying the bills, budgeting your money, saving for a rainy day, and saving for emergency situations.

Don't marry just for a change of scenery or to escape the parts of your life you are no longer happy with. Not being able to find a good job, make enough money, or get out of a bad relationship or other unfortunate circumstances do *not* make good reasons to marry a military man, or any man for that matter. If you are running to him to run away from something else, you are just creating a different set of problems. Chances are, when military life no longer seems romantic and becomes complicated, you will be ready to run from that, too. So why waste your time and his? Remember, you will be faced with insecurities in military life, so *do* make sure you are committed enough to the relationship to make it work when it happens.

3. MAKE LIFE DECISIONS A TEAM EFFORT.

Once you have made the decision to marry, there are countless other decisions to come. Now would be a great time to discuss with your honey the specifics of whether to live on or near the installation versus far from it, when to have children, whether to be a dual- or single-income family, and what level of involvement you will be expected to have. None of these questions have a right or wrong answer as long as you both agree on the decisions. Furthermore, the answers may change as your life circumstances change.

Living on post or off post. The military makes housing available to service members and their families through either an actual dwelling on base or through a basic housing allowance (BAH) to help cover the cost of living off post. Please understand a few things about this. First, nothing is free. Therefore, when you evaluate whether to live on or off post, you should thoroughly review your finances. Construct budget scenarios that clearly show your income and expenses in each case. If you live on post, you will not receive the BAH because it will go toward the cost of the home assigned to you. Second, if you live off post, you may need to add a little more to the amount you receive for BAH, especially in high cost-of-living locations. In most cases, the decision to live on or off post is strictly one of preference and how much you can get for your money in the local area.

No matter how much you ask around for advice, you will get responses on both sides of the coin. For instance, some people love it that everyone must keep up with certain standards on post, like maintaining your lawn, while others will hate the fact that someone else can tell you when you should cut your grass. Some will love the feeling of so many living as neighbors; others will want to create some space between home life and work life. You and your partner will have to do your research before you relocate and discuss what will work best for you.

"Doug and I decided to live off post every time we moved," Pamela says. "Not only did he want some 'space' from his work life when he left the office each day, but we could usually find a really great deal on rental property off post. There is usually plenty of housing reasonably priced right outside the gate because military homeowners who end up renting their property to other military families typically are very fair about the prices. However, when we moved to Hawaii, the off-post housing was small on size and big on cost. We were pleasantly surprised to find much bigger and better accommodations on post and in a quiet neighborhood. Together we agreed to change our normal living situation, and we enjoyed every minute of it. On the other hand, we had friends who felt like they had substandard housing on post. They lived in an older neighborhood and one where the housing was not as spacious as the newer housing."

When to have children. Again, this has got to be something you evaluate, discuss, and decide together. Some factors might be how long you will be assigned in one area, whether your honey is expecting to be deployed or away from home for training, whether you will be able to afford to have children at the time, whether you work and will be able to access convenient child care, and whether you have an established support system. These factors may change with each relocation, so don't get so stuck in your ways that you can't make adjustments that will better suit your family needs. Remember the earlier reference to adaptability being a quality of a successful MS. Female service members can enlist the help of the commanders or other leaders to help map out a family planning time line that will enable them to also meet their military career goals.

Being a single- or dual-income family. We've met loads of spouses who chose not to work outside the home. Some of their reasons included being home with the children when they are young, being home with the children when they are older, being able to keep the house in order, not having to worry about taking time off for school activities or military activities, volunteering in the military community, and simply making that a lifestyle choice. Depending where you are based, the available wages may be such that after child-care and work-related expenses, it just doesn't make sense to work outside the home.

Some of the reasons for working as a military spouse are being able to help with the family finances, build up the savings account, pay off the bills, do extra things like take vacations, or simply have more cash on hand. And, for some, it is a great way to get out of the house.

Your level of involvement in spouse activities. There's an endless debate over how much a spouse's involvement influences her man's upward career trajectory. That's something you two have to decide together. Before you agree, let's review what you'll be signing up for. Here's a list of the more common military activities that include spouse participation:

Family Readiness Group (FRG) activities: This group is an official program of the commander, so all the members of it belong to the same unit. Your FRG leader should reach out and contact you whenever you arrive at a new duty station. The purpose of the FRG is to be a reliable source of information and support, and it usually meets monthly to discuss important topics that will ensure a strong link between the unit and the family. For example, you can find out about upcoming deployments, homecomings, social events, training activities, and volunteer needs. The FRG also provides ongoing support for members of the unit (checking in on mothers who have given birth, helping new spouses transition into "the life," and being a referral agent to help you link up with needed services) as well as helps in emergency situations, especially when the service member is absent. Informal activities of the FRG can be social events like family holiday parties and get-to-know-you cookouts. If you don't live near an installation, ask your hubby to find out if the unit has a virtual Family Readiness Group (vFRG). These secure websites are reliable means of long-distance support and up-to-date information so you can feel more involved even if you are not living nearby.

Ceremonies: Traditional ceremonies occur when service members get promoted, retire, reenlist, and obtain or relinquish command or responsibility of a group of service members. They typically involve uniformed service members, marching bands, and official military speakers along with a very specific order of events.

Social events: Military balls are a formal social event. Most service members wear their uniforms, and their dates wear formal attire. Think prom night as an adult, but more "ceremonial." These nights include a social hour and color guard (flags being marched in to begin the formal part of the evening and removed at the end of it). There is a sit-down dinner and several official military speakers followed by the informal (and fun) part of the evening: dancing. Informal social events include coffee group activities, which are usually attended by women in the same unit, but don't necessarily include coffee. The monthly meetings might involve dinner or dessert, activities like scrapbooking or bowling, and plenty of talking and laughing. Simply put, it's just a night with the girls. Informal family events might include unit-sponsored picnics or parties that tend to be casual in nature and may include children. Sometimes these are held during the afternoon of a workday, making it mandatory for the service members to attend. If you are dating or engaged to a military man, the events at which you can get a taste of military life are the military balls and some of the ceremonial events. The ones not likely to be open to nonspouses are the FRG and coffee group activities.

Pamela's Pick: Know When to Say When: Determining Your Level of Involvement in Military Activities

Over the years we have found that my level of involvement in military functions is based on what is going on in our personal and professional lives. The factors that have impacted my level of involvement were whether I worked full-time, was continuing my education, and the number and ages of my children. I always attended the "big" military social functions

(I don't think there was a military ball I missed in all these years) and most of the family support meetings. But how much time I spent on coordinating events, attending parties, serving on committees, and the like was limited to commitments that would not be a detriment to handling my business at home and at work. If these two aspects of my life aren't in order, then I know I can't do anybody else any good. And lucky for me, unlike for some wives, my husband never put pressure on me to do more than what was manageable.

But some husbands do put undue pressure on their spouses and more often than not, it only has the opposite effect they are hoping for. You can always tell what spouses are doing things because they want to and which are doing them because they "have to." Those who begrudgingly take on roles and responsibilities often come across as very discontented with military life, themselves, or their relationship. And that can lead to trouble. Resentment is hard to hide and can easily develop into a general air of negativity, which can ruin your relationships with other spouses and make you and your hubby victims of the rumor mill. Needless to say, this situation can also quickly turn a marriage sour.

The truth of the matter is, your man's level of professional success is not supposed to be based upon your level of involvement. Now there are people who will argue until the end of time about whether that really is the way it works or not. But the bottom line is that the more comfortable and happy you are with military life, yourself, and your relationship, the better able you and he will be to determine what works best for your family.

4. MASTER COMMUNICATION DURING SEPARATION.
Whether he is five miles, five hundred miles, or five thousand miles away, be sure to put extra effort into using a variety of ways to stay connected. Rather than waiting for his call, initiate calls to him when possible. A quick e-mail note to say hello or share some good news can make his day. Reading and rereading handwritten

letters, greeting cards, and postcards are a great way for him to "hear from you" again and again, as is being able to replay tape-recorded messages. Send care packages with his favorite or much needed items, and don't forget to send photos. The fact that you frequently reach out to him will delight him and, subsequently, you will be delighted by how he reacts to knowing that you are thinking of him all the time. There's more specifics on Separation and Deployment in Chapter 3, but lay the groundwork for good communication as early as possible.

5. UNDERSTAND THE RANK AND STRUCTURE OF THE MILITARY.

The U.S. military, also referred to as the armed forces, is made up of the U.S. Army, U.S. Navy, U.S. Air Force, Marine Corps, and Coast Guard; these branches are controlled by the president as the commander in chief. The army, navy, air force , and marines fall under the Department of Defense (DoD), while the Coast Guard falls under Homeland Security, although it can be placed under DoD during wartime. Each of the branches has a different mission. The army has primary responsibility for military operations that occur on land and is the oldest and largest branch. The navy conducts its primary responsibilities in and on bodies of water, including seas, oceans, and large lakes and rivers. The air force, the last branch of the military to be established, uses aircraft to conduct its military functions. The Marine Corps primarily seizes and defends navy bases and operations in support of the navy as well as develops techniques and equipment used by land and water vehicles and is actually part of the navy. Finally, the Coast Guard protects the public, environment, economic and security in maritime (sea or ocean) regions.

Although their primary responsibilities differ, their hierarchical structures are similar. They are all based upon a pay grade and rank system that basically tells the world how long individuals have been in the military, at what level of responsibility they are, and how much money they make compared with others. Here is our "civilianized" way to explain the differences between enlisted ranks and officer ranks. Enlisted members usually sign up for a specific time of military service and generally have at least a high school diploma when they do so. They are considered the workforce. Once they move up in enlisted rank they are called noncommissioned officers (NCOs) and become first-line supervisors to the junior enlisted while at the same time working directly under the commissioned officers, who are the senior leaders. They generally have at least a four-year degree and are expected to provide guidance and training to NCOs as well as plan and manage the accomplishment of the mission. They are considered the managers.

Warrant officers (WO) are technical experts in their fields. They possess a high degree of specialization and extensive professional experience. Enlisted pay grades are E-1 to E-9, officer pay grades are O-1 to O-10, and warrant officers are W-1 to W-5. Each pay grade has a rank attached to it, such as private, sergeant, lieutenant, or general. Further complicating this name game are the symbols worn on the uniform that identify the rank and pay grade so that they can be addressed properly, *and* they all have abbreviations when you see them in print. For example, there is Seaman Recruit Jones and Tech Sergeant Smith as well as SSG (Army Staff Sergeant) and SSgt (Marine Corps Staff Sergeant). Be aware that each branch of the military differs and that it is not necessary to memorize the structure of them all. For now, just focus on being familiar with rank, grades, and insignia (symbols worn on uniform collar or shoulder) for your man's service branch.

TOP SIX THINGS TO KNOW
ABOUT RANK AND STRUCTURE

1. Metal bars signify a junior officer or warrant officer. Silver is higher ranking than gold.

2. Oak-leaf clusters signify midlevel officers. Silver is higher ranking than gold.

3. Eagle and stars signify senior officers.
4. Rank determines who salutes and who responds upon passing each other.
5. Every single item worn on the uniform tells something about one's military service such as combat, unit, deployments, awards, and so on. You don't have to know them all, but your husband sure will.
6. Spouses have no rank and should not wear their service member's, literally or figuratively.

Now, despite your best efforts to preclude embarrassing situations by becoming familiar with all this, there are always some tiny little details that can slip right on by. I'll let Pamela share one of hers:

"Shortly after Doug and I were married and finally living in the same residence, I made a trip to the commissary (military grocery store) to take advantage of the food prices that are always much lower than at the civilian grocery stores. As soon as I entered the parking lot, I noticed an empty space right at the front of the store reserved just for me. As I pulled into the space marked 'General Officer' I thought: I could get used to this. The next thing I knew, a little, old, gray-haired man with his face all torn up grumbled to me, 'Is your father a general officer?' I looked from side to side to find out who he was talking to, but I was the only one around. 'No, he is not, sir,' I replied, 'but my husband is.' And I walked away thinking: he had a lot of nerve. What business is it of his?

"As soon as I got home and told my new hubby about this, he laughed and shook his head. *You what?* I explained that I parked in a space for general officers. I thought that the word *general* referred to *any* officer, as in *no specific* officer. I had only heard generals referred to as generals, not as general *officers* and had no idea that *general officer* refers to one who has achieved any rank of general (brigadier general, major general, lieutenant general, or general). So Mr. Grumpy had every right to question me. He could tell by my youthful look that there was no way my husband had been in the military long enough to make it to the top echelon. But I bet he had. He was probably a general officer who had been in the military since before I was born twenty-one years earlier. And, had I parked where I was supposed to park, he could have had the spot that he had earned. Oops! I could not imagine how sorry I would have been if I had gotten a parking ticket or how embarrassed I would have felt if I told that story to a room full of other military people instead of just to my husband. My rank and structure faux pas was not the end of the world, and yours won't be either!"

6. UNDERSTAND AND ACCEPT THE MILITARY FOR WHAT IT IS.

Aside from its hierarchical makeup, the military is steeped in solid tradition. For service members, working for this type of structure can make it easy to adjust to new places, jobs, and people and lessen the learning curve. And it is always amazing to see that every single ceremony, promotion, celebration, and military ball is "dress, right, dress" (perfectly coordinated).

However, along with this hierarchy and tradition, there is *much* bureaucracy. And for family members, this can mean a lot of headaches from banging your head against the wall when no one is willing to think outside the box to resolve a problem. "Ma'am, that's the way we have to do it according to the regulation" is a sentence that you will hear more than you'd like to, but it is the military way; and you are not likely going to change that single-handedly with attitude, anger, frustration, or anything else. Trust me, many have tried—and failed. The most frustrating red tape will be when you are trying to get things done and everyone's hands are tied.

Jennifer, an air force wife in New Mexico, learned a costly lesson about filing claims for personal property damaged during relocation. "We never got reimbursed for about $2,400 worth of property that included a china cabinet, dishes, a hutch, and mementos because when they came to assess our losses, we had thrown all the broken items away. We had no idea that we had to keep them."

That being said, no matter how frustrating things might be, it is always a good time to practice abiding by the unwritten code of how military wives should act: with pride and composure. So, if you feel like screaming, scream in private. Then remember a famous quote that has been attributed to several people, including Eleanor Roosevelt, Franklin D. Roosevelt, and Thomas Jefferson: "When you get to the end of your rope, tie a knot and hang on."

7. COMMUNICATE OPENLY.

Don't keep your feelings to yourself. Talk to your mate about what scares the stew out of you and what you are most excited about. Opening up about your fears (not moaning and groaning about them) will help both of you start to identify ways to deal with them and the military services you may need to use (don't forget we are going to address them in Chapter 2). Sharing what you most look forward to can create excitement that will offset some of your nervousness.

And, sisters, please remember that as important as it is for you to express your feelings, your man needs to have the opportunity to get his off his chest, too. Listen to him! If you are always talking, he can't possibly get a word in edgewise. And if he chooses not to talk about things when you want him to, don't force it. Look for signs of how he feels in his body language and his actions without overanalyzing or taking everything personally. His thoughts and feelings may be different from yours and that's perfectly okay.

Now that we prepped you for the life ahead and you haven't decided to jump ship yet, here are some good suggestions for planning your wedding.

Planning Your Big Day

In the civilian world, weddings are planned six months to two years in advance. Deposits are paid, invitations are printed, and other arrangements are made to solidify the event; and these actions all but write everything in stone. However, you should be aware that in military life, there is no occasion that is safe from the ever-changing demands of Uncle Sam, including your wedding. That being said, if you are planning anything bigger than a courthouse union or a small event in the chapel on post, you could very well be upstaged by Uncle

Sam issuing your hubby-to-be a set of orders to be some place other than at the altar with you.

After Doug proposed to Pamela in June of 1989, they decided to give themselves a full year to plan and prepare. That quickly turned into six months when they found out that he would be going to Korea for thirteen months. In retrospect, they're convinced that having a small military wedding, using military resources and the help of friends, was one of the best decisions they ever made.

At the time, Doug was stationed in Maryland for training, and Pamela was finishing her last year of college in Boston. He contacted the chaplain on his very small training post and a local wedding planner who told Pamela to send the invitations, buy a dress, pick the flowers and cake, and just show up. And that's exactly what they did, pulling off a beautiful, though short-planned traditional military wedding.

A military chaplain performed the ceremony in the post chapel, and a group of fellow soldiers helped Doug and the planner pull everything else together. They ushered, decorated, and ran prewedding errands. They donned those sharp dress blue uniforms and formed the Arch of Sabers (called "swords" in the navy, Marine Corps, and Coast Guard) for Pamela and Doug to transition into their new life, even catching her off guard at the end of the line with the traditional swat on the rear with a saber and a hearty "Welcome to the army, ma'am." After the ceremony, they were chauffeured to the club on post, where they helped with the reception and never missed a beat all the way up to cutting the cake with a saber and cleaning up their own mess at the end of the night! To top it all off, they were not left with a mountain of debt to begin their life together.

Just a word to the wise here, ladies, weddings planned with short notice can still get complicated. For example, if your future husband is stationed at a large installation, the simplicity can quickly turn into a complex protocol puzzle. From a guest list that includes every military person associated with your fiancé, to addressing the invitations properly, to seating and standing arrangements, the whole event can become daunting. And who needs that when this is supposed to be a time of celebration and fun? If you want to eliminate a lot of stress from planning your nuptials, these strategies will help:

1. Pick the right planning partner. You need someone by your side to be the sounding board for your ideas, who knows you well, who

will delegate for you, and who won't take it personally at times when stress gets the best of you. If possible, try to find a planner with military experience.

2. Talk to other women who have had military weddings. Experience is the best teacher, so capitalize on what they learned and get a heads-up on what situations might arise and how to handle them. Check out chat rooms and websites to post your questions and get advice.

3. Set a budget and stick to it. More is not always better. Once you make decisions, don't be easily drawn into reevaluating your options just because there are more of them.

4. Patronize the military shopping resources for the biggest discounts. Visit the exchange on post or online (www.aafes.com and www.navy -nex.com) for prices that beat most any retail place you will find. Believe it or not, some posts are large enough to offer you almost everything you need: flowers, cake, arts and crafts center for personalized wedding party gifts, alterations and dry cleaning, catering, and more. And if they don't have it on post, they have relationships with the best local vendors to meet your needs. Finally, don't forget to check with the staff at the Tickets and Tours Office for great deals on trips for your honeymoon.

5. Find out where on post you can get help with protocol. Every base has a protocol office. The chaplains and their assistants can also be great resources for helping you figure things out and avoid protocol snafus.

6. Consider purchasing wedding insurance. What happens when you do plan ahead and have to cancel or postpone because your man has to ship out before the wedding? If you have wedding insurance, you may be able to recover your deposits on the wedding site and other items so you can afford to reschedule the event. Just like any other insurance, the cost for wedding insurance depends upon how much coverage you want. Make sure you know what is already covered in your vendor insurance policies before you make any payments.

7. If you decide to have a civil ceremony, your options for inexpensive or free picturesque locations on many installations may be plentiful. Consider the golf course, parks, lakes, and enlisted or officer's clubs for the ceremony, the reception, and the wedding day photo backdrop.

8. Remember the reason for the occasion: you and your intended are making a lifetime commitment to each other. Let that be the focus; no other planning detail should ever supersede the importance of that.

WALKING DOWN THE AISLE, MILITARY STYLE
∽ A WEDDING PLANNING CHECKLIST ∽

- Set a date, taking into consideration his military schedule (field duty, training, etc.).
- Set a budget within your means.
- Visit chaplain's office for information about premarital counseling, performance of ceremony, and local resources and referrals.
- Select and notify desired wedding party members.
- Compile your guest list keeping the budget in mind; consult with protocol for inviting military personnel.
- Check out possible wedding and reception venues on post.
- Consider purchasing wedding insurance once you clarify with vendors their policies on date changes and cancellations.
- Consider using save-the-date cards to give people advance notice even if details are not finalized.
- Choose invitations.
- Research wedding registry options that are available online since family and friends may not be local.
- Shop for dress and appropriate lingerie for a perfect fit.
- Shop around for a photographer and/or videographer.
- Shop for flowers, cakes, and wedding party gifts, starting with the exchange on post and its catalog.
- Select wedding day transportation.

The Mocha Mix
Real Talk on the MS Life

★ ★

Red tape . . .

My biggest anxiety was having to deal with the military system. I heard horror stories of having to deal with paperwork, trying to make appointments, and being given the runaround for anything you needed to get done, from IDs to opening a bank account on base.

—MICHELLE, AIR FORCE, GERMANY

I was clueless . . . I did not know I should be nervous beyond the fact that I was getting married.

—SUMMER, ARMY, TEXAS

Leaving friends and family and my entire support network and living in a foreign country.

—JUANITA, ARMY, GEORGIA

FRGs and other spouses . . .

I used to go to FRG meetings, but I thought they were more gossip-fests than much else. Plus, I found that they would give us one piece of information, but when my husband called he would tell me something completely different.

—ARMY WIFE, FORT BRAGG

I found that officers' wives got together more than enlisted wives. Also, compared to other enlisted wives I was much older and more mature and had different interests.

—LAUREL, FORT SUMTER

I learned the most from . . .

Other military spouses, families, and my own life experiences. Getting involved has been very helpful and participating in any training available; i.e., Army Family Team Building (AFTB), Family Readiness Groups (FRG), etc.

—JEANNETTE, ARMY, GEORGIA

My fiancé is very open and honest with me about everything that he goes through. I've learned all of what I know from him and from researching on the Internet some of the things that we've discussed.

—ANGELA, NATIONAL GUARD, MARYLAND

People in the military. They were willing to "show me the ropes" and share with me what they wished they had known at the beginning of their careers.

—JUANITA, ARMY, GEORGIA

Unspoken expectations . . .

I felt that at all times spouses served as the unspoken ambassadors to the U.S. Armed Forces and as role models to whomever was watching. I had fun perfecting it and learning from others who have already received their MS (Military Spouse) degree.

—KATERIA, ARMY, MARYLAND

I always thought a military wife does not work, especially for officers. [You] take care of the children and be the ideal soccer mom. [You] support your spouse's career and network, especially as your spouse moves up the chain of command. Some of my feelings were correct and some were not. There were professional military spouses and some soccer mom military spouses.

—VERONICA, ARMY, ALABAMA

I have always heard that if the military wanted you to have a family, they would have issued you one, but this varies from post to post. At some places they want the wife to feel involved and be knowledgeable about what's going on. At others it's like as long as you have a spouse, she'll be there to run the household. We need you (the soldier) on post, in the field, deployed, etc.

—NICOLE, ARMY, TEXAS

The expectation is still there for wives to actively participate in all FRG functions. However, I think the leadership now realizes spouses need and want to work.

—CARLA, ARMY, MARYLAND

We were led to believe that we attend all functions and coffee groups and not to voice too many opinions about our husband's military comrades. This is not true at all. No one makes you attend functions, but by attending them you learn more about your husband's life and what the military has to offer you.

—DEIDRE, ARMY, FLORIDA

What Military Men Want and Winning at Love and Marriage

As soon as you start seriously dating a military man you should try to get a basic knowledge of military rank and structure and really understand how little control a soldier has over his assignments—especially in the early days. Once I was given an assignment in Qatar and my girlfriend was, like, "Why didn't you tell them that you didn't want to go?" She was very upset with me and I'm, like, she has no clue that it doesn't work like that at all. You go when and where you're told to go.

I've seen a lot of military families going through divorces and it's very sad. You need strong family values, to really know each other well and be prepared for long absences. I've been married twice during my military career, and both my marriages ended due to the infidelity of my wives. I was in Guam and my first wife was unfaithful with another soldier. After I retuned, I ended up working with him! In other situations I've seen, the woman assumed the man was cheating, so she decides to cheat. I've also seen women who are too dependent on their husbands and when he's gone there is a huge void they can't fill for themselves and they start looking for others to fill the void.

A military wife needs to be a strong person. When the man leaves, she has to take on everything and hold it down. They have to take on the parenting, helping the kids get through the deployment, and managing the household. It's a lot.

Lastly, I think it's important for a wife to understand that a black man's military experience is very different from a white man's experience. There's segregation and racism in the military too, and sometimes higher-ranking black men can be your worst nightmare. So she needs an extra level of understanding and support than other wives.

—JOHN, RETIRED AIR FORCE TECHNICAL SERGEANT

CHAPTER TWO

Surviving the First Year

Your Induction into the MS World

Congratulations! You have that military man on your arm, the ring on your finger, and the marriage certificate on file. These things make you a wife, but they won't make you an official military spouse (MS) just yet. But first, let's address you as wifey.

The first year of any marriage can be rough. There's a reason why statistically more couples divorce in the first year than any other. I've been married twice, and I can remember each first year's struggles like it was yesterday. Adjusting to living with someone takes time; understanding who's doing what when it comes to household chores may have been taken for granted without having a clear conversation, and don't even get me started on possible in-law drama. My second husband of six years, with whom I have my two children, was the typical baby boy with five older sisters! Between the sisters and his mother it was a virtual drama-rama all the time. The most important thing I can say about marriage in general is to always have each other's back. Every man wants a "ride-or-die chick" as it were, and you need to be that for your husband and he should be that for you. That means nothing or no one comes between you two.

Keep your bond tight and let no one in. Here's some other wifey-to-wifey advice from Pamela and me:

1. Give yourselves time to adjust and be willing to work through the rough spots.

2. Communicate about life decisions. Discuss long- and short-term goals, how you will handle finances, the division of labor at home, and if and when to have children.

3. Learn how to live with your mate. Even if you have known each other for years, once you wed, your lives will change.

4. Commit to your marriage and mean it: ". . . in sickness and in health, 'til death do you part." There's a dangerous "I don't need this, I'm outta here" attitude in our society. And it frightens me. A marriage should be for forever; don't bolt at the first sign of trouble. You will have to sacrifice in many ways; be willing to do so for the sake of your marriage.

5. Communicate maturely. Arguments may be plentiful. Never go to bed or send off your spouse angry whether he is running to the commissary or shipping off to training. Fight fairly. Listen to your mate. Seek communication skills training from the chaplain's office.

6. Keep your private matters private. Don't involve friends, family, or his boss in your affairs (unless you are reaching out for help with an abusive relationship).

7. Remain friends. Have fun. Just because you have made a serious commitment doesn't mean you have to take life too seriously. Laugh, play, and hang out together just like when you dated.

Pamela's Pick: For a successful mocha marriage, check out the African American Healthy Marriage Initiative (AAHMI), which offers conferences, forums, and great resources just for us at www.aahmi.net.

Getting Your Props

Now that we've addressed you as a wife, you are almost ready to claim your status as an officially recognized military spouse. To really become "official" in the eyes of the military you have to get your name on "the list" of those who are eligible to receive military benefits and to get that coveted military identification card in your purse. And then, you can get your props, no questions asked.

"I was a twenty-seven-year-old woman who worked eleven-hour days, was active in my community, and sang semiprofessionally and in the church. My father took our family traveling all the time, so I have seen a lot of places," said Rhonda. "Two months after I married I moved alone from Las Cruces, New Mexico, to Columbia, South Carolina. My drill sergeant husband had already started his rounds on Fort Jackson Army Base. When I arrived there, I slept for two days. I was not only a new wife, but also unemployed, alone, and a military spouse. I decided that the commissary would be the easiest place to start to become familiar with military life. But I was quickly schooled after giving my social security number and it was denied. I was no longer Rhonda Y. Cherry. I was Sergeant Cherry's wife."

For new spouses, it can be difficult to adjust to the feeling of not being a person in your own right. It was bad enough being the girlfriend or fiancée and not getting any recognition, but then when you get married there is still a certain degree of feeling less significant than your mate. But the truth is, the military is not trying to shun you. It is simply using your husband's identity as collateral for your actions. If anything happens that should not, it can be traced right back to him and he will have full responsibility to rectify the situation.

But on the bright side, having your name on "the list" and an ID card as proof of your connection with a service member means you will have access to the commissary (military grocery store with better prices than you will find anywhere), the Exchange (military-run department store with great prices and no tax), fitness centers, medical facilities, and a host of other services on post that specifically cater to service members and their families—without having to be escorted around. And, off post, the military ID can get you countless discounts no matter where you are stationed. Wives who work the perks have gotten discounts at all kinds of stores in the mall, and at movie theaters, hotels, parks, and more. Just ask about it everywhere you go. The worst things they can say is, "We don't offer that."

To get your official status, make sure that your spouse enrolls you in DEERS (Defense Enrollment Eligibility Reporting System) the very first chance he gets. This will be the only way the military can verify that you are authorized to receive military benefits such as those listed above as well as medical coverage and your spouse's life insurance if anything happens to him. In fact, you may need to remind him to update DEERS anytime there is a significant change in your family situation that could impact eligibility, like military status, address changes, births, and so on. Any problems or mistakes in this system and you could have all kinds of issues getting your entitlements.

Take your original marriage certificate, birth certificate, social security card, photo ID, and your new hubby straight to the personnel office on post and handle your business. Well, actually, he is the one who technically has to do it, but you get the idea. If you are not on post and don't know the closest place you can accomplish this mission, visit the Defense Manpower Data Center (DMDC) online at www.dmdc.osd.mil/rsl to search by city, state, zip code, or country. Or contact the DMDC Support Office (DSO) at 800-538-9552. Make sure you call the phone number that is listed online or given on the phone before you go to the office. Military facilities are known to move around, so you will want to verify the location, contact information, and hours of operation.

Next, get that military ID. Where you enroll in DEERS may be the same place to get your ID, but if it's not, personnel will direct you to where it is located. Anyone in your family who is age ten or older should have his or her own card. When accompanied by an adult, some places will let children in without one, but you? Don't even think about it. In fact, don't get caught off guard trying to convince anyone that you have every right to be in the bowling alley, buy food from the commissary, or are eligible to use the medical facility if you don't show your military ID. There is no magic list they can look at, no exceptions to the rule without risking their job, and no sob story they will buy. Trust us.

One year right before Christmas Pamela took a day off work intending to start her holiday shopping at the PX (Post Exchange for army people; same as the air force's BX or Base Exchange, and the MCX for the Marine Corps, or the Exchange for the navy and the Coast Guard). She showed up as soon as the doors opened, but unfortunately, never got past them. When she handed her ID to the store associate with a smile, she smiled right back, took the card right out of her hand, and refused to return it because it had expired. "I'm sorry, ma'am, the regulation says . . ." There went all her hopes of taking care of any errands on post for the whole weekend. But looking on the bright side, since the ID card office didn't open again until Tuesday, her husband had to escort her around all weekend because he was the only one with an ID card, so she got some quality hubby time out of the ordeal.

The point is, get used to carrying your military ID card with you at all times, and make sure it is always up-to-date. Don't become frustrated when you are not allowed access to something if you don't have the card. Once you become better acclimated to "the lifestyle," you will love the benefits and realize that it really is in your best interest to ensure that access to services are limited to people who are entitled to receive them.

Pimp Your Ride

Obtaining a base decal for your car should be the next item on your list. To get on and off almost any military installation without hassle, you need to register your car and place the sticker on your windshield. This too has an expiration date, so take note of it and start the renewal process within a reasonable amount of time before then. Your sticker will indicate whether the car belongs to an enlisted or officer and will be saluted if it is owned by an officer. If you are driving, there is no need to salute back, just smile and wave as the gate guard allows you to enter. Always be prepared to show your military ID and driver's license or to submit to having your car searched, if asked. The military is taking every precaution to keep everyone safe, so be grateful for the "inconvenience" rather than be bothered by it.

Get the Power

Finally, visit the legal office on post with your mate in order to obtain a power of attorney (POA). This is definitely one of those things that is better to have and not need than to need and not have. It will allow you to conduct business on your spouse's behalf when he is away. When you first get married, it may take some time before your name is on everything and your hubby may get called away at a moment's notice. Without the POA or your hubby right by your side, you might be stuck without access to bank accounts, housing, transportation (the car is in his name and the tags expired), or who knows what.

A girlfriend once told us about a young wife who went to the grocery store to buy baby formula and was unable to get it because her name was not on the checking account. She and her husband usually went shopping together, but he had been called away. With a POA she most likely would have been able to work with the bank to have her name added. Instead, Army Community Service (ACS) and Army Emergency Relief (AER) staff helped her obtain a food voucher until the more senior spouses could facilitate getting her name added to the account by working through her husband's unit. Whatever you do, don't let your spouse be too busy to get around to getting a POA for you. And you should store copies in several different places at home just to be on the safe side.

Get Ready for the Road Ahead

Being a new military spouse, in a new location, with a whole new life ahead of you can be daunting. But not to worry, everything you need to help you with that transition is available to you . . . if you know where to find it. The moment you arrive at your first duty station, be sure to visit the installation's Family Readiness Center. You will be thrilled to see the vast array of services and information available under one roof. Make a point to review the listings of available services; get maps; sign up for the newcomer orientation, which often includes a tour of the installation; and check out the list of classes the center has to help you learn about every aspect of military life. From acronyms, to military culture, to protocol, to military benefits, to answering lingering questions like, why in the world does everyone on post stop in their tracks and face the same direction even if it means getting out of the car in the middle of the street every time that music begins to play throughout the entire base? There's a good answer for that. Through service-specific training, you will become indoctrinated into this life in no time. Look for the times and dates of Air Force Heartlink, Army Family Team Building, Marine Corps L.I.N.K.S (Lifestyle, Insights, Networking, Knowledge, and Skills) or Navy COMPASS, based on your situation. For more in-depth information about services that are available to you, you may also visit Air Force Crossroads at www.afcrossroads.com, Marine Corps Community Service at www.usmc-mccs .org, Navy Fleet and Family Support Centers at www.ffsp.navy.mil, or Army Community Service at www.myarmylifetoo.com.

Unfortunately, many of the wives who have been around for a while could share countless stories about husbands who tell the wives to stay away from the base, the activities, or the services. And so they do. If you find yourself in this situation, how do you convince him otherwise? One spouse suggested taking an approach that he can relate to. Tell him that when he is away you need to make sure you are equipped to take care of you and the kids no matter what happens. If there is a family emergency here at home or with either set of parents, you have to be able to step it up and know enough to handle whatever comes your way.

For those who serve in the National Guard and reserve forces and are not near an installation, be familiar with your Family Programs staff. They specialize in bringing together community partners to provide assistance and services to geographically dispersed families. The website for the National Guard Family Programs is www.guardfamily.org. Army Reserve Family Programs can be found at www.arfp.org.

Understanding Your Rank and His

In the last chapter, we discussed the general hierarchy of the military. Well, your spouse's unit is similarly structured. There is normally a senior commissioned officer and a senior noncommissioned enlisted for every unit no matter what level or size it is. Several smaller units make up a bigger one and so on. For example, in the army, a platoon is a small group of soldiers. Several platoons make up a company. Several companies make up a battalion. Several battalions make up a brigade. Several brigades make up a division. And so on. Ask your spouse to help you understand that structure and put names with the positions and ranks so you can understand his chain of command and be aware of who is who.

And you should strive to be equally aware of who you are not. Most people don't care to be bothered with a spouse who wears her husband's rank. In other words, you will be respected for who your spouse is in the chain of command, but don't ever appear to be using his rank to get what you want as if it is something you have earned. A service member is a service member and a spouse is a spouse, period. That being said, military spouses have a chain of concern (not a chain of command) so that they too will receive unit information and get assistance when problems arise. This chain of concern, along with your unit spouses' meetings or Family Readiness Group meetings are effective ways that you will be able to be in the know about what's going on and what's coming up that is most important to you and your husband.

Getting Set Up in Military Housing

As mentioned earlier, military housing on post may be available to your family. And deciding whether to live on post is strictly a matter of preference. When you arrive at your new post, you will have to check in with the housing office to put your name on the waiting list for accommodation. Some families prefer the luxury of not having to go house or apartment hunting, because moving the family is enough work in and of itself. Others don't like to consider living on post because they would rather not have to live in temporary lodging while waiting for housing and then have to move again when quarters become available.

Be aware that sometimes with government quarters, what you get isn't exactly what you expect or want, but the best thing to do is take what you get and move on. You won't be there forever. But in the meantime, here are some tips for making the best of it:

1. While living in base housing put your personal stamp on it and make it a home for your family.
2. Follow the rules and regulations; you will have them no matter where you live. And know that you *can* be evicted from government housing.
3. Don't balk at having to keep up the appearance of your property. That is a perfectly normal responsibility no matter where you live. Expect to get warning notices if you don't comply.
4. Treat it like you bought it.
5. Take the opportunity to pay off debts, put away money in your savings, or invest, since you won't have the additional living expenses associated with living off post.
6. Realize that some installations are now charging for electricity based on whether you exceed the average usage determined for your neighborhood.
7. Stay out of your neighbors' business and keep them out of yours.

Living in a small, close-knit community, there is a common tendency to talk. Don't let it be about you.

8. When it is time to leave, ask your neighbors whether the inspection is difficult to pass. If so, just pay an approved cleaning company and get on with moving to the next location.

YOU KNOW YOU ARE A MILITARY WIFE WHEN . . .

- Losing your ID card is more important that losing your license.
- You stand up for the national anthem before a movie starts even when you are at an off-base theater.
- You can tell how many times you have moved by the number of inventory stickers on the back of your furniture.
- You can say your husband is "only" going away for a few months.
- You know that "dependent" means anything but dependent.
- You have a picture of every child in a Pampers and huge combat boots.
- You know that 0100 hours is 1:00 A.M. and 1300 hours is 1:00 P.M.
- You remember milestones based on where you were stationed.
- You notice mistakes in movies that portray the military.
- All your children were born in different states.
- You have to reach for your social security card when asked for your number because you can't remember it.

Finding Sister-Friendly Goods and Services

We have already talked about the Exchange and the commissary, but there is more to know about shopping on post. Many installations also have specialty shops. There are flower shops, trophy shops, and dry cleaners. There are even salons and barbershops. But do they cater to us? YES!

"Personally, I think it is a misconception that we (black women) can't get good hair care services or products. I have lived in Korea twice and never had a problem. In fact, Japan and Korea have very experienced hairstylists and barbers on post. They do everything: braids, flat irons, relaxers, and cornrows," said Diane, a fortyish army wife of sixteen years. "In Korea, I have found a wide variety of hair care products and cosmetics for black women at the exchange and there are three salons on post that do black hair."

Other women have said that there was a time when products for black women were few, including the right color pantyhose, but according to several women we spoke with, times have changed quite a bit. No matter where you go, there is likely to be a Wal-Mart or Target that carries our products within driving distance. There are some exceptions, however. Plus, "regular" and highly specialized items can be easily purchased online. "I have found that some companies will even discount or waive the shipping cost when shipping to FPO (Fleet Post Office) or APO (Army Post Office) addresses. As I see it, with little or no shipping and not spending money on gas, ordering online comes out a whole lot cheaper," Diane added.

In some really remote places that won't carry our products, you may have to be more creative. "When I was deployed to Iraq, I got my hair braided. I would often have family members send me products from stateside since the local PX didn't carry that many African American products," says Jacqueline, a fortysomething soldier.

Shon Gables, a former army reservist turned nationally syndicated broadcast journalist, says her struggles to find suitable hair care products are still vivid. "I used everything from Vaseline to Crisco on my hair when I couldn't find our stuff," she says (read more about Shon Gables's military experience on page 58).

Michele, a fortysomething army reservist said, "The answer to every deployment was www.Drugstore.com. They ship to APO addresses. From toilet paper to relaxers and curling irons, they were my saving grace along with a network of family and friends to send me the products I love."

If you are new to the area, relocation assistance, employment and volunteer opportunities, and local resources may top your list of transition needs. At some places you will find that the Family Readiness Center offers things like a lending closet from which you can borrow the necessities until your household goods arrive. Many wives have used dishes, pots and pans, small appliances, ironing boards, and all kinds of things that make life easier when living in transit and you don't have the normal comforts of home. The center's employment resources will help you get a jump start on the local job market if you plan to work once you are settled in. Remember this service when you get ready to move again and you can start your job search campaign well in advance of the relocation. You can also make connections with volunteer opportunities, which might be just the thing you need to help you meet people at your new duty station.

"For those who have a hard time meeting people, I would suggest they spend as much time as possible volunteering in places where they enjoy going, like ACS, the library, the child care center, or the bowling alley," says one wife.

Finally, if you want to become familiar with the lay of the land without getting lost in the process, sign up for a tour on post to quickly learn where to find the commissary, PX, child development center, movie theater, bowling alley, fitness center, schools, and more.

Help for Emergencies

If you find yourself facing a personal or financial emergency, there are several aid societies that offer emergency financial assistance through interest-free loans and grants when military families are in need. Emergencies can include transportation, rent, food and utilities, child-care expenses, layettes, funeral expenses, survivor benefits support, budget counseling, essential vehicle repair, disaster relief, education funding, thrift shops, and more. Contact Army Emergency Relief (AER) at www.aerhq.org/ or 866-878-6378, Air Force Aid Society (AFAS) at www.afas.org/ or 800-769-8951, and Navy-Marine Corps Relief Society at www.nmcrs.org/ or 703-696-4904. For after-hours assistance, contact the Armed Forces Emergency Service Center at 877-272-7337.

The American Red Cross provides emergency financial assistance and communication, health and welfare referrals, volunteer opportunities, training courses and opportunities, and more.

Travel and Recreation

The Armed Forces Recreation Center (AFRC) provides luxurious resort lodging at many top vacation destinations, including: Orlando, Florida (www.shadesofgreen.org); Honolulu, Hawaii (www.halekoa.com); Tokyo, Japan (www.thenewsanno.com); Seoul, Korea (www.dragonhilllodge.com); and Garmisch-Partenkirchen, Germany (www.edelweisslodgeandresort .com).

Information, Tickets, and Tours (ITT) offers discounts for recreation and entertainment.

Military Lodging provides temporary, reasonably priced accommodations on a space-available basis for traveling and relocating families. Call for reservations and information:

AF: 888-235-6343
Army: 800-GO-ARMY
Navy: 800-NAVY INN
Marine Corps: www.usmc-mccs.org/lodging
Coast Guard: www.uscg.mil/lodging/Lodging.asp

Education and Career Assistance

Career resource centers conduct seminars and workshops as well as provide career counseling, employment opportunities, job search tools, computers, and other office equipment.

Education centers provide counseling and information on going back to school and funding college and training programs.

Family and Child Assistance

Exceptional family member programs provide information about local special education programs and medical services.

Family advocacy programs give confidential help with child abuse, child neglect, and spouse abuse.

Tax centers offer free tax advice and help with preparing tax forms.

Resources Outside the Gate

Just because you live on or near the military base doesn't mean that you should not venture outside the gates to check out local resources that may also be helpful. Corporate, nonprofit, and community entities want to learn about and help service members and their families. Find out which ones are most active in your area by asking the chaplain staff, family service center staff, or your other resource referral agents on post. You might also check out the website of your family service center, the post relocation office, or the base website to identify the trustworthy ones. Then, call them up and see what they have to offer military families. Again, don't wait until you need something to seek it out. The best approach is to know what's out there right now. A word of caution: be careful not to get involved with the wrong organizations. We strongly recommend only using agencies referred by a military resource.

Surviving the First Year for Service Members

Female service members, especially single ones, have shared lots of different approaches to adjusting to a new community. Since most of you are already familiar with your resources, you told us you prefer to focus on getting to know people in your new community and finding the right balance between work life and personal life.

Tina, a thirty-something air force major, shared her strategy:

"Before moving to my new location, I usually fly in to search for a home in advance. I try to find a home close to the base for convenience and safety, and usually there are lots of business establishments to keep me busy. Since I'm single with no children, I prefer to live in an area with other young, urban professionals like myself for an easier fit.

"I don't like to mix business with pleasure, especially due to the issue of fraternization, so I keep socializing to a minimum with my co-workers. Being a member of Alpha Kappa Alpha Sorority, Inc., I reach out to the local chapter and get connected so I can have an immediate support system. I also meet new people by visiting churches and attending social functions in the local area.

"My duty stations have all been in interesting places, so it's very easy to invite friends and family out for a visit to keep me company. I love to run, so running in my neighborhood also helps me learn about the surrounding area and meet others who are health conscious.

"It may take several months to truly fit in, but eventually the new city, country, or island becomes my 'no place like home,' equipped with learning the new culture, food, interesting sites, and entertainment. There are pros and cons to moving so frequently, but, overall, exploring the world at Uncle Sam's expense has been a rewarding experience for me. I've made friends that will last a lifetime and the memories are priceless!"

Debra, a forty-something army reserve captain, described leaving her twenty-year, well-established life in North Carolina when she was called to duty:

"I was mobilized in May 2005 to Fort Jackson, South Carolina, for twelve months. Although the mobilization was here in the States, it was still a huge burden on me and my family. You would have thought the scenario was simple: I am a single soldier, I have no children, and my family is located forty-five minutes from my assignment, but it was difficult to leave family, friends, and a twenty-year well-established life in North Carolina.

"I was thirty-five when I mobilized and I had recently met a nice man, I was settled at my job, and I was at peace with my life. When I mobilized, I had to start all over again in a new city, plus I had to put my existing life on hold for twelve months, which ultimately became eighteen months. The army did a very good job ensuring that I had nice and adequate lodging; however, there is no place like home—whether it is one hour away or a hundred hours away.

"Once I arrived in the Fort Jackson area, the relocation itself wasn't that bad, nor was it that hard to adjust to my work assignment. The major adjustment was in my personal life and balancing it with my military profession. As a civilian, you can date and see friends at your leisure and your time is not restricted; however, serving full-time in the military, while my personal life was still at home in North Carolina—it was a challenge. I realized my desire to have a personal life conflicted with my desire to have an army career because my time no longer belonged to me.

"As time went on, I was able to balance my army life and my personal life. And then, things became so much easier. And, since my boyfriend supported my mission and my ambitions to being an outstanding officer, the burden became a blessing."

Vernice Armour, Marine Corps. Captain

Vernice Armour has seen a lot of history. She holds the distinction of being the first Black female combat pilot and has served two tours in Iraq. What's more, her father and grandfather served in the military. The roots run deep. Still, from the vantage point of such a rich heritage, Armour sees something missing.

"Back during segregation, when Black folks traveled to a brand-new city, they would get off the bus and just stand there on the corner. They wouldn't go anywhere until another Black person walked up to them and told them where it was safe to go. That's because the last thing you wanted to do as a Black person was to wander off in a city on the wrong side of the tracks.

"I believe it used to be that way in the military, too. When you saw a new young couple trying to navigate the minefields of life or the military lifestyle, there were people waiting there to help them when they stepped off the bus," she said.

"But now there is a mentality that everything is equal, everything is fine, and that the playing field is a lot more even in the military world. So I don't think people view it as much of a necessity to reach out like they used to do," Vernice adds.

One thing that is extremely critical, Armour said, is recognizing that the ultimate responsibility for your success with military life lies with you. She offers this advice for any wife, fiancée, girlfriend, service member mother, sister, or aunt whose life is touched by military service.

Write your own book.

It is your life and you are sharing that life with your partner, spouse, and family. Even though you are making a life together, you have to bring something to the table. What is it in your life that you love or are passionate about that you can share with your family? Don't lose who you are. I can't tell you how many times I get, "Hi, I'm John's wife." I always say, "Hi, John's wife, what's your name?"

Strengthen the team without leaving your identity at the door.
You don't have to assimilate. Bring your thoughts, your diversity, and everything you are to the table. That strengthens the team and people should know what strengths you possess.

Bloom where you are planted.
Make the best of your situation. Sure, you may not like that duty station because it will take you away from your family, friends, and job. But are you going to hang on to that discontent and frustration or are you going to look for the lessons and opportunity at your feet? There are always opportunities; they don't go away, other people take advantage of them. Find the opportunity and blow it out of the water. Make that duty station or assignment the best one ever!

GET OFFICIAL
∽ USE THIS CHECKLIST TO HAVE EVERYTHING YOU NEED TO BE "OFFICIAL" AS AN MS. ∽

The must-haves
Marriage certificate
DEERS enrollment
Military identification card

The helpful-to-haves
On-post vehicle registration
Power of attorney
Name on all financial accounts
Passwords to online accounts
Ability to cite your spouse's social security number forward and backward
    (to access important information)
Ability to pack and move with little notice
Flexibility
Positive attitude

GET CONNECTED
FOLLOW THESE TIPS TO BE SUPERCONNECTED IN NO TIME.

- Attend unit FRG meetings to get unit information, but also to meet others who can introduce you to community groups
- Attend PTA meetings at your child's school; the members are usually very familiar with community organizations.
- Read the local paper for the surrounding cities as well as the free weekly base newspaper that is usually available at places you frequent on post, like the commissary, family service centers, the Exchange, the bank, and the rec centers.
- Attend community forums on post. Representatives from all organizations attend to provide updates on activities, events, services, and classes. Usually the forums are monthly or quarterly.
- Sign up for fitness classes, volunteer opportunities, or an arts and crafts class to meet people of varying interests.
- Visit the library on post and off post as well as the Family Readiness Center for listings of organizations.

GET YOUR STUFF
A GIRL NEEDS HER FAVORITE PRODUCTS; DON'T BE WITHOUT YOURS.

- Sally Beauty Supply, www.sallybeauty.com: Ships to continental U.S., P.O. boxes, Alaska, Hawaii. Does not ship to international, APO, or FPO addresses.
- Drugstore.com, www.drugstore.com: Ships to continental U.S., Alaska, Hawaii, U.S. territories, APO, FPO.
- Black Expressions Book Club, www.blackexpression.com: Ships to

continental U.S., Alaska, Hawaii, APO, and FPO addresses. Does not ship to international addresses.

- CVS, www.cvs.com: Ships to any valid U.S. address (including P.O. boxes, with some exceptions), APO and FPO addresses, U.S. territories of Guam, U.S. Virgin Islands, American Samoa, and Puerto Rico.
- Wal-Mart, www.walmart.com: Ships to fifty states, APO and FPO military addresses, American Samoa, Guam, Northern Mariana Islands, Palau, Puerto Rico, and the U.S. Virgin Islands.

Pamela's Pick: Keepin' It Tight

Now that you've got your man or your new service career, how can you keep yourself looking your best, which for us means feeling our best? I've asked some experts to weigh in on maintaining bouncing and behaving, healthy hair and glowing skin if you have a military lifestyle.

Hair

Who needs hair drama when you are dealing with the stress of relocation? Not me and not you. So I spoke with Lovie, a former salon owner, current hairstylist in Georgia, and wife of a former marine. She gave me these tips for getting the look you want no matter where Uncle Sam sends you:

1. Try a chain salon like Fantastic Sam's or Super Cuts. All the stores have the same standards so there should be a certain degree of consistency when it comes to quality and services they provide.
2. Use department store salons. Although they are usually high-end, they also spend more time with you.
3. Ask your stylist to recommend daily products that can be purchased in chain store drugstores like CVS, Walgreen's, and Rite-Aid.

4. Use natural products.

5. Ask around. Using word of mouth is always a good bet. When a sister's hair is tight, tell her so, and then ask her for the phone number of who hooked it up.

6. Purchase the goods online using the websites of your favorite beauty supply stores, like Sally Beauty Supply at www.sally .beauty.com, which, by the way, offers a military discount.

Other spouses said:

When people who you know will be traveling to a more populated area, ask them to shop for you. When we were stationed in Korea and I traveled to Hawaii, many people gave me money to bring back things from the hair supply store or from Wal-Mart. Then we would just purchase it in large quantities. There are always people, wherever you are, who have lived there awhile and know how to work things out to get whatever is needed. Just ask sisters who look like they use products similar to what you use.

—Von, twenty-year army wife.

I love a short haircut but I worry at every duty station whether I will find someone who can do my hair the way I like it. I get accustomed to someone every time, but they can't PCS with me so I have learned to improvise. I go through the ugly stage but I always maintain a fresh perm and am savvy with the curling iron. Sometimes I let it grow out and then fuss and complain until I start looking around (at other black women's hairstyles). One time, I ran across a store just to ask a lady where she got her hair done.

—Nicole Brown, eleven-year army spouse who has spent nearly four years in Germany.

More Than Skin Deep

To get the lowdown on keeping your skin healthy and radiant, I chatted with Frances Jackson, who is now an independent sales director for Mary Kay and the wife of a twenty-seven-year retired military man.

Pamela: *Based on your experiences as a military wife for twenty-seven years, why do you think we need to share tips about skin care with military wives?*

Frances: Military spouses place everyone's needs before their own. We tend to see the beauty in others and forgo our own. Forgetting oneself is to set oneself back so that others advance. After tending to others, we are too tired to do our own maintenance, and we can crumble.

Pamela: *Why is good skin care essential to being at your best?*

Frances: It keeps the immune system as well as your outer being healthier. And it makes you feel wonderful as well.

Pamela: *What do you say to women who tell you: "I just don't have time for a long, drawn-out beauty regimen in the morning; and by the time the day is over, I don't have the energy for one"?*

Frances: Don't you think you deserve to be pampered? You take care of everyone else; why would you not think of yourself as well? Once you feel the cleanliness of the skin you will feel reenergized and have a robust feeling.

Pamela: *What are the top five basic things every woman should do to get the healthy skin they deserve?*

Frances: Cleanse and moisturize day and night. Use antiaging products for your eyes and lips. Use products that contain sun protection with SPFs during all seasons. Have a healthy diet. And use exfoliation (like scrubs) to remove dead skin cells.

Mind, Body, and Spirit

There's no point being glamorous on the outside, if things aren't right on the inside. Dealing with stresses of separation, deployment, and uncertain times requires some serious mental and spiritual fortitude. Here's how to get yours.

Michele Spencer, a registered yoga instructor and twenty-two-year service member, shares her thoughts on getting to your authentic self through yoga. She was deployed to Baghdad during what was called "the killing season," a period of severely violent attacks between Iran and Iraq in the late 1980s. It was a very frightening time.

"When I was in Baghdad, there were people dying all around and helicopters falling out of the sky. It was very important to me to share that wherever we are at any given time, from Baghdad to Boston to Bakersville to Atlanta, we have to take a much needed mental escape. We were going a hundred million miles a minute and forgetting to breathe. We were forgetting to connect with ourselves because we were in a place that wants you not to be human. A war zone is not a very nurturing place. When you are wearing a uniform, in body armor, carrying around weapons all day, and riding around in armored vehicles, it is humanly degrading," she said. By teaching more than 150 yoga classes to more than twenty-seven hundred students in Baghdad, Michele feels like she brought energetic healing to that space. You can reap the same benefits.

How can yoga help military spouses?

"It's about stepping out of the cacophony of what's in your head," advised Michele. "Think about a monkey jumping from tree to tree. Does your mind constantly jump from thought to thought with all the things you have to do? Perhaps it goes something like this: feed the kids, pick them up from school, take them to tumbling and football, get your groceries, go to the post office, go back and pick up the kids, make dinner, get them to bed, pay the bills, start the laundry. . . . That's what is known in the world of yoga as the monkey mind," Michele says.

If you have been looking for a way to send that monkey packing, yoga is just what you need. By focusing on your breathing, you use it as a tool to remain in the present moment, rather than letting your monkey mind take over.

According to Michele, deep breathing actually gives your body more oxygen that it craves so you will be able to think clearer and recognize that even if you are in a stressful situation, you do have control by being present. And when you expand the breath through the mindfulness of presence and add a movement, as in a yoga posture, the movement creates the energetic flow for the body to really move, so that you can get an even deeper sense of your awareness.

"This opens up your heart and opens up your ears. That means you listen more deeply and have more compassion. Being able to open up your heart and speak your truth is the stress reducer because you are more authentic. Whenever you come from a place of authenticity, you are able to heal parts of yourself that are in need of healing. You are not trying to make up a lie, you're not trying to figure out how to say it better, you are just speaking from your heart," she says.

"This will help you get centered so that you don't freak out when things seem like they are caving in on you. We'd rather not really look at our fear and then move through it. But that is how we start to heal. Before you know it, you can let go of some of those habits that you thought you were attached to, like smoking, being overweight, having toxic thoughts of low self-esteem, draining friends and relatives, or a job that no longer serves you.

"So start now—BREATHE!"

Shon Gables, Army Private

Shon Gables is an award-winning, nationally syndicated television host, and by the looks of her camera-ready appearance and designer suits, you wouldn't believe she cut her teeth in the U.S. Army Reserves for six years. As a self-proclaimed "Private Benjamin," referring to the Goldie Hawn movie character where a spoiled and clueless woman naively joins the army, Shon credits the army for teaching her discipline, focus, and how to make a mean bed.

Shon shares her perspectives on surviving her rude awakening, using Crisco on your hair in a pinch, and dealing with natural desires when you're a sister soldier.

No Money for College

What drew me into the military was that I had a scholarship to attend the University of Oklahoma and I lost it in my freshman year. I lost my focus and went from being an honor student to failing. My mom said I couldn't come back home. I had royally screwed up a great opportunity, and I needed to do something drastic to make me appreciate what I had lost. I have six siblings, and four of them were in the military. They would call and say how much they hated it. I figured if I had a similar experience, then I would appreciate college. And miss college.

I called the recruiter for air force and army reserves. I decided to go with the army reserves and be a weekend warrior. Even though I tested well on the assessment test, which recommended that I pursue an officer route, I joined as an enlisted PFC. I was sent to Fort Jackson, South Carolina, for the twelve-week basic training and had the wake-up call of my life. I was the black female version of the movie character Private Benjamin, played by Goldie Hawn. Plus I had a severe defiant attitude against authority. The first day I got there, as we crossed the entrance of Fort Jackson, and the drill sergeant started yelling in our faces, I said loudly, "Um, excuse me, why are you yelling?" And it was downhill from there.

The Boot Camp Wake-Up Call

I had a lot of anger and blamed it on everyone but myself. I had a major transformation in basic training. They took this wild stallion of a twenty-year-old and tamed me. I began to respect authority, to recognize the value of team-work, to focus on integrity, and to understand the importance of honoring all contracts (financial or otherwise).

A Debt of Gratitude

I'm very grateful for the experience now. I have the discipline and persever-ance that I would never have without seven years of army reserves. I realize that the army is not just preparing you for war, but preparing you to be a good cor-porate and civic citizen. It is a character-molding experience.

The Harsh Realities

For one, segregation is as apparent in the military as it is in everyday life. The enlisted ranks are disproportionately black. When I was enlisted, there was always a depressing lack of goods and services for people of color. I've used baby oil, lotion, and even Crisco on my hair in desperation when I couldn't find our products in the locality.

Military career? Thanks, but no thanks.

I joined as a private first class and left as a private first class. I was only there to get money for college and had no interest in becoming a career reservist or service member. I turned down every promotion opportunity. But it wonder-fully leveraged for my career as a journalist.

Five Tips from the Wise

1. Understand your objectives. Are you in it for a career or not?
2. If this will be your career, seek a mentor who is a seasoned veteran.
3. Take the time to know your rights. As a female you are guaranteed certain rights and privileges. People will usurp those rights from you.
4. I advise every female to remain abstinent during basic and advanced training duties. This allows you to stay focused and not have the emotional baggage of dealing with a relationship that is probably not going to happen.
5. Have fun.

The Mocha Mix
Real Talk on Surviving the First Year
as a Military Spouse

★ ★

For me, it was not about surviving. It was exciting to do something new and different. I am ok with change. If you are not the type of person who likes change, it will be a difficult life.

—LaTanya, Air Force wife

My first deployment was very difficult. I had a new baby and I spent most of my time crying. After a few weeks, I packed up and went to stay with relatives in New York for about a month. After I got it together, every deployment has been easier and easier. Now, they seem to fly by!

—Lynette, Fort Bragg

Settling in to a new location . . .

Although this advice may sound too easy, it is really the truth: stay positive and open to making the moves. I have lived in Kansas, North Carolina, Georgia, and northern Virginia since marrying a military officer in 2000. We are now getting ready to return to Georgia. With each move I become an active part of the community by attending area churches and joining groups, many of which I have a membership or affiliation with already. For example, I am a member of Mocha Moms and Delta Sigma Theta Sorority, Inc., and both of these national organizations have chapters all over the country. So when I move, I can join the local chapters in my area. I am also an avid reader and published writer, so I join or start book clubs and even joined a writers group in Kansas.

I basically don't reinvent my life. I build on the life I already have when I move to different areas of the country. My interests and affiliations don't change, so I make connections based on who I am and what I like to do. I will admit that some assignments are better than others, but it is the open mind, sense of adventure, and knowledge that it is not forever that makes each move workable and manageable.

—LORRAINE, ARMY WIFE

Get lost, literally! With or without a GPS, I grab my telephone book and my trusty road atlas and go for a ride. Map out a few places that are about five to ten miles away from your house, starting with common places like banks, grocery stores, schools, malls, and my personal favorites, TJ Maxx or Ross. I make note of landmarks so I can find my way back home. It is important to understand how streets are directionally (N, S, W, E) and try to maintain your bearings. Take calculated risks when venturing out to new surroundings but do not become hostage to your home and workplace. Consult the Sunday paper for outings that the family can participate in—local community concerts, arts, and sports. Get involved!

—MICHELE, ARMY RESERVE MAJOR

Service Member Survival
I have been a member of the ROCKS association for years. The ROCKS is an organization comprised of black military officers. I always try to find a chapter when I relocate to make the transition smoothly.

—JACQUELINE, ARMY

Mrs. Evelyn McDew

Military life is full of challenges for spouses. Mrs. Evelyn McDew, wife of U.S. Air Force Lieutenant General Edward A. Rice Jr., shares how spouses can make the life work for them.

Learn Everything

My biggest passion during my many years as a military spouse is taking care of the Family Readiness Centers and I support them 100 percent. Every spouse, no matter how much or how little time she has been married to the military, must stay abreast of what services are offered and how to access them. Furthermore, we all have to take the responsibility to not only get educated ourselves, but to also share the information with our fellow military spouses.

There is no secret to learning all you can about what the military has to offer. Just walk into any Family Readiness Center on base and ask, "What do you have to offer me." They will go through all the programs, give you dates and times of activities and programs, and even sign you up for them on the spot. I got to the point that every time we moved, I would just drive around on base and go into different buildings and ask questions. I also would get a copy of the base newspaper each week, read it from cover to cover, and call around to ask questions about the things that caught my eye. I will never stop doing these things because no matter where we are stationed, I want to be a part of the base and I want to know everything about it there is to know. There will never be a time when you know it all because new things develop every day, and I want to know about them for me and for every other spouse I can tell about them. It can take a lot of time, but it's worth it. However, it's not enough to just get the overview; you have to go back to get the details about the resources and then, you have to use the resources.

Help Spread the Word

As for spreading the word, we need everyone's help in educating every single military spouse. We have a huge problem in getting spouses into the centers.

When we don't take this responsibility seriously, there are so many spouses and children who don't get what they need to thrive in this lifestyle despite the difficulties. I have seen and heard it all, from one spouse whose military ID card was about to expire and she thought she couldn't come on base to a woman with three children with a deployed dad and nothing to do all summer. The family thought they were not allowed to come on base to use the swimming pools, rec centers, day camps, youth centers, and other activities without being escorted by the service member or having proper military ID. This is not the case.

We have to earn the trust of our fellow military ladies, and the only way to do that is to go out and talk to them. Tell them what is out there and how to access it. Accompany them to the centers if we have to. The service members have a lot going on and just don't typically fill their spouses in on all the programs, so it is really up to us to join hands with each other and get the job done.

Connect on Base

Another great resource is the base information sessions. Although they may differ from place to place, the objective is to bring together representatives from different on-base agencies in an effort to provide information to help military families manage day-to-day issues as well as crises that may arise. One project I am particularly proud of is when I brought together the chaplains and a school liaison to talk with the spouses in confidence about what problems there were and how we could solve them. We provided dinner and activities for the kids to make sure we had as many participants as possible.

Getting involved will always be the key to knowing your resources, meeting new people, building a support system, and giving back to others, all of which are vital to managing and enjoying life as a military family.

CHAPTER THREE

When Honey Is Away

Dealing with Separation and Deployment

There's no doubt about it, deployment is the toughest part of military life. Being separated from the person you love, while you are left to raise the children, manage the house, and make sure life continues as "normal" as possible is a balancing act of mythical proportions. Of course, when you fall in love and choose a life with a service member, you understand that there will be deployments. But what you don't often get is how frequent these will be. And no one tells you that even before the actual deployment begins, your spouse will be away from home a lot in training to prepare for the deployment. And they certainly don't tell you that just when you've gotten over the crying spells, lonely nights, figuring out how to fix the garbage disposal on your own, and settling into a routine that works, your mate will return and quite likely throw everything into a tailspin. Uugghhh! After the initial welcome home, a military spouse's return can be as traumatic as his departure. Feelings of resentment and anger can be expected. You want a pat on the back for holding down the fort in his absence, but he may still be emotionally distant while dealing with whatever happened during deployment. You've been doing things your way, and now it's time to include him in the decision making and house operations. Trust us, from the moment he receives his orders until weeks or months after his return you will be living, breathing, eating, and sleeping the effects of deployment.

In this chapter, you'll learn about all the stages of deployment, what military tools are available to help, and what girlfriend advice is out there from other military spouses on making the best of all phases of deployment. We've gleaned a lot of experiences with separation and deployment. Not only have we surveyed hundreds of military spouses, but we have Pamela's firsthand experience. Just weeks after getting engaged, her husband-to-be, Doug, left her in Massachusetts, where she completed her senior year in college, to attend his officer basic course in Maryland. "A few months later, after graduation, I got on the Amtrak train one Thursday and we were married on that Saturday. While I still bask in the afterglow of that day, the realities of military wifehood came soon after the Kodak moments ended. I am certain that military marriage vows should certainly include something like . . . 'Dearly beloved, we are gathered here today to witness this couple . . . for better or for worse, in sickness and in health, in separation and deployment . . .' because what I thought would be a few months of separation turned out to be a whole lot more. Not only did we spend the first six months of our marriage living in two different states, Massachusetts and Texas (his first duty station), but when the day finally came for me to join him, he left two weeks later to attend training for thirty days in California! There I was in a brand-new state, with no family, no job, no friends, and no husband. Then, less than three months after his return, he was sent to Saudi Arabia for seven months."

This kind of separation is typical for an MS. And with an uncertain global future, deployments are more common than ever before. You've got to be ready. Now that you know we understand what you are going through, let's get you prepared for your own deployment dance.

Prepare Yourself

Ladies, this is the reality. Separation is not only inevitable in military life, but highly likely to be the norm as long as he wears the uniform. Olga Carson-Thomas, a thirtysomething military wife of ten years, experienced the same. "It would seem that since we got married we spend more time apart than together. I have been separated from my other half many times whether through deployments, field rotations, or TDYs. I feel alone, and at times I will jokingly tell my friends that I am a single mother. I know that he is always there for me, but sometimes I feel as if I am in this boat all by myself and I have to learn how to keep that boat afloat."

Like Olga, so many wives feel like single parents. And in reality, you are. And you won't always be a happy camper about it. Your life as a military spouse could be full of times when you look up and there he goes again, off to somewhere else, leaving you to handle the household *and* parenting responsibilities, in addition to balancing a well of mixed emotions. You will feel anger for having to do this again, fear for his personal safety, and ticked off because you know that as soon as he leaves, something, anything, will stop working or go wrong.

Seasoned wives know the drill. "For me, it was always the air-conditioning unit. It was so frustrating. One time I called in the repairman and paid $65 only to have the technician tell me that the circuit breaker had tripped and caused the A/C unit to stop working. I felt really dumb. Then I felt even worse when my husband called. He said, 'The technician must know that a man is not in the house because that is the first thing we would have done.' I was completely upset. And my husband's comments didn't help. I am trying to do the job of two persons and if it was not for the children I probably would have just given up this whole life," says Carson-Thomas. That kind of frustration can happen.

Becoming the CinC

Don't give up. Breakdowns will inevitably happen; just do your best to manage the appliance kind and try to prevent the personal kind. Instead, take a deep breath, and have confidence that you can handle whatever situation you face. Know that you are not the first or the last woman to face the complicated world of military wifehood, and you can be successful as others have. The reality is that you will have to "wear the pants." You are now the CinC of the house. In military speak, that means commander in chief.

It doesn't hurt to learn how to do simple repairs and even car maintenance before your spouse leaves. Many wives have learned how to check the oil and handle the lawn mower, and Pamela even got a little better acquainted with the septic system.

One evening an alarm sounded at Pamela's house and she had no idea what it was. She searched high and low for hours trying to figure out where it was coming from and finally discovered an unfamiliar box and switch downstairs in the same room that houses the hot water heater. "Who would I call to fix it if I didn't even know what that box was?" Pamela says. "First stop, my dad. Well, he had no idea what the box was, but he suggested I open all the windows just in case my husband had installed some high-tech carbon monoxide detector.

Next? When my son's friend's father came to pick up the boys, he looked around with me and all the kids in tow. He had no idea either. Next? I called the company that handles our yearly heating and air-conditioning maintenance and even they didn't have a clue. At this point, the best I could do was turn off the annoying sound of the alarm, say a prayer, and send my husband an e-mail.

"It was almost midnight here and around 8:00 A.M. in Iraq so I hoped he would respond by the time I woke up. A couple hours later, both he and God answered my prayers with a 'rescue call' from Iraq. And of course my hero told me the source of the problem and who to call to get it resolved. I slept like a baby once we completed a two-way call with a twenty-four-hour repair service that would send someone over first thing in the morning," Pamela recalls. "I try my best to resolve it, but if I can't, I ask my husband for help."

The most important thing we learned from talking to wives is that they have to learn to ask for help. I think this is a problem with black women in general. We often suffer from the Strong Black Woman syndrome (SBW). We try to do all, be all, and fix all with a big S on our chests and a red cape blowing in the wind. It's exhausting and unhealthy. Being an SBW means being strong enough to know when to get assistance. It also means being strong enough to say no without guilt to energy-sapping, emotionally draining demands or people who take you away from your core responsibilities. You can't save everybody all the time. And knowing that makes you a very smart SBW.

Next you have to trust your instincts. Sure, you'd love the luxury of having a second person to share in the decision making, but the reality is that if you waited for your husband's call or e-mail to handle all matters, a heck of a lot of problems would pile up. As the CinC of the house, sometimes you have to make executive decisions. To make the best ones, take an honest look at "how you do business." Look at how you plan and organize, how you manage the children and your life, and how much support you have.

Time for a Little Self-Assessment and Managing Expectations

How you do business can also include how you take care of yourself. With so much riding on your decision-making skills and support, don't take it for granted that your judgment will be sound if you don't take time to take care of you, including proper rest, good nutrition, and some serious me time. Then and only then will you be able to manage everything else. Then and only then will you be in the best shape to support him in his mission and have a stronger relationship.

As any military wife will tell you, the key to surviving deployment is learning as much as possible and then managing your expectations. So what can you expect during deployment? Brace yourself for an emotional roller-coaster ride. You know the one. When you walk into the park and buckle yourself in, you fully understand that you're about to go through stomach-churning ups and downs. But you also know that you will never get the full effect of the ride until you are in the front, no matter how many times you've been on it. Long-term separation due to military deployment can be the same way. The best thing you can do during this potentially emotional time is to understand the cycle of emotions you will encounter during the five specific stages of deployment and get in the front seat.

These stages are known as predeployment, deployment, sustainment, redeployment, and postdeployment. By being prepared, managing your expectations, and giving yourself and your husband "permission" to experience and overcome the full range of emotions, you will decrease the level of stress you both may encounter and significantly increase your ability to cope.

Predeployment

Predeployment basically covers the time frame from when you find out he will be deployed to the time that he actually leaves. And it's hardly ever predictable. The time frame could be months or it could be weeks; the call just comes when it comes. And when it does, denial, disbelief, anticipation of loss, and even anger are all normal feelings.

Carson-Thomas recalls a time when her husband was told that he would be exempted from a deployment to Iraq. She was relieved because otherwise it would be their first deployment to a war zone. But it didn't take long for the tables to turn. "We were having dinner one evening when the phone rang and he was told to start packing because he would be moving out with his soldiers within two weeks' time. I was mad at him even though I knew it was not his fault. I was really angry. In my opinion, I could see no reason why he or anyone else had to be sent (over) there, and all I could think about was that he would be gone for an entire year. It just was not fair," she says.

Once the denial dissipates and spouses realize that things are not going to change, most of them want to bond more with their life partners, but instead feel frustrated by the fact that it seems like the service member wants to bond less. In addition, an increase in training and preparation for the deployment requires more hours at work and therefore fewer hours at home. However, once a spouse truly understands that the training is absolutely necessary for the safety of the service members when they are "on the ground," it does make sense.

But in many cases there might be something deeper going on. "I used to get offended when my husband started acting so cold and distant right before a deployment until he explained to me that disconnecting from us emotionally and mentally was his way of dealing with the fact that he had to leave us," said Von, a forty-five-year-old mother of two.

At this time you might feel resentment and then guilt for feeling like you wish they would just hurry up and go. You might feel like it would be easier to cope with their being away than their being home but not really being "psychologically present."

"Just be patient with him. He's not mad at you, and there is nothing wrong with your relationship. He's just doing what he needs to do to let go. My husband never sleeps in our bed the night before he leaves. His ritual is to stay up all night packing, tending to business, and things like that. I have just come to accept it," said Von.

HANDLING HOUSEHOLD BUSINESS

At this point, it's time to settle into the reality that a plan for handling household business needs to be in place and the emotions need to move to the back burner. Before your service member departs, make sure you discuss and organize financial, legal, and other matters that will have to be taken care of solely by you. (See our checklist on pages 74–76.) One helpful way to do this is to make sure all important documents are in one place. For example, Pamela's husband created a three-ring binder that contains items like life insurance policies, general and special powers of attorney, last will and testament, vehicle registration information, and military points of contact. On the financial side, he set up automatic payments of many bills, making bill paying one less thing she had to do. The binder also had most of the purchase, warranty, and repair contacts for things like appliances and vehicles for easy reference.

Also, as mentioned earlier, make sure everyone in the family is properly enrolled in the Defense Enrollment Eligibility Reporting System (DEERS). It is the only way you will be able to receive TRICARE medical benefits. And make sure that none of the family military identification cards are going to expire while he is deployed. Getting a new one always seems much easier when the husband is around. Explain deployment to your children and how it will impact their life. Prepare yourself to understand the indicators of deployment-related stress in your child and make plans for how you will deal with it.

"You never know how they are going to react. My youngest child took it really hard when his dad left the first time. He cried a lot and he was moody and always upset. My older one became withdrawn and would act out in school at times. I handled that situation by making each day all about them. We went on excursions and I made their days fun and filled with activities. This kept their mind off the deployment. The days were hectic and tiring but they were happy and coping with daddy being away," says Carson-Thomas.

Once all these things are in order, it may be easier for the more personal and intimate things to come back into play before he departs.

Dealing with the Anxiety

Planning for the last of your special occasions together and trying to make each one of them "the best," as well as trying to be together romantically, seem like the right things to do, but sometimes the exact opposite happens. While striving to get everything "just right" and coping with the "transition of authority," the anxiety that is created by the feeling of loss can lead to a *big* argument or two. Even the closest couples have them, so don't be too hard on yourself or your hubby if this happens. The stress of this difficult time is the culprit, not you, and not him. But there are steps you can take to make this easier.

"Start taking over the responsibilities little by little as soon as he finds out he has to leave. By the time that day comes, you will have worked out the rough spots, been able to ask for his help with understanding or learning new things, and already be used to shouldering the responsibilities alone," Von advises.

Establish and *Use* Support Systems

Plan to ask for help. Like I said, we sisters have a tendency to want to do it all and not ask for help, but at a time like this, you have to have people to fall back on. In no way are you showing any sign of weakness by doing so. Establish your support systems before the deployment—just in case. And if need be, don't be afraid to ask an available mother, grandmother, sister, or friend to live with you until he returns.

Family and friends can provide much needed help during this time. They want to help, but they may not know what would be most helpful, so don't be shy about telling them. If they live close by, they can help with the logistics of parenthood, so ask for it instead of trying to do everything. Now is the perfect time to coordinate carpools and playdates. If they live far away, let them know that just having their ear when you need it or getting a call to see how things are going will be just as helpful as anything else they can do.

Pamela's Pick: Family Support

When my husband, Doug, was preparing to deploy I was fortunate to have my dad around. He bought a house six miles from our house in Georgia and eventually relocated from Massachusetts in order to be front and center, ready to help us. Doug would be stationed more than three hundred miles away for the entire year leading up to his fifteen-month deployment, but would commute the almost four hours home to see us on every weekend he could. My dad helped me out in so many ways over those few years (and he still does) I probably couldn't count them if I tried. He did everything—from helping me shuttle around our children and their friends to their activities, to yardwork, to minor repairs, to staying at my house with the kids when I left town on sometimes too frequent business trips. Other friends and family called to check on us and to offer help. There's nothing like knowing that people in your support system are there when and if you need them.

Be prepared, though, to set boundaries with some of your family and friends if needed. "I have had family members call each time they watched the news and saw or heard that bombs went off to ask if my husband was okay. This was very stressful for me and I had to put a stop to it. I told them I really do not watch the news that has anything to do with the war because it traumatizes me and the children. In a nice way I told them not to call and tell me about bombs going off and my motto was "no news is good news." As long as no one rang my doorbell, he was okay and that kept me going on a daily basis," says Carson-Thomas, whose husband spent nearly two years in Iraq.

Be sure to create an additional support system for your children by explaining the situation to their teachers, coaches, and other caregivers who will spend a lot of time with them. Experts agree that it's important for them to be aware so they can be supportive. For instance, if your child's behavior changes, the teachers, coaches, and other caregivers might notice it before you do. After all, they spend a lot of time with your child, too. It helps to have several sets of eyes and ears on the lookout for these changes so they can be addressed before they develop into bigger problems.

CHECK IN ON THE CHILDREN

Make sure your children understand as much as possible about why your mate will deploy. "When my husband was first sent to Iraq, our daughter tripped out," recalls Nicole, mother of three. "I had to sit her down and explain that when Daddy is here on post, he is training. What he does when he is away at war is his actual job. I told her that he protects our country and defends our freedom. Even though it's hard, and she hates to see him go, she understands that she has to do it. Now that she's twelve she loves to share her daddy with her friends when their dads are gone. And they do the same for her."

GATHER FRIENDS AND FAMILY

It's easy to view deployment as a downer. And for good reason. But your husband (and you!) may actually enjoy gathering friends and family together for a big celebration before he leaves. Finally, your hubby might well benefit from having a big celebration before he leaves. Gathering friends and family can offer so much more than just a party. Being with friends and family creates fun memories that he takes with him, allows him to feel the love before he heads off, and reminds him of all the people who can support his family in his absence. That's a welcome respite from a time filled with much stress and uncertainty. Such get-togethers have always been important for Pamela's family, and it always gives Doug a chance to show off his grill skills.

Predeployment Checklist

You've got a lot on your mind, so use the following list to make sure all the necessary bases are covered.

- Decide, *together,* where you will live. For some, it will be better to stay at the location where you are stationed because you will get unit information more easily and there are others to support you. For others, going back home where family support is strong is a better decision. Either way, you could be in for constant conflict if you decide on your own after he leaves and he disagrees with your decision.
- Get your man's official mailing address while deployed and e-mail it to other family members. That will cut down on potentially having to repeatedly reply to e-mails requesting it.
- Make sure you have all the contact information for the rear detachment personnel (military people left behind to liaison between families and unit).
- Know who will be e-mailing updates from the unit, and make sure your name is on their e-mail list.
- Make sure you have emergency numbers in one place and that both sets of parents know who to call in an emergency.
- Make sure at least several other spouses and neighbors have phone numbers for a few of your relatives and know how to contact you if you leave town.
- Attend any meetings, briefings, or get-togethers prior to the deployment so you will know what to expect and form some relationships that could become part of your support system.
- Inform your children's teachers and coaches about the deployment.
- Obtain an up-to-date copy of the post information booklet that contains organizations available on and off post and emergency contact numbers.
- Give a trusted friend or neighbor a duplicate set of house and car keys.

- Find out if the local law enforcement on or off post will complete a safety check of your home. Make sure you or they check all detectors and alarms. Purchase replacement batteries so you have them on hand when they need to be changed.

- Have all vehicles fully inspected and repaired if needed. Join an auto club like AAA or Allstate or make sure your insurance covers towing. Decide what repair shops should be used.

- Gather all warranties and other paperwork for major appliances, determine who will repair them, and locate all customer service numbers and keep them in a handy place.

- Review safety, emergency, and natural disaster procedures with your children. Be careful in your presentation of this review; the last thing you want to do is give them something else to worry about (i.e., not only might Dad be in danger, but something could happen to us, too).

- Develop a family budget taking into account the change in income, whether it be more or less than the usual. For the most part, active component personnel will receive extra pay. However, reserve component personnel could have a decrease in pay if their civilian job pays more than their military one. Don't forget to decide how to handle emergency expenses.

- Know all the financial and computer passwords, especially for accounts online.

- Set up automatic payments for regular bills, if you are comfortable with the amounts not potentially exceeding your deposits. That's twenty fewer things on your plate each month. Make sure you have all credit card information and access. If the card expires while hubby is away, payments can't resume until authorization is received; if you are not an authorized user on the account, this could turn into a real pain in the neck.

- Gather all important documents that require annual renewal or other action; for example, car registration (on and off post), income taxes, insurance paperwork, warranties, and so on. Keep a copy at home and a second copy in a safe deposit box or with a relative. (Make sure someone you trust, other than your mate, has access to the safe deposit box in case of an emergency.)

· Draw up a will and power of attorney just like your spouse did in the unlikely event something happens to you while he is away. Determine who will step in to help in any emergency situation and go over the documents with him or her.

๏ PREDEPLOYMENT CHECKLIST FOR SINGLE MILITARY PARENTS AND DUAL-CAREER COUPLES ๏

Complete a family care plan to designate who will take care of your children if you both have to deploy. Then, prepare your caregivers with the following:

· Complete all-about-me forms with favorite foods, toys, pastimes, fears, sleeping habits, allergies, illnesses, medications, doctors, dentist, and so on.

· Discuss rules with caregiver and children together.

· Discuss with children how to communicate with you. Provide e-mail address and purchase stationery, stamps, envelopes, and so on.

· Organize birth certificates, immunization records, power of attorney, guardianship paperwork.

· Set up financial means to care for your children.

· Sign proper legal documents to stand in for you.

· Consider the benefit of "practice" by allowing children to stay with their caregiver prior to your departure, if possible.

· Compile a list of all activities, contacts, and schedules.

Deployment

During the deployment period, which is the first thirty days of your husband's departure, you may continue to experience mixed emotions. Some spouses report feeling relieved in some ways, at first, that they no longer feel the pressure of getting prepared for the deployment or putting up the strong-military-spouse front. But it's not long before numbness kicks in as a direct result of the hole left by your husband's departure. Many wives also report feeling overwhelmed and disoriented when their loved ones leave. They have difficulty sleeping at night worrying if they will be able to handle it all, and worrying about their husband's safety. Given the fact that it may be weeks before your service member can make the first call home, it might take some serious restraint not to sound resentful and angry. Just think about how difficult it is for him to want to call you and not have access to a telephone. How excited he will be when he gets to one and can dial your number; be careful not to ruin it.

When you get that unexpected call from him, the time will go by much too quickly. Those few minutes can be exhausting, because you might experience a lot of intense emotions packed into a phone call that will likely last only a few minutes. Surprise, joy, uncertainty about what to say, worry about fitting in everything you wanted to say, and anxiety about everyone in the family being able to talk to him might be a few of the feelings you encounter. If the call is made from a "morale line" (or a special military phone for free fifteen-minute calls to family), the call is dropped, gone, dismissed, like a cheap cell phone service, after fifteen minutes—whether you are finished talking or not. And there is a delay between the time something is said and the time the other person actually hears it, so be patient because you will get used to it. Besides, this minor frustration is the trade-off for a telephone call that costs you nothing. If your husband uses a commercial phone to call home, then the call might last a little longer, but you can expect the bill to be very high, and you will probably still be frustrated because no amount of time will ever feel like enough time to connect. It's important to remember that any negativity, real or imagined, that is shared during these calls can be damaging to both of you—to your confidence and to your coping skills.

For example, if either family member recounts all the things that are going wrong, the other might become more stressed or angry. "When speaking with your loved one on the phone, keep the conversation stress free and speak of fun things. It will make them feel less stressed," says Camille, a new military wife in North Carolina.

The following are more tips on initial communication with your loved one who is deployed.

Be patient when waiting for the first call. He will surely call the first chance he gets and has no control over when that will be.

Keep negativity in check. Vent to someone in your support system if you are having a hard time adjusting to his absence. He doesn't need to be worrying right now or feeling guilty about leaving you.

Share as much about your daily activities as possible to help him feel connected. No matter how insignificant something might seem to you, it may be a huge deal for him to hear about it.

Don't be frustrated that he keeps asking questions and not sharing what's going on with him. He wants to hear as much as possible about home in that brief phone call, and it's highly likely that he cannot, for security reasons, say certain things about what's going on over there.

Keep a list of what you want to share during his calls. Just check off the items as you go along and keep adding to it after the call. You will never have too much to say. And don't forget to jot down the important questions that might come up about household business.

Don't feel guilty if you miss a call from him, because you have no way of knowing when it will come. And he knows that you have to live life while he is gone. Although he may be disappointed, he will leave a message and try again later. He would much rather have you out and about living than sitting around waiting for a phone call.

Stay away from news reports about "the war" or other world events that might impact your coping ability. If you are all stressed out about what you see on TV, he will hear it in your voice. And again, it's not the time for him to be worried or feeling guilty. He must remain focused on his safety and the mission.

Sustainment

The sustainment stage lasts from the thirty days into the deployment to thirty days from the anticipated return. This is the majority of the time your loved one is away, and therefore it is the time for you to get your stuff together and get into the groove of coping with the deployment.

MILITARY SPOUSE SURVIVAL KIT

Being a TSF (temporary single female)—that's our moniker, by the way, not an official designation—means being able to fend for yourself if necessary. Don't take on the expense and hassle of arranging for others to take care of minor repairs, small home decor projects, or life's other minor uh-ohs. Instead, here are some useful items to help you take matters into your own capable hands.

- Tool kits
- Emergency roadside kits
- Tape measures
- Cordless screwdriver
- Hammer (big and small)
- Putty
- 24-hour repair numbers
- Flashlight
- Jumper cables
- Wrench set
- Box of multisize screws and nails
- Industrial plunger
- Hedge clippers
- Lawn edger
- Lawn mower
- A good corkscrew
- Rubber gripper (to open jars—rubber glove will do in a pinch)
- A gas grill
- User manuals for all appliances (remember, you can access most of them online if you can't find the one that came with the equipment)
- Batteries in all sizes
- Home warranty service: a service contract that covers the repair or replacement of certain appliances for a monthly fee and service

> fee upon incident using approved contractors. Just call toll free or submit a request online. For example, visit www.ahswarranty.com or www.homewarranty.firstam.com or www.bhwc.com.
> - Check out the girly version of tools. There are even a variety of colors available these days like pink, yellow, green, orange, and more. Visit www.tomboytools.com and www.ladiestoolsonline.com.
> - Your spouse's T-shirt sprayed with his favorite cologne.

You're Pregnant, He's Deployed. Now What?

In addition to the many war stories military wives told us of the birthdays, anniversaries, and other special occasions missed by their deployed mates, there are also many women who shared stories about being pregnant during most or all of their mate's deployment. Given the nine months of pregnancy and the new frequency of deployment, it's more likely that if you're expecting, you will spend some of your pregnancy alone. You will definitely need a strong support network given the unpredictability of pregnancy. Thankfully, the same great use of technology can help keep your man in the loop with your pregnancy. First, get your support together. In my first book, *The Mocha Manual to a Fabulous Pregnancy*, I offer the following suggestions for women who are single (permanently or temporarily) and pregnant.

Establish your own circle of support—sometimes the family we create for ourselves can be stronger than the one we were born into.

Have someone go to doctors' visits with you—"pregnancy brain" cannot be trusted. Have someone else there to hear what the doctor is advising. If that's not possible, take a pen and paper and write down questions and answers.

Keep the father involved—men don't always respond to pregnancy the way we do. That doesn't mean he's not happy; there's a lot of fear for men that comes with a new baby. Be understanding when he doesn't read all the books and e-mails you send or listen to every heartbeat, video, or sonogram recording you record and share.

Have a plan. Create a labor and delivery plan well in advance as you may be relying on others to make it all happen. Prepare a list of contact numbers and make sure everyone involved in the plan has the information.

Also, use these nifty ideas, culled from military wives all over, on how to keep your man involved in your pregnancy even when he is far away:

1. Tape-record his voice reading stories or talking about himself and play it for your belly and new baby. Have him make new cassette tapes and send them to you.

2. Record the heartbeat and mail it. You can also have it recorded electronically and then save to a DVD or e-mail the file.

3. Send pictures of your expanding profile, and write e-mails of all your pregnancy news. Keep a month-by-month journal of all the little things and send it to him once a month.

4. Webcams are great for pregnancy. Many wives have set up a live one for the delivery, too!

5. Stay close to the FRG and sign up for the live telecasts so your spouse can see you and the baby.

6. You can also contact the Red Cross at least forty-five days before delivery and they will verify your due date and send a message to your husband's chain of command requesting his presence. It rarely happens but give it a try!

DEALING WITH LONELINESS

Let's be honest. No matter how strong you think you are, there may be times when you are lonely as hell. But Diane, a sixteen-year army wife suggests, "If you don't have a busy life, make one! Take on a cause or challenge, or learn about something that interests you. I have been thinking about adoption so I have been trying to learn all I can about it."

Now is the time to stop making excuses for not doing some of the things you would like to do. Stop blaming your husband, the last duty station, and the possibility of relocation. Just do it. Learn a language. Get on the treadmill an hour a day. Enroll in school. Volunteer. Pick a hobby. Do something to fill your time constructively and with activities you enjoy.

"I am so busy that my neighbors want to know where I work, and I am an at-home mom!" Diane added.

But be careful, the wrong thing to do is to fill your time with activities that can put your marriage or your health at risk. Hanging out in the club, going out with someone who is "just a friend," or overindulging in food, alcohol, or drugs is not the way to go. These things are sure to eventually put you in a compromising or dangerous situation. If you love yourself, your hubby, and your kids, it's just not worth it.

"We made the commitment to each other when we married. And even though sometimes the course changes and you are faced with things you could have never predicted, we remain committed," said Diane. "And with that, we must change with the times and with our husbands, through all the difficulties we might have. We have to be willing to support him and grow with him. And that has nothing to do with being a military wife; that has to do with being a wife, period," she added.

So what are some ways you can cope with the loneliness when it rears its head at night? Diane spoke to her hubby through letters: "By the time I am settling into bed at night, I am ready for some pillow talk. But since my hubby isn't there, I write him a letter as if I was talking directly to him. Nowadays we are so stuck on computers that we don't write good old-fashioned letters anymore. But I did. And they made me feel much better. Most of the time it wasn't a letter a day, I wrote him a letter of the week. I made short and long journal entries to tell him what the kids did, what was going on in my world and that I wished he were here."

An added benefit to letter writing: when he gets lonely, he will be able to read her letters over and over again. Keep sending letters, e-mails, and cards even when you might not get many. Remember, his resources may be much more limited that yours.

A Woman's Got Needs, Too!

Now, just to put it out there even more, there's loneliness, and then there's *loneliness*. Which is often closely followed by lustfulness. A thirtysomething female service member openly shared her story with us.

"Some may say it's the devil that puts sinful sexual thoughts in your mind, but I say it's human nature. As a female in the military I'm always surrounded by men. Not just your average Joe but your decision makers, your planners and thinkers—you know how attractive that is. Being in the presence of intelligent men is a turn-on; being deployed makes them even more attractive.

"During my first deployment I was single and my only screening criteria was that they were not married. To be honest, though, I've fantasized about being with a few married men. For my recent deployment the tables have turned just a little. I'm now married and my dilemma is that I am still in the company of intelligent men and I'm getting turned on. For example, today I attended the first of a three-day military class. The instructor, an ex-military man, was fine as hell and very smart. When we spoke on the phone several times prior to the class, I couldn't help but think that he sounded sexy. When I start to feel guilty for my thoughts, I usually convince myself that there is nothing wrong with looking and that I will be home in less than thirty days for Rest and Relaxation (R&R) with my loving husband and that it will be okay. As far as I'm concerned, it's human nature, and right now this Latino instructor is definitely the object of my desires and the main character in my mental fantasies. Will I act on my desires? Naaaaaaaahhh. Will I continue to lust? Yeah. Will I drive my husband crazy when I return? Oh yeah. Will I tell my husband? He will never know!"

Some sex therapists say having sexual fantasies, either about your spouse or someone else is normal and healthy. In fact, there's a growing consensus and mounting evidence that sexual fantasies are not a sign of sexual inadequacy or deprivation but are a sign of a healthy, happy sex life. Of course, not everyone agrees. My girlfriend insists fantasies should only be about your mate or people like Terrence Howard, who you aren't likely to ever meet in your lifetime. Anybody else that you could possibly act on under the wrong circumstances—too many drinks, one bad argument, a lapse in judgment—should be off the fantasy radar. Others argue that marital relationships will only be damaged by more lenient attitudes about fantasies. Either way, everyone agrees that fantasies about other men belong in your head. Acting on them is definitely a no-go area.

Fantasizing about your own man, however, is definitely all good. There is nothing wrong with thinking about everything you want to do when he returns. Think back to your most intimate times and relive the emotional and physical satisfaction he brings you. Whatever you do, many spouses discourage watching sexual movies or going to clubs and opt instead for viewing comedies, sharing a night with the girls, or completing a home or hobby project. When you just have to let your imagination loose, write a tantalizing e-mail or letter to your man or write down your fantasy and share it with him on his next call home. Record a sexy message and mail it to him. When all else fails, some say you may have to take matters into your own hands. You know what you like, go for it!

Besides your sexual urges, there will be a whole host of other feelings to deal with. Some may be negative. But there will be plenty of times when you feel like, "Hey, I've got it going on!" "I can do this!" and "It won't be long before he returns." There will be times when you hang up that phone and feel energized by the call, smile and laugh out loud to that e-mail filled with his personality, and generally feel pride in what he and your family are doing for our country. That, my dear military spouses, is what it's all about!

There's no doubt about it, deployment is tough. And no matter how many times you experience it, you may never get completely used to it because every deployment will be different. Those differences could be based upon the number of children you have, the people in the unit, the conditions of the place your husband is in, and whether or not it is a wartime situation. No matter the differences, note there is one thing that will be consistent: don't take it for granted that your hubby will always be there—get all your business in order now!

EGO WORK

Ladies, we all know that men want to feel needed. Even the most self-evolved man still has some old-school patriarchal ideas about protecting and providing for his family. Needless to say, every savvy wife, military or not, knows how to make her man feel good on the inside. Military wives have a tricky tightrope to balance between holding down the fort so he can focus on his mission and holding down the fort so well that your man feels he's not needed or missed. If this is your dilemma, try these suggestions:

Have your husband show you how to do some things around the house or with the car before he leaves. Then, the minute you use something he taught you, let him know his expertise came in handy.

When you are getting ready to take on a project that is not urgent, send him an e-mail and ask for his input, advice, and ideas. Let him know how it is going and how it turned out, thanks to him.

DURING SUSTAINMENT: REST AND RELAXATION (R&R)

"Everything they told me and everything I expected when he returned was just not true," said Carol. "They say, 'Everything's going to be fine. It will be perfect.' But that was not true. The first day he came home, when we met up it was hugs and kisses; but when we got home he just shut himself up. He was in his own world. There was no communication. He said he was fine, he just didn't want to talk. I wanted to know what was wrong with him, but he wasn't ready to talk. It took until that night for him to open up and tell me what was wrong with him. But there wasn't anything I could do about it because it already happened.

"I tried to let him know it was going to be okay and that it was okay to cry. I told him not to keep it all bottled in; he could talk to me. Just to see him like that hurt. I couldn't do anything about it when it actually happened. He was telling me things about guys who were killed three or four months ago and he was bringing it up now. It's too late to ask 'What do you remember about him?' I wished I could have asked when he needed it the most. Now I could talk about it, but there would be so many guys who died to talk about. I don't know what finally got through to him out of the conversation, but the next day we woke up and he was back to normal. I don't know if he just needed to get it all out, but we got the kids and went on vacation.

"He didn't say anything else about being deployed again. He e-mailed his soldiers to let them know he was thinking about them and told them to take care. He finished his two weeks of vacation and when it was time for him to go back, it was harder than it was when he initially deployed. It was hard for me because I heard what happened the first seven and a half months. I knew about everyone who was killed and injured, and some of them I had previously met. Just to see that they were nice guys and it happened to them, what's to say nothing was going to happen to my husband? So, it was hard for me to let him go back. But I knew I had to support him. It was hard for him because he knew I was scared and didn't want anything to happen to him."

Redeployment

Excitement and anticipation will be in the air, as will apprehension, during the redeployment stage that occurs about one month prior to the service member's return home. Many wives talk about engaging in the same "nesting" activities as when the birth of their children drew near. Cleaning the car and the garage and redecorating the house, buying all the favorite foods, getting a personal makeover, and planning for visitors are among the common get-ready-for-your-baby-to-come-home things we do during this stage. The apprehension arises with the uncertainty of whether hubby will love the household and personal changes as much as you do, will still favor the favorite foods, and will want visitors, when, and how many. Just when you had gotten over the difficulty of making decisions on your own and the new roles have been in full swing, you may start second-guessing yourself now. The best thing you can do for everyone's sake is to relax and follow these tips:

- Do what you can and focus on the most important things only.
- Don't make drastic last-minute changes to yourself or to the house; even you might not like the way they turn out.
- Don't make plans for his return that cannot be changed. Arrival dates often get moved several times.
- Be prepared to relinquish control and some of your independence.

"Right before Robert came back from one of his nine deployments I had been e-mailing him each time I assembled something at home," said Connie. "I put together a computer desk, a book shelf, and some chairs. By the third time I e-mailed to tell him of my accomplishment, he wrote back, 'When I come home I won't have anything to do.'

"I told him, 'Yes, you will because I am giving it all back.' Sometimes it's harder than we think for them to fit back into the family plans and daily goings-on."

Pamela's Pick: Halted Homecomings

Planning for the homecoming day won't be perfect, easy, or on schedule, for that matter. Chances are your spouse's arrival time may change again and again. Be prepared to be flexible and remain positive, especially so the kids will do the same.

One time, the kids and I were so excited that we would be taking the four-hour drive to Fort Stewart to welcome our soldier home from Iraq. But the plan was thwarted when two hours before I was going to leave to pick up the kids from school so we could get on the road, my husband called. Instead of telling me all was going as planned, he told me that the flight had been delayed until they could replace the engine on the plane. I was glad that he hadn't taken off in a dangerous airplane, but still disappointed at the delay. The twelve-hour delay turned into another one and then another one, and eventually, several days and many telephone updates later, we were finally heading to meet him. Instead of leaving to get him on Wednesday, the final change had us not leaving until Friday because he would arrive at 2:30 A.M. on Saturday.

We headed out right after school at around 4:00 P.M. and should have arrived by 8:00 P.M., giving us time to get almost a whole night's sleep before having to head out to the parade field where he would arrive by 4:30 A.M. Well, about an hour or so from our destination, I had to pull over to the side of the road and check out something that just didn't sound right in the car. My dad told us right away that the fan belt was broken. So I called our auto club company, who then called a tow truck operator, who told us that there was no one in that town or anywhere near who would fix this at 7:00 P.M. on a Friday evening. We would have to wait until Monday or Tuesday. To top it off, the car auto club representative told us there was nothing more they could do to help. What they didn't know was that when my man got off that plane, we were going to be there, with or without their help.

I had to take matters into my own hands. I searched for and located an auto part store on my GPS. I called them to see if they had the fan belt we needed and asked them to stay open so we could get there and buy it. And it was close. By the time the tow truck came and drove us thirty minutes in the direction from where we had just come, it was exactly one minute before closing time. We purchased the fan belt, my dad used his tools to put it on with the help of the store manager, and by 11:00 P.M. we were back on the road.

The four-hour trip had turned into an eight-hour trip. But as far as the kids, Dad, and I were concerned, we could still squeeze in a two-hour nap. However, twenty minutes after we arrived at our hotel room, my husband called to say they were in Virginia and were taking off for the one-hour flight to Georgia and we needed to be ready to leave the hotel in an hour. There went our two-hour nap, but we did get an hour in before the forty-five-minute drive to the parade field only to be told the troops would arrive in an hour.

And even still, we smiled, and sang along with the band, and talked to all the other families who were just as happy as we were because, despite the obstacles, we would be hugging and kissing our hero in less than one hour.

Homecoming Checklist

- Stock up on his favorite foods.
- Plan a welcome home party.
- Wash and fold all his clothes, since they have sat around in drawers for twelve or more months.
- Purchase all new toiletry items, socks, and underwear (throw in a few sexy ones).
- Purchase the kind of lingerie he likes to see on you.
- Plan meals and shop ahead for at least the first week he is home to cut back on the running around when he arrives.
- Prepare at least one or two dishes you can refrigerate or freeze (lasagna, gumbo, chicken and dumplings).
- Hook up your hair and nails with cute, but low-maintenance styles.
- Wax, but not too close to arrival if you tend to be red or sensitive afterward.
- Put all his tools back in place.
- Give the home an extra special cleaning and add a touch of fragrance.
- Get the cars detailed, checked, and serviced.
- Make sure the yard is in good condition even if you have to pay someone.

- Have fresh sheets, new pillows, loungewear, and slippers.
- Set up a couples massage.

If your husband has been feeling a little displaced and feels like everyone is getting along just fine without him, try to show him how he is needed at home. Discuss with your husband what future projects you two can tackle when he returns. If there is a project he had his heart set on before he left, facilitate his being able to complete it by expressing your enthusiasm for it, buying him a special tool or supplies he may need, or by purchasing idea books and how-to books on the subject. You might even send one or two to him while he is still deployed.

Postdeployment

Postdeployment, also known as homecoming, usually spans at least a few months after your loved one's return. Although a happy time, it can also have challenges. For a long time you have maintained certain rules and routines. And his coming home and trying to take charge right off the bat might interrupt that flow and pose a *big* problem.

Everyone in the family must realize and expect that this will be a transitional period. In addition to expecting that hubby's arrival date is almost sure to change several times and with little notice, it is completely realistic that the arrival itself might be awkward after the initial "honeymoon" phase. Remember how during the predeployment phase you felt that although he was "in town" he was not "psychologically present"? Well, you may eventually have similar feelings in that it may be a challenge for the two of you to reconnect emotionally.

Sometimes your best efforts may not be good enough. A military wife shares the challenges she and her service member experienced upon reunion and reintegration.

"We had our personal problems when he returned from Iraq the first time," she said. "This was the first time that we had been apart and the communication was not strong (limited phone calls from me). He felt that he was not needed. That he was not important to the household since I held it all together all this time without getting his input. My objective was to give my husband 'peace of mind,' as he went and put his life on the line every minute of every day he was overseas. Never did I want him to feel any panic or concern, but in my husband's mind we just went on with life without him.

"So during his second deployment, we had a house built and I had a plan to make sure he came home feeling needed. We did not decorate, we did not put up pictures, we did not put up bathroom racks for towels, and I left boxes that I knew he wanted a hand in unpacking. That really worked when he returned, but he was only home for six days before having to go to Oklahoma for a training class and that is where enough is enough: the uncontrolled male machismo came over him and into our home.

"In retrospect, I think my husband needed time to bond with his family again. He needed to be refueled both emotionally and physically. He needed my touch as a wife and my kids' touch solidifying his reason for living and *why* he loved to be a family man. Six days was just not enough, but it was an open door for disaster—another woman. I will never know what actually went on, but the lines of respecting our marriage and being a faithful husband was out the window. And, the more sufficient I became for my family's sake, the more of the silent penalty I received.

"Not everyone that is a soldier is meant or able to deal with the civilian life. Not every spouse that marries a soldier is meant or able to handle the military life. My husband and I are now separated and there was truly nothing I could do (short of losing my sanity) to prevent our current situation. Am I special? Am I the norm? Do I represent the general population of a military spouse? Is my story similar? The answer is yes to all. The divorce stats speak for themselves."

Yes, reintegration and reunion can be quite an interesting tap dance. You may struggle to maintain your current independence and control while your husband may want to regain his former control. "I have learned that you have to make a conscious effort to move out of the way, relinquish some of the control, and allow him to step back into his role," says Evans. "It's my job to make his reintegration easier even if that means explaining to him what has changed rather than correcting him on everything he does," she adds.

Believe it or not, resentment might rear its ugly head here, too. As the one who kept it all together, you might even find yourself wanting to be appreciated for your own heroism in taking care of the kids, the home, and everything

Lost That Loving Feeling?

After a long time away, it's easy to feel like strangers. Whenever couples have trouble, experts always recommend going back to basics—getting back to what attracted you to each other in the first place. Then, they say, start dating. Here are nine great suggestions collected from your sister military spouses on how to get that groove back in your relationship:

1. Give yourselves time to court each other and the rest will fall into place.
2. Hold hands.
3. Write a poem to your spouse.
4. Download all the songs you loved as a couple when you dated and put them on a CD for the car and bedroom as well as load them to his portable listening device.
5. Kiss. Hug. Touch. Snuggle. Whisper in his ear.
6. Share a milkshake or other drink with two straws.
7. Lounge in the bathtub together.
8. Say, "I love you" or "I am glad you are back with me."
9. Exchange foot rubs and back rubs.

else on your own. And you have every right to feel that way; just make it known in a positive way. Don't wait until you feel terrible or are in the midst of a disagreement to add fuel to the fire.

Your husband doesn't need to constantly have it thrown in his face that you've handled everything just fine without him. He does need, however, for you to understand that his life has changed, too. He has to adjust to a new way of living also. And the more helpful and accommodating you can be, the better the chance for a smoother reintegration.

Stress is a normal part of this phase. Here are a few stress-driven situations that are likely to occur and what you can do about it.

You want the homecoming to be perfect: don't worry about every little detail. As long as you are together again and he is safe, nothing else really matters. A touch of cheerfulness and some sense of humor will go a long way.

You are nervous about your relationship: although you keep hearing how your interaction will be a little rocky in the beginning, accept it and don't worry about it. Just talk about your feelings with your mate and agree ahead of time not to get all wound up about any of it. Give yourselves a "grace period" to get back to normal.

You are concerned about the sex: it's just like riding a bike. Since you haven't done it for a while, it will take "a minute" to relax, but you'll be off and rolling again in no time.

You wonder how the kids and he will interact: it is very likely that he will be much more lenient than normal and the kids will know it. As frustrating as it may feel for things to be shaken up a bit, just realize that their relationship takes time to get back to normal, too. Loosen up for the time being.

The bottom line: everyone will have changed during the deployment. Talk openly about your feelings and encourage everyone else to do the same. Recognize all family members for their parts in getting through the deployment. Foster patience and understanding among all of you. Don't be in a hurry to get things back to "normal." Celebrate the homecoming with a party, and then let things slowly settle down.

It also needs to be said that your husband may return a changed man. You don't know what he's seen being in a combat zone and how he's been affected. Be alert to danger signs such as increased anger or violence. You won't hear this at the monthly coffee meeting, but there is a problem with domestic violence on some bases, or to use the military euphemism, the "spousal aggression issue." As it turns out, the rate of domestic violence in the military is two to five times higher than in the civilian population. In the summer of 2002, four wives were murdered at Fort Bragg, North Carolina, the largest military base in the country, allegedly by their husbands or ex-husbands, in a six-week period. During that time, it was statistically more dangerous to be an army wife than a Fort Bragg soldier. The point is, do not be afraid to get help for yourself and your spouse if you notice any warning signs of depression or posttraumatic stress syndrome (see Chapter 11 for more info).

Connie Tolbert: Finding Strength in the Lessons of Deployment

"We were living at Fort Hood, Texas, when my husband (Robert) was suddenly deployed to Panama. He was shining his boots and I was at the table watching TV and talking when he got a phone call. He was told that the next morning some of his soldiers would be deploying to Panama. At 10:00 P.M. he put on his BDUs and went into the office. He called me at 2:00 A.M. to tell me he was one of those soldiers. By 3:00 A.M. he had showered and packed. By 5:00 A.M., less than eight hours later, on that December 9, he left.

"The colonel's wife called a meeting later that day. My son was angry. He cried and cried. She told us that she would be there for us, but I thought, 'Yeah, right. She has five kids of her own.' Unbelievably, that strong army wife proved me wrong. She kept us busy with activities for the whole six to eight months of deployment. After that, my thoughts about her and about what I could handle had changed completely. I figured if I can't show support to someone else, too, then I have failed."

Now, after nine deployments, each ranging from six to fifteen months, in almost thirty years of military life, Connie Tolbert has many other lessons to share about finding strength in deployment. "A deployment can happen at any time. If you are not prepared in every way possible, that's when you could fall in many areas of your life," she said. Here are her other words of wisdom.

Rule number one is to **stay connected to spouses in your husband's unit**. Many times when a spouse finds herself without her man, there is the tendency to isolate herself from others. But experts warn against doing so, because isolation can lead to depression. Other spouses isolate themselves from the military and their support resources by moving home. Now, in some cases, moving home can help the situation because friends and family members can offer much needed assistance with the kids and household duties.

However, in other cases it can make it more difficult to get through the deployment.

"When a spouse moves home, the experience of deployment is totally different in that her connection to the unit is not as strong as it would be if she stayed. She often misses a lot about what is going on back here and with her husband's deployed unit. For instance, the Family Readiness Group meetings and other gatherings are often the primary way that information is disseminated. Also, during the FRG meetings the group might show video clippings that the unit has sent back home, video teleconferences may be arranged for families to directly interact with the deployed service members, and if there is no military post close to home, the free morale calls would be unavailable. Finally, she misses her military family connection. Nobody understands what you are going through better than other spouses who have similar experiences. Therefore, the support of other military wives can be unmatched."

Stay strong in your marriage. You have to work on your marriage every single day, whether your spouse is home or away. "If your husband leaves and you are having problems, they will only get worse," said Connie. "If you two are in good standing, then you can get through it. The two of you have to want your marriage to succeed."

Stay connected to your faith. "During that Panama deployment my husband missed Christmas. It was my very first Christmas away from my family and my husband wasn't even there. I cried that morning. And over the years, there were plenty more times I cried at night, but the Lord shows me that everything will be all right. People have always said that I look so strong, but a lot of times, it was a farce. I did what I had to do to get through the day and be able to help others so I had to look the part. Deep down, my real question was: 'Who do I turn to for a shoulder to cry on?'" Connie turned to the Lord.

Stay connected to your children and help your hubby do the same. "It will be up to you to stand in the gap for him with your children." They will miss their daddy, who is physically absent. They don't need to be burdened with Mommy being psychologically absent while he is gone. "At times, I felt myself getting sick, but I knew I had to keep it moving because if I allowed myself to get sick, who would take care of my kids? They were always my focus. And I was theirs. But when Dad came back home, I had to realize that I needed to make his transition back into the family a smooth one. The kids were used to coming to me about everything and I allowed them to continue to do that for a certain period of time, but then, I needed to gently direct them to their dad to even it out and help the family function well. Sometimes, it can be harder than we think for them to fit back into the family operations."

The Mocha Mix
Real Talk on Sex, Infidelity, and Resisting Temptations

★ ★

As a military spouse, the sponsor is often away. Carrying insecurities and flirting with other men is the gateway to hell. Learn how to be alone and be okay with it. Learn to masturbate and how to love and appreciate yourself. And don't fool around just because you found out that he did. It won't fix a single thing. If you want to stay married, you have to work at it.
—MILITARY WIFE

Infidelity and emotional and physical abuse is very prevalent in the military world. We have our own police, courts (superiors), and jurors, [and I believe] that those statistics go unreported. My husband was married before and infidelity was the main issue that ended their relationship. It takes a lot of commitment for a military marriage to work.
—LESLIE, MILITARY WIFE

I was able to put my marital needs in a so-called time box. Our intimacy was very healthy, wonderful, and complete once needs were understood. I focused on the love I had for him and the love he showed me. There was no one who could do me like my husband and I was not interested in finding out. If my husband was to be gone for six months, my time box was eight months.
—MILITARY WIFE

The truth is, sex, like any natural activity, is required and should be maintained. "Use it or lose it" is my saying. A woman deployed, if not into gratifying herself, may seek pleasures that can be compromising. Basically EVERYBODY is game—married men are known as Temporarily Divorced for a Year (TDY). Infidelities run rampant; sometimes relationships at home and abroad are pathetic soap opera dramas. Any person with a significant other can/will be tempted—acting on the choice of refraining or not will always be entirely a personal decision.

—FEMALE SERVICE MEMBER

One joke about deployed females is the "Desert Fox" syndrome/stereotype—that means back home this woman would probably be categorized by men as a "2" but during a deployment with very few females she becomes a "10"—thereby getting all the action she wants . . . Booty call action that is!

—FEMALE SERVICE MEMBER

Keeping my legs closed during this deployment is my least worry. My issue is dealing with the provocative thoughts. As long as I keep telling myself that it's human nature, I am comfortable. If I bring God into this, I will feel as if my soul is ruined and that I am the biggest sinner running around on this military base. So how do I deal with not being with my hubby in an intimate way? Well, I just think of how I would feel if my husband was to cheat on me while I'm here, and I do the right thing. With lots of phone calls and e-mails, exchanging photos, and constantly redefining our long-term goals we have managed to stay strong. I will never cheat. It's also important as a leader to let my soldiers see me practice what I preach about being faithful and committed.

—FEMALE SERVICE MEMBER

You have to be a complete woman before marriage and before deployment to survive a military marriage. I see women who are so dependent on their man for every interest and activity, and even their sense of self, that when he is gone, they don't know how to fill the void. That's when trouble seeps in as they start looking for others to complete them and give them what their man can't because he is away and what they can't give themselves.

—ANN MARIE, ARMY WIFE

A Soldier's Story

We asked Pamela's husband, Lieutenant Colonel Doug McBride Jr., to share his thoughts on our family deployments and here is what he had to say.

Recently, I was separated from my family for two years and, so far, have been on three long deployments (Desert Storm, Korea, Iraqi Freedom) totaling approximately thirty-six months. The key to success has been educating my family on what Dad was going to do, letting them know what the mission was, and showing them where I was going to be located.

The kids would do the research and locate my deployment destination on a map or globe. They read about the culture and what is available at the site. This is critical as far as them having somewhat of an understanding of the lifestyle that Dad would be living for the rotation. They saw how far away it was from home and what other countries were in close proximity. We discussed R&R leave and what that entailed. This ensured them that although the deployment was long . . . they would see Dad at some point during the deployment.

The key and essential component of sustaining the family during a prolonged deployment is open communication on a predictable schedule. With the increase in technology with Internet and a webcam . . . there is really no excuse not to stay in touch with your loved ones. I was able to write e-mails to my wife and kids daily just to let them know that Dad was OK and to see what was going on in their lives. We spoke on the phone most Sunday evenings . . . their time. I allocated time for each child and my wife to share with me without feeling left out or competing for time.

I encouraged my family to continue to live life to the fullest while I was deployed. Life doesn't have to stop, nor should it, because of deployments. The key is to share those experiences with your deployed service member to include triumphs and shortfalls.

I encouraged my family to continue to pursue their passions and make the best of a challenging period of separation. My wife wrote two books while I was deployed for fifteen months. My son and daughter maintained A averages in school and competed at a high level in sports. My kids missed their dad but they understand that freedom isn't free and that they had to share their dad in service with the country to ensure that the liberties we hold so precious remain intact.

The support systems at home are critical as well. Both sides of our family helped either directly through assistance with the kids and house, like my father-in-law . . . or indirectly by just calling once per week like my mother, and other friends and relatives. My sister-in-law sent me care package after care package. Don't get me wrong . . . there were challenges at home, as well as for me while deployed, but nothing to the point where it caused any serious issues. We all established some proven coping mechanisms to get us through.

This sounds corny but my family, especially my children, embraced the "Army Strong" mentality and believed that in order to be Army Strong we had to be family strong.

We maintain a silent covenant to stay strong as a family all the time and during periods of separation . . . and it strengthens our bond. I can honestly say that my family is stronger today, as we close out another long deployment, than before we began it.

Triple Exposure: Air Force Service Retiree, Husband, and Son

Terry Smith has been attached to the military all his life. He grew up as an air force child, entered the air force himself, and is married to a woman who is nearing air force retirement. Here is what he had to say about separation and deployment in each of his roles.

Military Service Member

Based on my experiences, the toughest part of deployment for most men is the fact that they are physically not there to protect or be there for their families. To them, it seems like they are a million miles away from their family, and they just keep hoping their spouse can handle any problems that arise and not have to be dependent on someone else back home to do the job the service member would do if he was home.

Being a Deployed Military Husband/Father

Being separated from your family is tough because of all you miss back at home and the little things that you don't think about, but are so important to your children.

My advice for separation, no matter how long or short it will be, is to get your business in order in plenty of time before you leave and don't wait until the last moment to do things. This affects the last couple of days/weeks of quality time with your family, not to mention the stress you put on yourself knowing you left things for them to do. They don't deserve that.

The relationship between my wife and me also grew stronger because we were able to talk emotionally and appreciate each other more.

Being the Husband of a Deployed Wife

I would wish she were there. My relationships with my children got stronger because I was fortunate to see a lot of things as a father that I would never have experienced otherwise. We relearned each other and understood our respective points of view. But then, I would find myself wishing she were there to experience it with me. My wife and I have always been a team at home, so it was a trying time for my kids and me. Can you imagine playing on a football team with only half your team?

It was challenging to not have a voice of reason to talk to, not being able to hold an adult conversation, going to sleep every night to an empty bed, nobody to hold, nobody there to pick you up when you're down, trying to be strong at all times so your kids think everything is going to be all right when you're not sure.

I think the fact that I knew we were always thinking of each other helped me get through the times when I felt sad, lonely, empty, and even abandoned. The strategy that helped most over the total of three years of separation was breaking down the time in fractions and celebrating the completion of each part we got through.

Military Son

I was a military dependent for eighteen years and then a military parent for twenty. The biggest challenge(s) I had to face were when I was moving and making new friends as a child and changing jobs as an adult. Even if I wasn't the one moving away, my friends were. I learned the value of family this way. I learned that even though you may think your friends are the best thing that ever happened to you, by no fault of anyone, they may soon leave. As sad as reality is, the good news is I also learned family will ALWAYS be there.

No matter what role you are in, cherish each day as though it were your last one.

THE "OFFICIAL" FAMILY DEPLOYMENT CHECKLIST

The National Military Family Association has the following deployment checklists that can be downloaded at www.nmfa.org.

Although extended deployments are never easy on the family, the hardships need not be increased by the failure to plan ahead. A carefully prepared and executed predeployment checklist can save you and your family from giant headaches in the future. It is very important for you, as a military family, to have certain documents in your possession. Military spouses are often required to take over the family during the service member's absence; therefore, it is important that both of you sit down together to gather information and documents named in this checklist. You are encouraged to keep originals or copies of all listed documents in a special container (safety deposit box) in a location you can find immediately and is known to both you and the sponsor.

- Marriage certificate _____
- Birth certificates of all family members
  Wife _____
  Husband _____
  Children _____ _____ _____ _____
- Divorce papers _____
- Death certificates _____
- Medical (shots) and dental records of all family members (including pets) _____
- Citizenship/naturalization papers _____
- Adoption papers _____
- Passports, visas (remove only when needed for international travel) _____
- Insurance policies (Note: company, policy #, and amount of payment) _____
- Real estate documents (leases, mortgages, deeds, or promissory notes) _____
- Copies of installment contracts and loan papers _____
- Current list of immediate next of kin, personal lawyer, trusted friend (include phone # and address) _____
- Car title (registration should be in car) _____

- Last LES (Leave Earning Statement) ____
- Discharge papers (DD Form 214) ____
- Allotments (updated with correct amount, name, address, account #) ____
- Social security number of each family member ____
- Current address and telephone numbers of immediate family members of both spouses ____

  The Following Should Be Completed Prior to Deployment:
- Next of kin informed of rights, benefits, assistance available ____
- Family budget and business arranged (See Financial Section for Budget Worksheet) ____
- Emergency data card updated in military personnel record ____
- Joint checking/savings account arranged (list all account numbers) ____
- Parents informed of how to make contact in case of emergency ____
- Armed forces ID cards (Renew if ID card expires within next three months. Rear detachment commander can sign for ID replacement after soldier deploys.) ____
- Emergency services explained and located
  - Red Cross/Army Emergency Relief (AER) ____
  - Medical facilities/CHAMPUS ____
  - Army Community Service (ACS) ____
  - Legal Assistance Office ____
- Security check on house ____
- Problems with cars, household, and appliances identified and resolved ____
- Power of attorney ____
  - **General**: Allows holder to act in all matters on sponsor's behalf
  - **Special**: Allows holder to act on sponsor's behalf in special transactions
  - **Medical**: Authorizes holder to obtain medical care for family members under eighteen years of age
- Wills for both spouses ____
- Orders ____
- Copy of emergency data card ____
- List of all credit cards and account numbers ____

- AAFES Deferred Payment Plan (DPP) (to use, spouse must be listed as an authorized user or hold sponsor's general power of attorney) ____

- Federal and state income tax returns (last five years) ____

HOUSE CARE CHECKLIST

Take a ten-minute walk through your house. Carry this checklist to help you truly see your home. The idea behind this walk is to look for fire hazards. You don't have any? Are you sure? Perhaps this list will change your mind.

Kitchen

- Are curtains, dish towels, or paper items kept away from stove? ____
- Is stove's exhaust hood and ductwork clean of grease? ____
- Do you have a working fire extinguisher close at hand? ____

Living Room, Dining Room, Bedrooms

- Is fireplace spark screen always closed? ____
- Are electrical wiring/circuits/outlets adequate to handle load? ____
- Is there sufficient space for air circulation around TV/stereo? ____
- Are ashtrays available in home occupied by smokers? ____
- Are matches and lighters out of reach of children? ____

Attic, Closets, Storage Room

- Do you keep oily cleaning rags in tight metal containers? ____
- Are you using only nonflammable cleaning fluids? ____
- Do you avoid accumulations of paper and combustible materials? ____

Workshop

- Are combustible materials kept away from heat sources? ____
- Are paint thinners, paints, and solvents kept in their original containers for identification purposes? ____
- Are the furnace, heaters, vents, and chimneys inspected and serviced regularly? ____
- Are fuses of the proper size for the circuits they protect? ____
- Are the dryer lint trap and vent kept clean? ____

Garage And Grounds

- Is gasoline for the mower stored in a safety can? ____
- Have you removed accumulations of trash and paper? ____

- Are oil-soaked rags in tight metal containers to prevent combustion? ____

- Do you use commercial starter fuels (not gasoline) for barbecue fires and are barbecue mitts ember-proof? ____
- Are there dry leaves under porches or wooden stairs, in windowsills, or anywhere else close to the house? ____

Self-Check
- Do you know where the electrical box (fuse/circuit box) is and how to replace fuses? ____
- Do you know the location and procedure of shutting off water/gas master control valves in case of broken or leaking pipes? ____
- Do you inspect electrical cords frequently and keep them in good condition? ____
- Do you use extension cords only for temporary convenience, never as permanent wiring? ____
- Do you enforce a "No Smoking in Bed" rule? ____
- Do you and your family avoid using hair spray near open flames or while smoking? ____
- Does everyone in the family know how to call the fire department or dial the operator? ____
- Does each telephone have the fire, police, and ambulance numbers close to it? ____
- Does your family have a fire escape plan and has your family drilled with it? ____
- Do you make sure your children are not left unattended and instruct baby sitters about emergency procedures? ____

NOW IT IS TIME TO ADD UP YOUR ANSWERS.
To how many of the questions did you answer no—one or two? Your home is pretty fire safe. But remember, just one accident can cause a tragedy! If you had 5 or 6, you are risking the safety of your family. If you have more than 6, you are asking for trouble. **Take action NOW!**

Smoke Detectors
Buy a battery-operated smoke detector. It is one of the best and most inexpensive forms of fire insurance. It will not prevent a fire from starting, but it may save your life! Be sure to check the smoke. detector on a regular basis.

Home Tool Kit

____ Flashlight and extra batteries ____ Hammer

____ Assorted nails, screws, and tacks ____ Screwdrivers

____ Masking tape ____ Scissors and/or knife

____ Pliers ____ Wrench

____ Furnace filters ____ Extra lightbulbs

Financial

- Who will have the checkbook and who will have the cash card? Remember it will take a week or longer for mail to be forwarded to the spouse's new duty station. Plan on paying bills in a timely manner. ____

- What types of accounts does the family have with what banks? Do the current accounts allow family members access to funds? ____

- Where are the bank books and account numbers? ____

- Are all the credit card numbers written down and in a safe place? Are the numbers and company addresses recorded in case of loss or theft? ____

- Are you knowledgeable about check writing? How will you determine if there are insufficient funds and what is your plan in case this happens? ____

- If allotments or checks to the bank are delayed, who can you contact? ____

PREDEPLOYMENT CHECKLIST

Turn into company prior to deployment.

Does Your Spouse Have The Following Paperwork?

- A current ID card? ____
- A current passport? ____
- Access to a checking account? ____
- Enough money to manage household while you are gone? ____
- A current power of attorney? ____
- Current ID cards for children (in good condition)? ____
- A driver's license? ____
- Up-to-date car registration? ____
- Up-to-date immunization record for children and pets? ____
- Current chain of concern phone roster? ____

- Phone numbers of battalion rear detachment commander? ____
- Does your family have any special medical problems? (If so, get a statement from the doctor.) ____
- Is your wife pregnant? ____ When is she due? _____ (If so, get a statement from the doctor, especially if it is expected to be a problem pregnancy.)

PLEASE CHECK ALL QUESTIONS, SIGN, AND DATE.

NAME: _____

COMPANY: _____ PLATOON: _____

SIGNATURE: _____ DATE:_____

Lieutenant Jamis Merjae Seals

As the only, or one of the few, active-duty black female helicopter pilots in the navy (and certainly the youngest), Lieutenant Jamis Seals is in a class of her own. That's quite an accomplishment for the twenty-six-year-old D.C. area native. Admittedly, I may be only slightly biased since Lieutenant Seals and I are second cousins, but I think her track record—West Point grad, search and rescue officer in Kuwait, and helicopter aircraft commander—speaks for itself. Plus, girlfriend flies the MH-60, aka the "Knighthawk," the navy's newest, state-of-the-art, multimission helicopter.

Jamis shares with us about navy life, the challenges of being a single sister and female pilot, and what it really means to be navy strong.

Looking for Discipline

I wouldn't say I actually chose a military career. I was looking at colleges and was drawn to the military service academies largely because of their rigid structure (I'm easily distracted). The summer before my senior year I visited the big three, navy, air force, and army via their summer programs.

I decided that the navy felt the best, had the major I wanted, and I was impressed by the senior design projects. I knew I would have to serve in the military, but I don't think I fully understood what that meant until halfway through my time there.

Navy Perceptions Versus Navy Realities

Initially I took it too seriously. I bought into all the talk of courage and commitment. That is very important, but sometimes people look at the military and put it up on a pedestal. While it's true we're held to higher standards, we're all just people doing a job. It's not a nine to five and we're responsible for millions of dollars of equipment at relatively young ages, but we're not drastically different from some of our peers except in the sacrifices we make.

Surviving West Point

The Naval Academy is what you make of it. It's not an easy place to be. There are a lot of freedoms that normal college kids have that you aren't allowed. There are also a lot of responsibilities that come with that. The summer of my junior year I was responsible for training the new class of freshmen. I was a squad leader of eleven people. I trained them physically and mentally for the challenge of a military life. I was only nineteen.

Females have come a long way at the Naval Academy. I didn't endure nearly any of the harsh treatment that the first class of females did in 1976. There are still people around who don't believe women belong at the Academy. Some of them were my classmates, and some were older alumni from the 1950s. I can't think of a time I was singled out and treated differently there because I am a woman.

Taking Flight

The pilot thing was kind of an accident. Every summer you're required to do different blocks of training. One summer I went to Australia on a boat that went to Japan with a three-day stop in Saipan and I loved it. I was determined to live the life of a surface warfare officer aboard ship.

The following summer I was attached to a helicopter squadron in Jacksonville, Florida. I flew one time for about fifteen minutes and spent the rest of my weeks there at the beach and the bars. Somehow I viewed that as the life of a pilot. When it came time to select my service, I remembered those weeks in Jax and decided why not? I haven't regretted it yet.

Mama Said, Say What?

My mother wasn't onboard with the pilot thing at first because she feared for my safety. She still worries, but she's either a lot more comfortable with it or has gotten better at hiding her feelings from me. My friends have all reacted positively. Most of them think my job is pretty cool. I happen to agree.

Living Under Navy Rules

Right now I miss the fact that I won't spend the holidays with my family. I don't like not having control over my schedule. I can't take vacations without clearing it through my commanding officer. There are countries that are off-limits to me because the navy says so. I hate that I can't be friends with people I work with outside of work simply because they're enlisted and I'm an officer. One of the things I missed most on my last deployment was making my own food. Little things like that come up a lot.

Facing Fears

Last year I was flying over Iraq and, long story short, the pilot that was with me almost flew me into the ground. We recovered from about a 2,000-foot-per-minute dive from 300 feet at 30 feet. I never said a word.

Life in a Man's World

I always worry about being considered on a level playing field with the guys. I try and approach my day as a pilot and officer who happens to be black and female instead of the other way around. I find that if initially people had reservations, they abandon them after they've interacted with me for a while.

There are still a lot of people in the navy who are "old school" and not necessarily used to working with women or for one. There is an overwhelming feeling of having to prove yourself time and again, and like with any other job there are always "haters." If you spend more time doing well at your job and less time worrying about those who don't want you to do well, then you'll ultimately succeed. Unfortunately, you also have to be mindful of people's perception of you as well. Never give anyone a reason to think you're acting improper. Be mindful of being behind closed doors when being counseled by a supervisor or when counseling a subordinate. Perception is reality.

Life as a Single Sister

It's tough being a sister, let alone a single sister. I was on Facebook not long ago and was talking to another pilot who did some sort of research or report on black female pilots. It turns out that after her research was over she discovered that I was the only active-duty black female helicopter pilot in the navy. She flew another aircraft, and another female we know flies the same one she does. It's something I kind of knew, but it's a bit of a lonely feeling. My squadron only has three female pilots out of over fifty pilots. One of them is a close friend, so I have a female to talk to, but there is only one other black pilot besides myself. He's of a higher rank and a different deployment cycle so I haven't really seen him much. It's tough when nobody understands why I'm so frustrated that on the island of Guam nobody knows how to do my hair. I've been in predominantly white school since I was in sixth grade so I'm used to it, but I'd be lying if I said it didn't bother me once in a while.

As far as being single, it does become trying at times. The married people don't have to worry about who watches their car or house while they're out to sea or who pays the bills. In addition, it's hard to meet other single people partly because of the long hours we work. (It doesn't help that Guam is barren when it comes to a supply of single people outside of the ones you work with. The problem is for men and women alike.)

I dated a navy guy while I was in Pensacola. We broke up for different reasons, but I don't think we would've survived the distance thing. He moved to San Antonio while I was in Pensacola and he ended up in Hawaii while I've been in Guam. That's as close as you can get but that's still a $1,000 flight. I wouldn't be opposed to dating another navy guy. One of the benefits is they understand your lifestyle. I wouldn't rule out a civilian, either, but some guys are intimidated by what I do.

What's Next

I haven't decided what's in my future. I love flying, but eventually it becomes about working your way up the ladder and that's more involved than just working hard.

Words of Advice to Other Female Service Members

1. Don't take work/life too seriously.
2. Get in a little bit of trouble every once in a while, it makes for a great story.
3. Find a way to say yes. My first squadron skipper said that. There's always a way to tell your boss you *can* do something. You may have to phrase it in terms of things that need to be sacrificed to accomplish the job, but a yes with a lot of contingencies is always received better than an outright no.
4. Never turn down an invitation from a friend. I've lost a few and I wish I had more memories.
5. The best thing I've learned is to pick your job/warfare community based on the people you want to work with. If you love what you do but hate who you do it with, you'll never enjoy a day at work. If you

hate what you do but like the people you do it with, at least you'll have something to look forward to when you come to work and people to commiserate with afterward.

Living Your Best Life

Don't let anyone tell you that you *can't* do something or a goal is out of your reach. And finally, look after yourself. Nobody cares about you like you do, with the exception of maybe your mother.

CHAPTER FOUR

Social Studies

A Lesson in Protocol, Pomp and Circumstance, and the Social Scene

It was a night Catherine Lewis will never forget. "As a new military wife, I remember my first dining-out experience, which is a dinner for both military and civilians. I was so nervous. It's a very scripted event; this means that a set pattern of events takes place and any misstep is duly noted by the proper officials. The entire event is formal and dignified and is a way to initiate newcomers into the world of military tradition while enhancing camaraderie by poking good-natured fun at each other.

"My husband's entire unit was there, and most of them had brought a guest; I'd say there were about a hundred people. Everyone was in formal dress, as is required for these occasions; my husband was in his dress blues. I had chosen a light yellow satin gown.

"I remember that the food was delicious; we were served filet mignon with all the trimmings—baked potato, asparagus tips with hollandaise sauce, tossed salad, and tea, water, and wine, all in beautiful crystal goblets. Being young and new to military life, I knew nothing about toasting at dinner parties, especially the military kind. I didn't know it but that night there was a general in attendance, and after we were finished eating, a toast was announced in his honor. I was so caught up in all of the events that I didn't even hear the toast being announced. The next thing I knew, everyone around me was standing, lifting their glasses. I felt very embarrassed sitting there in my chair in the midst of everyone else standing around me. My husband looked down at me in panic, which made me panic. I jumped to my feet and as I did I grabbed my wineglass, causing several other glasses of water and wine to come crashing down. The table was soaked and so was my dress. There I was, the center of a lot of unwanted attention. For this infraction, my punishment was being sent to the grog bowl at the front of the dining hall. The grog bowl is a huge punch bowl filled with a nauseating mixture of all kinds of beverages (nonalcoholic). You have to fill your cup and drink it all."

That was Catherine's introduction into the military social scene, her first experience with the military rules, written and unwritten, and understanding just how important these rules are. Social gatherings are an integral part of military life. Research shows they date back to old frontier outposts where army families lived on difficult and often dangerous frontiers where they only had one another for companionship and protection. In those days, the post really symbolized community and security. Today, many military families still enjoy the tradition of entertaining in their homes. The monthly coffees and parties offer a chance to get to know others better despite the constant state of flux of military families. These are great opportunities, as are the hail and farewells and more formal balls—but they do require learning some social graces and protocol.

Now, let's be real. We black people have created our own system of social protocol, which ranges from our stereotypical CP time to the ever important unspoken rule to never bring your greens to another's home in a dish you need to get back asap! But seriously, although we may not have a personal historical attachment to social etiquette and protocol, it has existed in our community for decades. In fact, in 1940, Dr. Charlotte Hawkins Brown became known as the "first lady of social graces" after she appeared on national radio and published *The Correct Thing to Do, to Say, to Wear* as a textbook for manners originally created for the students at the school she founded, Palmer Memorial Institute. The advertisement for her book said, "In our day, good manners are almost outmoded, but in this book, we will find an opportunity to renew the art of fine manners as a means by which we can climb the ladder of success, whether it be companionship or commercial achievement."

This sentiment could also be applied to your man's military career and your military social experience. Nobody is saying you have to become Miss Military Manners of the twenty-first century, but it doesn't hurt to learn a few important rules. Who knows? You might even find it fun!

Of course, no matter how hard you study, there's a good chance that you'll still experience your first social faux pas as Catherine did. Or maybe you already have. After all, there are lots of unwritten rules you can't know, you just have to learn them as you go along. The best thing to do is to concentrate on learning the written rules, and the unwritten ones eventually will make themselves known to you.

We will, however, let you in on one unwritten rule that's really important: socializing is absolutely critical to your service member's career. You won't find this in any official handbook, but our military wives tell us that it is unequivocally a rule of play. In fact, not until 1988 did the DoD stop the practice of incorporating commentaries on a wife's behavior in a husband's job review. Right or wrong. Like it or not. Service members who socialize and throw parties are seen as good for boosting the morale among fellow soldiers and their families. To earn your stripes as an MS, you'll need to support his efforts. This also makes you look good as a spouse.

Call it what you like, but the military hierarchical structure and by-the-rulebook ways seep into the social scene as well. You should know that there are rules prohibiting "fraternization" between officers and enlisted service members and, to some degree, between junior and senior ranks. These rules also apply to reservists. Now, there aren't too many hard-and-fast rules on what classifies fraternization, but the general idea is that officers and senior enlisted are supposed to keep a healthy, professional distance from the junior service members they train and supervise. We feel confident in saying that getting drunk with your subordinates is pretty much a no-go area, but for some wives who may befriend the wife of a subordinate of their husband, the issue gets a bit trickier. If you are close friends with the spouse of someone from the opposite rank, can you invite her husband over for dinner? Technically, these rules don't apply to family members. But you may want to talk to your hubby and decide on a case-by-case basis.

In all seriousness, the hierarchy of the military is there for a reason. In combat there is no room for democracy. Orders have to be swiftly given and responded to for everyone's safety. A ranking officer's authority cannot be compromised, so anything that could lead to decreased respect or increased resentment in the workplace cannot be tolerated. This is one unwritten rule you must respect.

To help you get more familiar, read on.

The Social Graces and Your Husband's Career

These rules are unwritten, but very important for you to know. First and foremost there is military conduct. Your husband is expected to know it and demonstrate it, as well as educate his family on the subject. All military personnel must demonstrate loyalty, self-control, honesty, and truthfulness. It is important for him to always set a good example for those around him, especially younger people and nonrated personnel. By acting in a military fashion at all times and putting the good of the military before his own personal likes and dislikes, he will be setting that good example, and you as a military wife will be expected to follow suit.

As a military spouse you should understand that you *are* considered a public relations vehicle for your particular branch of service. That is, how you conduct yourself in public is considered part of how others form their opinion of the military. The military life is a life of service; know this going in and you'll have fewer surprises. You're expected to work with your husband as his partner to ensure that all of your relationships reflect this goal.

The first step in proper decorum is to address all military personnel by their title and/or rank. Military courtesy is based on mutual respect for those in this unique profession. In any social occasion, the simple rules of etiquette apply as well. Always be on time; it shows respect and responsibility. Conduct yourself in a mature and honorable fashion at all times, doing nothing that will draw undue attention to you. This level of behavior is expected of your husband, and of you as well; when it isn't given, it will be duly noted. Trust us.

Pamela's Pick:

Every military wife needs to be a chest woman. That is, you have to learn to read the "chest candy"—the rank insignia on your service member's and everyone else's shirt collars or shoulders. A service member's chest candy spells out his rank and résumé. As a quick primer, "stripes," or chevrons, mean he is enlisted; metallic bars are for a junior officer or warrant officer; oakleaf clusters are for a midlevel officer; eagles or stars for a senior officer. Turn to pages 118–122 for some detailed pictures of rank insignia from the Department of Defense (DoD).

THE UNITED STATES MILITARY
ENLISTED RANK INSIGNIA

 OFFICER INSIGNIA

Service members in pay grades E-1 through E-3 are usually either in some kind of training status or on their initial assignment. The training includes the basic training phase where recruits are immersed in military culture and values and are taught the core skills required by their service component.

Basic training is followed by a specialized or advanced training phase that provides recruits with a specific area of expertise or concentration. In the Army and Marines, this area is called a military occupational specialty; in the Navy it is known as a rate; and in the Air Force it is simply called an Air Force specialty.

ARMY — * For rank and precedence within the Army, specialist ranks immediately below corporal. Among the services, however, rank and precedence are determined by pay grade.

NAVY/COAST GUARD — *A specialty mark in the center of a rating badge indicates the wearer's particular rating. ** Gold stripes indicate 12 or more years of good conduct. *** 1. Master chief petty officer of the Navy and fleet and force master chief petty officers. 2. Command master chief petty officers wear silver stars. 3. Master chief petty officers wear silver stars and silver specialty rating marks.

The **U.S. Coast Guard** is a part of the Department of Transportation in peacetime and the Navy in times of war. Coast Guard rank insignia are the same as the Navy except for color and the seaman recruit rank, which has one stripe.

	ARMY		NAVY / COAST GUARD	MARINES	AIR FORCE
E1	Private		Seaman Recruit (SR)	Private	Airman Basic
E2	Private E-2 (PV2)		Seaman Apprentice (SA)	Private First Class (PFC)	Airman (Amn)
E3	Private First Class (PFC)		Seaman (SN)	Lance Corporal (LCpl)	Airman First Class (A1C)
E4	Corporal (CPL)	Specialist (SPC)	Petty Officer Third Class(PO3) **	Corporal (Cpl)	Senior Airman (SrA)

Leadership responsibility significantly increases in the mid-level enlisted ranks. This responsibility is given formal recognition by use of the terms noncommissioned officer and petty officer. An Army sergeant, an Air Force staff sergeant, and a Marine corporal are considered NCO ranks. The Navy NCO equivalent, petty officer, is achieved at the rank of petty officer third class.

	ARMY	NAVY / COAST GUARD	MARINES	AIR FORCE	
E5	Sergeant (SGT)	Petty Officer Second Class (PO2) **	Sergeant (Sgt)	Staff Sergeant (SSgt)	
E6	Staff Sergeant (SSG)	Petty Officer First Class (PO1) **	Staff Sergeant (SSgt)	Technical Sergeant (TSgt)	
E7	Sergeant First Class (SFC)	Chief Petty Officer (CPO) **	Gunnery Sergeant (GySgt)	Master Sergeant (MSgt)	First Sergeant

At the E-8 level, the Army, Marines and Air Force have two positions at the same pay grade. Whether one is, for example, a senior master sergeant or a first sergeant in the Air Force depends on the person's job. The same is true for the positions at the E-9 level. Marine Corps master gunnery sergeants and sergeants major receive the same pay but have different responsibilities. All told, E-8s and E-9s have 15 to 30 years on the job, and are commanders' senior advisers for enlisted matters.

A third E-9 element is the senior enlisted person of each service. The sergeant major of the Army, the sergeant major of the Marine Corps, the master chief petty officer of the Navy and the chief master sergeant of the Air Force are the spokespersons of the enlisted force at the highest levels of their services.

	ARMY		NAVY / COAST GUARD		MARINES		AIR FORCE	
E8	Master Sergeant (MSG)	First Sergeant (1SG)	Senior Chief Petty Officer (SCPO) **		Master Sergeant (MSgt)	First Sergeant	Senior Master Sergeant (SMSgt)	First Sergeant
E9	Sergeant Major (SGM)	Command Sergeant Major (CSM)	Master Chief Petty Officer (MCPO) ** ***	Fleet/Command Master Chief Petty Officer ** ***	Sergeant Major (SgtMaj)	Master Gunnery Sergeant (MGySgt)	Chief Master Sergeant (CMSgt)	First Sergeant / Command Chief Master Sergeant (CCM)

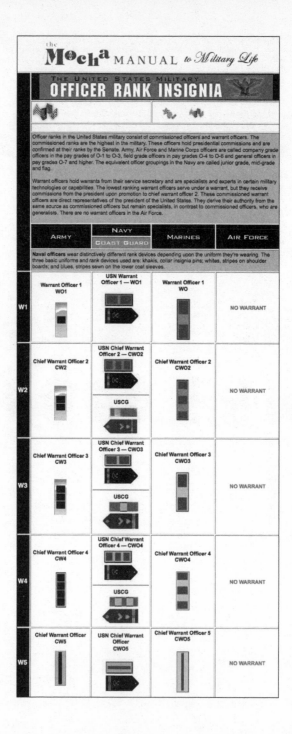

the **Mocha** MANUAL *to Military Life*

THE UNITED STATES MILITARY
OFFICER RANK INSIGNIA

Officer ranks in the United States military consist of commissioned officers and warrant officers. The commissioned ranks are the highest in the military. These officers hold presidential commissions and are confirmed at their ranks by the Senate. Army, Air Force and Marine Corps officers are called company grade officers in the pay grades of O-1 to O-3, field grade officers in pay grades O-4 to O-6 and general officers in pay grades O-7 and higher. The equivalent officer groupings in the Navy are called junior grade, mid-grade and flag.

Warrant officers hold warrants from their service secretary and are specialists and experts in certain military technologies or capabilities. The lowest ranking warrant officers serve under a warrant, but they receive commissions from the president upon promotion to chief warrant officer 2. These commissioned warrant officers are direct representatives of the president of the United States. They derive their authority from the same source as commissioned officers but remain specialists, in contrast to commissioned officers, who are generalists. There are no warrant officers in the Air Force.

	ARMY	NAVY / COAST GUARD	MARINES	AIR FORCE

Naval officers wear distinctively different rank devices depending upon the uniform they're wearing. The three basic uniforms and rank devices used are: khakis, collar insignia pins; whites, stripes on shoulder boards; and blues, stripes sewn on the lower coat sleeves.

	ARMY	NAVY / COAST GUARD	MARINES	AIR FORCE
W1	Warrant Officer 1 WO1	USN Warrant Officer 1 — WO1	Warrant Officer 1 WO	NO WARRANT
W2	Chief Warrant Officer 2 CW2	USN Chief Warrant Officer 2 — CWO2 / USCG	Chief Warrant Officer 2 CWO2	NO WARRANT
W3	Chief Warrant Officer 3 CW3	USN Chief Warrant Officer 3 — CWO3 / USCG	Chief Warrant Officer 3 CWO3	NO WARRANT
W4	Chief Warrant Officer 4 CW4	USN Chief Warrant Officer 4 — CWO4 / USCG	Chief Warrant Officer 4 CWO4	NO WARRANT
W5	Chief Warrant Officer CW5	USN Chief Warrant Officer CWO5	Chief Warrant Officer 5 CWO5	NO WARRANT

	ARMY	NAVY / COAST GUARD	MARINES	AIR FORCE
O1	Second Lieutenant 2LT	Ensign ENS	Second Lieutenant 2nd Lt.	Second Lieutenant 2nd Lt.
O2	First Lieutenant 1LT	Lieutenant Junior Grade LTJG	First Lieutenant 1st Lt.	First Lieutenant 1st Lt.
O3	Captain CPT	Lieutenant LT	Captain Capt.	Captain Capt.
O4	Major MAJ	Lieutenant Commander LCDR	Major Maj.	Major Maj.
O5	Lieutenant Colonel LTC	Commander CDR	Lieutenant Colonel Lt. Col.	Lieutenant Colonel Lt. Col.

O6	Colonel COL	Captain CAPT	Colonel Col.	Colonel Col.
O7	Brigadier General BG	Rear Admiral Lower Half RDML	Brigadier General Brig. Gen.	Brigadier General Brig. Gen.
O8	Major General MG	Rear Admiral Upper Half RADM	Major General Maj. Gen.	Major General Maj. Gen.
O9	Lieutenant General LTG	Vice Admiral VADM	Lieutenant General Lt. Gen.	Lieutenant General Lt. Gen.
O10	General GEN Army Chief of Staff	Admiral ADM Chief of Naval Operations and Commandant of the Coast Guard	General Gen. Commandant of the Marine Corps	General Gen. Air Force Chief of Staff
	General of the Army (Reserved for wartime only)	Fleet Admiral (Reserved for wartime only)		General of the Air Force (Reserved for wartime only)

WHEN TO STAND

- When a senior officer walks in, everyone stands. This applies to both enlisted and officer ranks.
- In a dining-out situation, stand when a toast is made, if the toastmaster stands. Don't stand if the toast is being made to you or "to the ladies."
- Stand when you are introduced by someone speaking from a podium and when someone older or more senior in rank comes to speak to you.
- When the colors (the flag) are posted or retired.
- During the national anthem.
- During invocation—a prayer used at the opening of a service or a ceremony.
- When flags pass in review.
- During retreat—this is a bugle call played at 5:00 P.M. as the flag is lowered, marking the end of the day on base.
- During reveille—the bugle call played at 6:00 A.M. that awakens troops in the morning, marking the start of the day.

WHEN TO PUT YOUR HAND OVER YOUR HEART

- The national anthem, "The Star-Spangled Banner," is sung.
- The American flag passes by.
- Always when outdoors under preceding circumstances; it isn't necessary indoors, but you may do so if you wish.
- Retreat is sounded on the base at the end of the day—everything and everyone stops. Whatever you are doing, wherever you are, stop and face in the direction of the flag or the music and stay there until the music stops.

Volunteering

One of the great things about the military is the vast array of opportunities for volunteering. There are so many organizations that need your help, and there are great ways to show your love of country while helping your husband's career.

Volunteering is not so much an expected thing at the enlisted level as it is in the upper echelons—the top three levels of enlisted personnel and the officer ranks. Officers' wives are expected to pitch in and help make all sorts of events happen.

If your husband is enlisted and you want to get involved, the Family Readiness Group is a great place to start. This group helps spouses and families that are geographically separated from military installations.

An FRG group can help new military wives on all levels, especially one whose husband has just gone to basic, and she's left to cope with a new life, maybe far from home and family. Even if family is nearby, she still needs contact with other military spouses, and FRGs supply that need by establishing lines of communication between service members and their families.

The Social Graces

ISSUING INVITATIONS

When sending invitations, use the following guidelines:

- Don't use initials or abbreviations, except in obvious ways like Mr., Mrs., Dr., and RSVP.
- Write all titles, ranks, and names in full; for instance, Second Lieutenant, Sergeant Major, and so on. Always write the person's rank first, then their first and last names.
- Spell out dates and hours on formal invitations, but only capitalize the day and month; you don't need to put the year (e.g., Saturday, the first of August, seven o'clock).
- Always put RSVP in the upper left-hand corner of your invitation.
- Respond to the invitation with a yes or a no; if no, you can give a short explanation, but it isn't necessary.
- Give your response within forty-eight hours of receiving the invitation.
- You should call or write your response to the invitation. If you write it, do it like this: Captain and Mrs. Sharon Webster accept the invitation of Lieutenant and Mrs. Smith.
- If your invitation reads "Regrets Only," only reply if you can't attend.

- You may "regret" at the last minute in case of emergency.
- Place your "regret" in the bottom left-hand corner with your name and phone number.

Hostess Gifts

- A hostess gift is not required, but is a nice gesture.
- Follow up any occasion with a thank-you note later.
- Bringing wine to a dinner party is acceptable, but it may or may not be used since the dinner beverage may have already been planned.
- Flowers can be brought to a dinner occasion as well.

For Dinner Parties, Casual to Formal

For large dinner parties, place a table diagram showing the seating arrangement near the entrance to the dining room. Your goal should be seating that will stimulate conversation. For instance, don't sit people together who you know have opposing religious or political views. These rules apply for larger dinner parties of ten or more.

For smaller dinner parties, use escort cards. These will have the man's name on the outside of the envelope, and his guest's name on a card inside. Put the cards on a table close to the door to be picked up as guests arrive.

Men should assist ladies to their chairs. The man pulls the chair out and the lady enters from the left side and departs from the right. Men don't sit until all ladies and senior gentlemen are seated.

At a small dinner, wait to eat until your hostess begins eating. This doesn't apply to large dinner parties; there you can begin to eat when people around you have been served. When in doubt, just watch your hostess.

Seven Steps to a Great Dinner Party

I. Welcome your guests. Not in that hurried, oven-mitt in one hand, still halfway dressed way that I answer the door. Party planning experts say your party should start about thirty minutes before your guests arrive with you taking a deep breath. Don't welcome your guests frantic from last-minute chores. Make sure your dinner music is on and check the atmosphere you're creating for your party.

2. Answer the door. As the hostess, you should answer the door and personally greet every guest.

3. Focus on the foyer. Most of us don't have elaborate homes with cavernous foyers, but regardless of its size, think creatively to make sure guests have a place to set down keys, gloves, and purses while removing their coats and wraps; a mirror for quick fixes to windblown hair; a place for wet footwear or umbrellas; and a clear path to the dinner area.

4. Anticipate hostess gifts. Have a clean vase, scissors, and a candy dish available for any flowers or chocolates you receive from guests.

5. If you have invited people who don't all know one another, prepare an introduction with a conversational hook that encourages conversation. Something like, "This is _____, they just moved here from _____."

6. Sit pretty. Plan in advance where you want people to sit. "Sit anywhere you want" sounds good in theory, but it can be a little awkward for guests. If you are using a rectangular table, you or your hubby should sit at the head of the table.

7. Enjoy your dinner party along with your guests.

RECEIVING LINES

The purpose of a receiving line is to make sure that all of the guests at a function get a chance to meet and greet the honored guests and hosts. The military receiving line consists of an aide (known as an adjutant), the hosts, and the guests of honor. The adjutant will take your name and introduce you to the host.

- You shouldn't eat, drink, or smoke while in line.
- A wife goes in line before her husband, and he gives her name to the adjutant.

- If you happen to be late to the event, be sure you make a point of speaking to the hosts and guests of honor.

Three Basic Rules of Introductions

1. The woman's name is said first, and men are introduced to a woman by saying her name first.
2. Say an older person's name first. If two people are of the same sex, introduce the younger to the older by saying the older person's name first.
3. Always say the senior officer's name first. This rule also applies to a senior officer's spouse, and it's acceptable to introduce yourself to a senior officer's spouse.

Toasting

You should always stand up and be a part of the toasting. Even if you don't drink, you can have water in your wineglass and raise it to your lips.

Don't drink a toast to yourself; if you are toasted, stay seated. A toast is initiated by the host, except for dining-in occasions.

Departing

It's considered good manners to wait to leave until the senior person or guest of honor leaves. This rule does have exceptions.

Mrs. Jean Ellis, wife of Army General (Ret.) Larry R. Ellis

When you are a person of color and living overseas (or dealing with people from places with little diversity), you may encounter people who have had no interaction with African Americans; their perceptions are based on what they have seen on TV or in the movies. And oftentimes, those are negative images. When they meet you, sometimes they are not quite sure about you because you don't quite fit the stereotype they have for you. Even when not verbalized, it can affect how someone will interact with you. Handling that gracefully means being gracious; be yourself and pay attention to how the military prepares you well for the local culture.

I remember at a social event hosted by a wealthy businessperson and attended by a lot of affluent Germans, a man asked me where I was from. When I told him the United States, he told me I did not talk the way he thought I would. When I engaged him in conversation, I learned that he had had no interaction with African Americans so his perception was different from the reality of being with me and my husband.

Etiquette Faux Pas

- Don't be a name dropper. In other words, don't mention important people that you know.
- Don't refer to your husband by his rank.
- Don't refer to your husband's orders as "our orders" unless you are also a service member.
- Don't show public displays of affection unless you are at a homecoming or a good-bye; this includes holding hands and kissing.

NONMILITARY FUNCTIONS YOU MAY BE EXPECTED TO ATTEND

Teas and coffees: These are held to get to know incoming spouses and to say goodbye to outgoing spouses. They are the civilian version of a hail and farewell. A tea is a more formal affair than a coffee and is usually held in the afternoon. A coffee may be held any time of the day or evening. Casual attire, which includes dresses, slacks, or skirts, is acceptable.

Teas and coffees may sound simple, but this is where the social scene can get tricky. The MS streets are littered with stories of cliquish, gossipy coffee klatches. Or groups of women you can't relate or connect to. Boy, have we heard some stories! One thing we learned from the women we interviewed is that, like any other situation, it helps to go into a tea or coffee with a plan for what you want to get out of it. If you're looking for information, go in there, be friendly, and ask questions. If you just want to put in face time because you feel it will help your husband's career, then put on your game face and get in there. If you're an officer's wife, there may be a stronger expectation that you attend. Many wives said they felt the pressure to attend. Others who had their own careers said that the events were always at an inconvenient time.

Spouse club membership has declined for many reasons, some good some bad. One of the key reasons, tossed about the message boards, is the backlash of being a "joiner." Everybody wants to be independent and different, and to some, joining the spouse clubs and groups strips you of your individualism. You may have heard this kind of talk from other spouses. While I'm still working on my honorary MS degree, I am a woman and a strong individual and I don't think there's anything wrong with connecting with like people in like circumstances. Everyone needs support, especially during stressful times like deployment. Don't let trendy language or fear of being labeled one way or another prevent you from making friends and getting the resources you need.

Pamela's advice on this one is pretty straightforward. She says it's up to you and your husband to decide what level of involvement you are both comfortable with. If he knows why you're joining, not joining, attending or not attending, then he can have your back should any murmuring begin.

Pamela's Pick:

Teas and coffees don't have to be so formal anymore. Depending on the social vibe at your base, teas and coffees can be game nights, movie nights, spa nights, or other themed get-togethers.

Blood drives: These are held fairly often, and spouses are expected to participate by helping to organize them and make them successful.

Open houses: This is an event where the military base is opened to the public. Booths are set up and manned by military and spouses alike, with the goal being to educate the public about what goes on at the base and about the military in general.

Flag Etiquette

Many aspects of flag etiquette are required by federal law. For instance, don't ever use the flag for any type of decoration or advertising purposes; this goes for costumes and athletic wear as well. The flag should be raised briskly and lowered slowly and ceremoniously. Ordinarily it should be displayed only between sunrise and sunset and when you display a five-by-eight-inch or larger flag, it must be lighted at all times, either by sunlight or another appropriate source of light. If your flag is smaller than five-by-eight it doesn't require lighting.

The flag of the United States of America is saluted as it is hoisted and lowered. The salute is held until the flag is unsnapped from the halyard (the rope used for hoisting it), or through the last note of music, whichever is the longest.

Never attach any kind of mark or insignia to the flag. Never dip the flag to any person or thing, and when it is lowered, no part of it should touch the ground. Don't ever carry the flag flat unless it is properly folded, or horizontally, otherwise only carry it unfurled and flying free. Clean and mend the flag when necessary, and never use it to carry or deliver anything.

When displaying the flag from a window, a balcony, or the front of a building, place the union of the flag (the stars), at the peak of the staff, unless you are flying the flag at half-staff. To fly the flag at half-staff, bring it all the way up, and then lower it ceremoniously to half-staff.

Always display the flag on legal holidays and other special event days like Memorial Day and the Fourth of July. Women and men not in uniform should remove their hats and place their right hands over their hearts as a salute to the flag. You may fly the flag on any day you wish.

Ceremonies You Should Be Aware Of

Flag ceremony: The flag ceremony is performed at least twice a day, every day. At reveille in the morning, the raising of the flag signals the day's beginning, and in the evening, at retreat, its lowering marks the end of the day.

Military funerals: If the funeral is for a member of your husband's unit, the entire unit will attend. You should wear normal funeral clothes.

21-gun salute: These are done at funerals to honor bravery in battle and/or uncommon valor. These rules apply to enlisted or officer ranks. Spouses should wear normal funeral clothes.

Ruffles and flourishes: This isn't really a ceremony, but more of a musical salute done for generals and heads of state, presidents, and high-ranking military and civilian personnel. When the person enters the room, music is played and everyone stands at attention; these could be at a dining-in or a dining-out or at a hail and farewell.

Promotion: You will be expected to attend these if it is your spouse being promoted. Proper dress is semiformal.

Retirements: Required attendance for retirements includes most officers from a unit and their spouses, as well as the top three enlisted ranks and their spouses. The dress and location of a retirement is dictated by who is retiring, but it's safe to dress semiformal.

Change of command: These occur when a unit officer is leaving. The entire unit and their spouses will attend, and dress is semiformal.

Hail and farewells: This ceremony takes place when a group of people in a unit are leaving and being replaced by a new group. It's a good-bye to the outgoing personnel and a welcome to the incoming. Dress is informal for all, and spouses are highly encouraged to attend.

Graduations: You will, of course, want to attend this ceremony if it's your spouse graduating and if you are able to and if it's within reasonable travel distance. For a tech school graduation, dress is casual; for a leadership school, dress is semiformal.

Dining-ins: These are get-togethers held on base for military only; spouses do not attend. They are for camaraderie, morale, and fellowship of the military.

Dining-outs: These gatherings can be held on or off the base and are open to civilians and military; spouses are highly encouraged to go, and dress is formal. These are usually a lot of fun, and it's a great time to see everyone in their finest military dress (you know you love those men in uniform).

Unit functions: Any get-together that your husband's unit has will be something in which you should participate. A good example is an open house, which allows the general public to come in and learn about the military. This is a goodwill gesture to show the public how the base operates. Dress is very casual for this event, but that does not mean any T-shirts where your breasts are falling out or miniskirts that leave nothing to the imagination.

Command-sponsored picnic or potluck: Wear nice shorts and clean sneakers. If you expect to swim, limit your bathing suit exposure and bring a wrap or cover-up. Don't wear clothes that will limit your ability to play sports or will show all your bizness if you do. P.S. Nobody wants to see your thong bikini straps. Ever!

Attire

Okay, ladies, it's time to keep it real here. We know as black women we like self-expression in our clothes, our hair, and our style. We like to do our own thang! I'm sure you've already picked up that this doesn't always fly in the military. One key area where this doesn't work is with dress and grooming. The military has strict rules for what is acceptable attire, and let us tell you, hoochie shorts are never on the list. Pamela's list of "oh, no you didn't" wardrobe mishaps that she's personally witnessed is way too long.

Most invitations will have the attire noted in the bottom right-hand corner. Sometimes this is not the case, and definitions are needed. Attire ranges from very casual to formal. Follow these general guidelines to avoid any unnecessary embarrassing moments:

- *Very casual* is shorts (not Daisy Dukes) or blue jeans, tennis shoes, sandals, or flip-flops for men and women.
- *Casual* is dress slacks, like Dockers, for men with button-down shirt and loafers or other casual dress shoes. Skirts or slacks for women, such as a pantsuit, or knee-length skirt and blouse, and closed-toe pumps are appropriate.
- *Informal* is business casual. For men, this means sport coat and tie, sport coat before 6:00 P.M., suit after 6:00 P.M.; dress or suit for women, such as a matching skirt and jacket (business suit), or nice dress (Sunday best) and closed-toe pumps.
- *Semiformal* indicates service dress for the military member—for non-military men, a dark suit and tie; for women, an evening gown and heels or flats.
- *Formal* means military personnel wear service dress uniform or a military tuxedo. Civilians wear tuxedos; women wear evening gowns with comfortable heels or flats.

Remember, too, depending on where you are in the world, the preceding designations could mean absolutely nothing. For example, when Pamela was stationed in Hawaii, she had to rethink everything. The whole culture is casual; Hawaiians don't dress up for anything. Pamela says outfits like khaki pants, flowered shirts, and sandals were acceptable at military events that would typically require a button-down shirt and proper shoes. Bottom line: it can't hurt to check in with other folks on what's locally acceptable. That's where the teas and coffees come in handy.

The Mocha Mix
Real Talk on Social Faux Pas

★ ★

When attending my first military function, I was determined to be the best military wife ever, and so when my husband stood up and saluted his commanding officer, I did the same. You should have seen their faces.

—TERI MILLER, EIGHT YEARS AS A
MILITARY SPOUSE, AIR FORCE, SAN ANTONIO, TX

At our first dining-out, we were late and missed the ringing of the first bell that tells everyone to enter. Because of this we were made to wait outside until the second bell was rung. It was quite humiliating.

—SUSAN LARUE, SAN ANTONIO, TX

Our answering machine recording included our favorite old-school hip-hop song in the background. When my husband's commanding officer called to leave him a message, he heard the song and made a point of letting my husband know how inappropriate it was and that he needed to change it.

—JENNIFER COWLING, FOUR-YEAR
MILITARY SPOUSE, FT. LAUDERDALE, FL

I had a little too much to drink at a party one night when I openly planted a big kiss on my husband in front of everyone, including his commander. I have yet to live this down.

—KATHLEEN GARRISON, WIFE OF RETIRED
AIR FORCE OFFICER, WICHITA FALLS, TX

During an awards ceremony, I was enjoying myself, talking to everyone around me. When Steve's commanding officer came up to us, I made the ultimate faux pas and addressed him by his first name.

—Joanne Knight, twelve-year
military spouse, Boca Raton, FL

When I was in the hospital for the birth of our second child, I received some beautiful flowers from the section commander and his wife. In the flurry of activity surrounding a new baby, I completely forgot to acknowledge the flowers until some weeks later. I was very embarrassed.

—Janessa Taylor, eight-year
military spouse, Killeen, TX

One day, I needed to go to the base Exchange to do some shopping. I was in a big hurry and parked my then 1969 Dodge Dart in the generals' parking space. Suddenly I was surrounded by Military Police with very alarmed looks on their faces. They gave me a stern warning to never make that mistake again; I never did.

—Joleen Rush, Army wife,
Ft. Hood, TX

My husband's first promotion to E2 was a casual affair, but not as casual as I had thought. I showed up in a pair of cutoffs and a tank top and really got some dirty looks.

—Brianna McDonald, military spouse,
San Antonio, TX

We were just getting settled into a new base and I wanted to go downtown and look around. The only problem was I forgot to take my military ID card with me, and I couldn't get back onto the base. My husband had to be called out of work to come and vouch for me; I never made that mistake again.

—Anne-Marie Getty, Army wife, Ft. Hood, TX

At my first coffee, they asked us to bring a favorite "recipe." I took the time to find a recipe, wrote it on pretty paper, only to learn that I was supposed to actually cook and bring the "dish" of my favorite recipe. Since it was my first coffee, I was exempt from bringing a dish anyway and no one was rude, but I was very embarrassed.

—CHERYL AYERS, WIFE OF RETIRED SOLDIER

CHAPTER FIVE

Here We Go Again!

Mastering the Military Move

Moving definitely lands high on the list of life's most stressful events. By most expert assessments, it falls somewhere in between losing a job and losing a loved one in death. That makes life particularly challenging, since military service and moving often go hand in hand. In fact, most service members and their families relocate as often as once every eighteen months, and typically every three years, sometimes to completely different areas of the country or even the world. And sometimes on very short notice. Diane Wiggins, an army wife of sixteen years stationed in Seoul, Korea, says she's moved seven times in sixteen years, including two overseas moves.

That was then. These days the military says it is trying to move families less often. Still, one-third of all military families move every year. Your first move will likely be the most stressful as you try to navigate your way through the bureaucratic process. After that, every move gets a little easier. Most wives just become so used to it, and those with their advanced MS degree even actually look forward to it. So learning how to minimize the stress, cost, and hassle of moving can go a long way in enriching your military life. Try not to stress too much.

Of course, moving affects all in the family, from the children to the pets. Recently studies have started to look more closely at the impact of relocation on the children of military families. Not surprisingly, one study found that teenagers have a more difficult time settling into a new place than younger children, as they are more likely to have deeper friendships and connections to their current community. The study also showed that personality, confidence, family support, and the amount of change between old and new location (e.g., moving from the city to the suburbs), all also affect how well a child settles in.

But it's not all bad news. The same research found long-term positive effects on children who move frequently. Children of mobile parents are often more mature and independent and have better relationships with their parents than children from nonmilitary families. And as for the adult partners, the moving around is all part and parcel of the military lifestyle.

Instead of viewing it as a majorly stressful event, think of moving as the next leg of your lifelong adventure as a military wife. Plus you have more exciting stories to add to your MS file, like the time Pamela moved from Virginia to Rhode Island in 1999. She was seven months pregnant with her daughter at the time and about to take off on an eight-hour road trip. At the time, they had one of those conversion vans with a comfy bed in the back. Good thing. The only way her doctor would give the okay for the long trip was if she spent most of it lying on her side on that bed plus stopping every hour to walk and stretch her legs. Somehow they made it, and baby girl arrived safely months later. There's a moving adventure made for the scrapbook.

The point is, even if you're pregnant and stuck in the back of the van, you can survive every move that comes your way. And with the right tools, the right tips, and the right planning advice in this chapter, you'll be actually looking forward to your next move. Moving frequently is one of the best—and worst— parts of military life. Knowing how to approach a move can minimize the hassle and expense and help the whole family to enjoy the adventure.

First Things First: Moving On Base or Off?

In any military relocation, one of your first decisions is whether to live on post in military housing or off base in a home you rent or purchase yourself. There are advantages—and disadvantages—to either choice. Having experienced both on- and off-post living, Pamela says that off-post living gives some separation between home life and work life. That's something she and her husband consider to be very important.

And let's keep it real, the stories of bad, outdated, dreary on-post houses are bountiful. We've met plenty of women who lived in those environments.

Pamela actually had a much different experience—though I must preface this by saying her only on-post experience was in Hawaii, of all places. And that was because the cost of living there was too expensive off base. "I remember back in 2000, a gallon of milk cost five dollars in Hawaii! Those were ridiculous prices at the time," Pamela says. "Because the cost-of-living adjustment was so steep, we were looking at renting a very small place that would be in our budget, but it required putting nearly all of our stuff into storage. And then the phone rang. The housing office on base called and said we must immediately come see a new home that had just became available. As it turned out, a more senior couple just turned down a very large house on base because they felt a family would get better use out of it. And that lucky family was us—the house was beautiful with a big yard and lots of space. It was a dream for on-post living." We're not at all suggesting that you should expect to be so lucky, but you may be pleasantly surprised.

If you want some more nitty-gritty details of each arrangement, here are some of the advantages of living on base:

- Living costs are covered in exchange for a BAH (basic allowance for housing), including utilities. The BAH is calculated based on standard costs of living in your area and based on your status as an enlisted or officer member and how many, if any, dependents you have.
- You save time and transportation costs because your man is close to work.
- Your family has easy access to post facilities such as the commissary, BX or PX, MWR centers, and more.
- Military Police and on-post security offers peace of mind for personal and family safety.
- You'll have built-in camaraderie and support from neighbors in base housing who understand your lifestyle.

On the other hand, there can be downsides to living on a military base. When your military relocation order comes through, base housing may not be available where you are going. There may even be a waiting list, so even if you want to live on base, you may have to find temporary housing elsewhere until something on base becomes available.

As you think about settling inside the gates, be aware of the following:

- Housing on base may not be as new as off-base housing. Although some military bases have modern housing, many do not. Base housing may be outdated and dormitory-like.
- Base housing is assigned based on family size and other parameters. This means that some assigned housing may be cramped and inadequate for family needs.
- Base housing is closely supervised. There are rules for everything—including the height of your grass and the placement of your children's toys. Be prepared.
- Privacy can be an issue. Your military housing neighbors may provide a support network, but sometimes they are too close.
- Living on base tends to isolate you from community involvement that can lead to contacts for present or future jobs, friendships, and community resources.
- From a financial point of view, living on base offers no opportunity to build equity and take advantage of the benefits of home-ownership.

Although many military families choose to live on base, many others like the opportunity to become part of the local community and school system. Whatever you decide, either moving option requires advance planning.

Plan Ahead

I may not have personal experience with military moves, but because my ex-husband was British, I've moved my whole house overseas to London and back, twice, with a small child. I won't even discuss my domestic movements. So I do know that moving is drama, but there are lots of ways to help make your household move easier, and with less hassle. The key, I've found, is planning, planning, planning. In fact, some of the spouses say the best planning happens long before a move is even on the horizon. Moreover, some of the planning can be done before you say "I do" to life as a military spouse. What do we mean? Well, whether you're a bride-to-be or a seasoned military wife, it is always a good idea to consider the military lifestyle when buying furniture, knickknacks, and other household items. I'm not sure if the military lifestyle is best suited for collecting antique teacups or glass figurines. After all, these items may not be able to endure frequent packing and moving. The two most important factors to consider when stocking up on your household inventory are, can it withstand the likelihood of frequent moves and would the size possibly cause a need for storage?

Of course, that doesn't mean that military spouses can't have the finer things in life like good china and crystal. It's just about getting the right kind that will be able to handle being moved every three years or so and, possibly, not by the gentlest of creatures. When these guys come in, it's a quick-moving mission. I've heard of movers going so fast and furious they packed up the dinner pot that was on the stove! You need durable stuff for these guys and a healthy dose of detachment. Most wives recommend never becoming too attached to anything you own. To move-proof your belongings, select durable china patterns such as Wedgwood, with colors that are baked in instead of painted on. Patterns with gold rims may look durable, but gold paint often chips off in the dishwasher. Also, choose thick crystal instead of the delicate thin kind.

You can also stay prepared for your inevitable move by keeping nonessential items, like outdated clothes and good ole junk to a minimum. Every three months, make your entire family review their clothes, toys, and other belongings and give away anything that has not been used in the past year. Not only will this improve storage and packing time, it will force every family member to think twice before buying something.

WATCH YOUR WEIGHT

Also keep in mind that permanent change of station (PCS) moves come with a weight allowance for all of your belongings. Whatever is over your weight limit is your responsibility. Your weight allowance increases with your rank and years of service. For example, an (entry level) E-1 level soldier would have 1,500 pounds as a single person and a 3,000 allowance with dependents, whereas a top-level officer could have as much as an 18,000-pound weight allowance. One rough estimate is to figure 1,000 pounds per room (not including bathrooms), then add on the estimated weight of your large appliances. Estimate at least about 150 pounds each for things like washing machines or dishwashers, and don't forget about the stuff in the shed, garage, basement, or other storage units.

So, in the early days of climbing the rank and pay grades, it may be best to keep it simple—or plan and budget to do a partial move yourself.

Harriet Staten, a now retired service member and army quartermaster officer, says she started off small, but as her and her husband's ranks increased, she ignored all the advice about her belongings. "I bought everything I thought I wanted because I knew the army was going to move it. For the first ten years when I moved, it was always my husband and I organizing the move together. Later, he was actually deployed at the time of moving, and I had to do it by myself. It was majorly depressing. I had two children and was trying to get everything set up on both ends."

RELOCATION AND MOVING
↝ AUTHORIZED WEIGHT ALLOWANCES ↜

Two factors govern the weight allowance for household goods that may be shipped at government expense: pay grade and dependents. This allowance includes the weight of household goods you ship, place in storage, or send as unaccompanied baggage. *You*—not your transportation officer or the carrier—are responsible for staying within weight allowance. If household goods exceed the weight allowed by the Joint Federal Travel Regulations, members will be required to pay all charges associated with the excess weight.

For this reason, it's a good idea for members to estimate the weight of their household goods shipment. An easy and fairly dependable method for making this estimate is to figure 1,000 pounds per room (not including bathrooms), then add the estimated weight of large appliances and items in the garage, storage rooms, and the basement to that amount. The following table outlines the weight allowances authorized by pay grade.

JOINT FEDERAL TRAVEL REGULATIONS WEIGHT ALLOWANCES IN POUNDS			
Grade	PCS Without Dependents	PCS Weight Dependents	Temporary Allowance
O-10	18,000	18,000	2,000
O-9	18,000	18,000	1,500
O-8	18,000	18,000	1,000
O-7	18,000	18,000	1,000
O-6	18,000	18,000	800
O-5	16,000	17,500	800
O-4/W-4	14,000	17,000	800
O-3/W-3	13,000	14,500	600
O-2/W-2	12,500	13,500	600
O-1/W-1	10,000	12,000	600
E-9	12,000	14,500	600
E-8	11,000	13,500	500
E-7	10,500	12,500	400
E-6	8,000	11,000	400
E-5	7,000	9,000	400
*E-4	7,000	8,000	400
**E-4	3,500	7,000	225
E-3	2,000	5,000	225
E-2	1,500	5,000	225
E-1	1,500	5,000	225

*Over 2 Years   ** Less Than 2 Years

❧ REMEMBER: EXCESS WEIGHT CAN COST BIG MONEY ❧

The total weight of property shipped and stored cannot exceed your authorized allowance. Exceeding your authorized weight allowance on a domestic or international move can cost you a lot of money. Charges for excess weight can range from several hundred to several thousand dollars.

❧ VERIFY ACCURACY OF EXCESS COST ❧

The way to avoid excess weight charges is to stay within your authorized weight allowance by estimating early and disposing of unnecessary possessions. When you receive a notification for exceeding your weight allowance, check it carefully. You may not have received credit for professional books, papers, and equipment (PBP&E), or some other entitlement. If you have any questions concerning your excess weight, contact your transportation office.

Source: Per Diem Committee

DECORATING WITH MOVING IN MIND

Military families also tend to live in base housing or rentals, and that means a lot of white walls. Despite your best decorating intentions, you are not likely to paint so it's better to strategize a solid decorating theme that will look good whether you're stationed in Japan, California, or Washington, D.C.

When buying your first pieces of furniture, select a general color scheme for the entire house. Every time you buy a new piece, make sure it fits into that scheme even if it is for a different room. In a few years, all of your furniture may wind up in the same room together, so it should somehow all coordinate.

- When you buy furniture, try to avoid neutral color schemes like white, beige, or black. Your walls always will be white or beige, so you'll need to brighten things up with color.

- Buy wooden picture frames and shelves that can be painted. It's a great way to spiff up white walls.
- "Keep small movable pieces of furniture," says Shawn Sironnen, a wife of an army chief. If you have larger pieces, make sure you have insurance before moving or you aren't too worried about the inevitable knicks and scratches that happen during a move.
- If you have upholstered furniture, choose patterns that will fit in almost anywhere. Then accessorize and accent-ize using inexpensive tablecloths, curtains, and decorative pillows to make your look more casual or formal.
- Wood antique or foreign furniture are great collectibles, inexpensive, and capture the memories of where you once lived.
- Consider buying a mirror instead of a large poster or painting. They're less expensive than good art and fit in with all decor.

There's always a chance that you'll be moving to a smaller space, which always begs the inevitable question of, what am I going to do with all this stuff? Well, of course, I would first refer you back to rule number one about military life, which is accumulating a lot of stuff is not in your best interest. But my second response is, don't fret too much, my dear; there are some ways to fit an entire house full of furniture into an apartment without giving half of it away. Here are some tips:

- Invest in a quality sofa bed. It is more expensive than a regular sofa, but you can put it in the living room or a guest room.
- Use laminated bookshelves that are put together and taken apart for easy storage. Buy one neutral color, such as black or white, so the items may be mixed and matched in any room. And they don't have to be used for books; they are suitable for bathrooms, children's rooms, or clothes storage in closets.
- For holding china, consider buying corner cabinets instead of traditional rectangular monstrosities that take up an entire wall. Triangular in shape, corner cabinets hold a lot more than you think and can fit in almost any room. They're harder to find, but usually you can buy them at any good furniture store.

- When choosing bedside tables or end tables, select those with drawers for extra storage space.
- Get a library card. Books are surprisingly expensive, they require a lot of storage, and their accumulated weight takes up too much of your allocated shipping weight.

If you must give away furniture and sundries, make an effort to give it to another military family. In the end, you will be keeping it all in the community.

Preparing for a Move

Good preparation helps avoid mistakes that can cost money, energy, time, and your sanity. Shanice, a marine wife, says she shifts into "wedding planner" mode when it's time to move. "It's all about the master clipboard and the superlists," she says. Shanice starts on moving lists as soon as the orders are certain, and she has a detailed time line for when everything—from garage sales to charity donations—should happen.

You too, can get your life, your possessions, your kids, and yourself organized and ready to go. The other good thing about military moves is that, as you would expect with the military, the process is laid out for you. All relocations are handled by your Personal Property Shipping Office (PPSO) of the Traffic Management Office (TMO). Base officials may use either acronym when talking about who handles your move, so be aware of them. When you get your orders, you will also get a checklist that tells you every office you need to go to, every form you need to complete, and every task you need to tackle. There are plenty of people at those office stops to answer your questions and direct to the next step. You are not alone in the process.

Whether you're having a full military move or are moving items on your own because you're over the weight allowance or have delicate items, you still need to be organized. The Housing Office has plenty of tips and helpful advice for relocating military families. This may not be so easy with little notice—we've seen families move with a few weeks' notice, but you can still keep the drama to a minimum with the right attitude and a few good tips.

GET WHAT YOU DESERVE

As I said, the good news about moving is that you do have assistance from the military. Some of that help comes in the form of cash—or at least, reimbursement. That can be a comforting thought during a move, especially if it's your first move. Contact the Housing Office to learn the monetary benefits available for military moves, and ask for the maximum benefit possible. For example, the burden of initial housing expenses can be minimized by obtaining an advance BAH (basic allowance for housing). In the set-aside program, the deposit is waived and the monthly rent may be lowered since rent is paid via direct deposit to the landlord. These programs offer the most benefit *before* signing a lease or paying a lot of expenses out of pocket.

Make sure orders include DLA (dislocation allowance), if applicable, to help with moving costs, and ask that it be issued in advance. Unlike advance pay or advance BAH, which is withheld from pay in monthly increments through the next twelve months, DLA never has to be paid back. Moving is a highly emotional time and, in the stress of a move, many decisions can be made on emotion and not on fact or logic. Military families have many options available for moving, but know the benefits and drawbacks of each major choice. Ask neighbors, talk to the TMO, and be realistic about your own situation.

Many people decide on a Do It Yourself (DIY) move because it appears to cost less and you can avoid some of the scheduling hassles that come with moving on the government's timeline. There is a cash incentive from the government for moving yourself that may seem enticing. Remember, though, that may not always be the case, and there are a lot of ways to mess up (see Pamela's Pick). Basically the government estimates its costs to move you, based on your weight allowance, then pays you 95 percent of that cost to move it yourself. You can get the money in advance to help offset the cost of truck rental, packing supplies, and the like. Before committing to a full DIY move, take careful inventory of the real cost (using some of the following tools and tips), including relational, physical, emotional, and financial factors. Check and double-check prices: one-way truck rentals can be extremely expensive, and a DIY move may not be as profitable as you think. Add on extra expenses like storing the shipment or paying additional rental time for the truck until housing is ready, and a DIY move may not be so money-saving in the end.

Pamela's Pick: DIY oh my!

Here's where some people get caught out with DIY moves: when you use your car or rental truck for a DIY move, you are expected to weigh your empty vehicle in advance and then again at an official truck-weighing station (you know the ones you see alongside the highway with lines of tractor trailers waiting) to get the exact weight of your stuff. The weight can't include a towed car. But be careful, if you overestimate the weight during counseling and get some cash in advance and then find out you have *less* weight when you get to the truck-weighing station, you will have to pay the government back. They are not that generous.

If you're doing a full or partial self-move remember these tips:

Make a list: Rule number one: Write everything down! From your to-do list to your inventory list, you can never have too many. Well-organized lists are the linchpin to an organized move. You'll thank yourself later. Pamela's moving lists include such details as when to do the final loads of laundry, a list for when to disconnect and connect utilities and security systems, when to transfer magazine subscriptions, and when to start cooking and eating the food items they can't pack. Having lists is even more critical when there is little advance notice of a move.

Before you pack even one box, create a simple record keeping system for your belongings. The military movers will provide you with an inventory sheet, but you should create your own first. If you don't trust the movers to pack certain special items, make a computer-printed list of numbers with a space to write the contents of the boxes. Or have a spiral-bound notebook for the job. Then, place a number on *every* box you pack and list the contents on your list. When describing the box contents, be specific—"A-D files" is better than "files," and "Tulip dishes" is a lot more helpful than "Misc. kitchen."

The military has great inventory checklists, plus helpful hints and lists, at www.usps.com.

Have ample supplies: There's nothing worse than trying to move without enough boxes, tape, bubble wrap, and other supplies. Find out about local suppliers who may offer discounts to military families. Check your local paper or with other newcomers on base to see if anyone has empty boxes they want to get rid of.

Utilize wardrobe boxes: These tall boxes are perfect for bulky, lightweight items such as comforters, pillows, and blankets, as well as clothes that need to remain hanging. Call your mover to ask the width of the wardrobe boxes they'll be bringing. Then measure the clothes in your closets (including coat closets) to see how many wardrobe boxes you'll need. You can also use them for closet storage boxes, shoe boxes, and other bulky items such as fabric bolts, large baskets, or gift wrap tubes.

Don't make the boxes too heavy to lift, however. I heard one funny story of a quick-moving military spouse who put a bowling ball in a wardrobe box! When the box was lifted off the truck, the bottom gave way, sending the bowling ball down the ramp, across the street, then down a hill where it finally landed across the road in a ditch.

PROTECT YOUR BELONGINGS

Once you know all the stuff you have, it's equally important to protect it. Let us say this: we think the most important tool to mastering military moves is the right mind-set. What we've learned from wives is that you should never get too attached to anything you can't stand to lose. Hey, we all like nice stuff, but getting too attached can only lead to disaster. But we also think it's smart to protect your belongings with some basic insurance. Yes, the government will reimburse you for anything lost or damaged, but as you may have heard, the government moves very s-l-o-w-l-y.

Remember this point: buy renters' or personal property insurance policy *before* your DIY move. Ask around any military community and you will hear stories of movers leaving furniture out in the rain and then putting it into storage for two years, packers boxing porcelain collectibles without any paper or padding, moving trucks catching on fire or driving off mountainsides—these are rare but real occurrences! When Pamela lived in Hawaii, she distinctly remembers her neighbor's moving truck pulling up. The very first crate they opened, water came pouring out of it and all over the place! Everything was ruined.

Insurance is a bargain when weighed against the cost of replacing the contents of even one room. Most policies cover a lot more than loss by fire or disaster. For example, food that spoiled during a prolonged local blackout was claimed and reimbursed under renters' policies, which allowed families in this situation to replace their groceries and not go into debt. Often, the benefits received for one claim cover the cost of an entire year's premium. (Remember that, in today's insurance climate, too many insurance claims may cause your insurance to be canceled.)

Keep the policy even after the move, since the coverage is crucial in any military housing or rental, and the small expense is worth it. Renters' insurance may be able to reimburse damages in days, versus the weeks or months it may take to collect from the government. In addition, personal insurance also usually requires a lot less paperwork and hassle than the documentation required by the government. Less time spent on researching replacement costs means more time spent replacing the item and getting on with life in a new location.

USAA has insurance policies that are specifically suited to military needs. The company can be reached at www.usaa.com or 1-800-531-USAA (8722). Many other insurers also offer coverage.

> ### Pamela's Pick:
>
> We have been insured by USAA since we entered the military. We not only have had renter's insurance through USAA, but also car insurance and homeowner's insurance, and we've financed our cars through the company. Fortunately, none of our claims have been claims for losses during moves, but the ones we did have were handled swiftly, efficiently, and extremely professionally. Recently the company expanded its service availability to widows and widowers of military members who were killed in action, retirees, and honorably discharged veterans.

CUT THE FAT, REMOVE THE CLUTTER

Moving isn't all about the actual packing. Some important steps can happen before you crack open a box. In fact, the packing process can be simplified with a little prepacking preparation (say that three times really fast!).

1. Start with the "search and seizure" process: this is a term used by Lauren Jackson, based in Columbus, Mississippi. It involves aggressively going through all clothes, toys, and other belongings to

find anything that hasn't been worn or used in three years and then throwing it out or giving it away.

2. Start collecting important papers such as passports, insurance policies, marriage or divorce certificates, property deeds, and tax returns. Put them in a safe location, like a box that can be carried with you.

3. Use a digital or Polaroid camera to take pictures of anything of value that is going with the movers. You can document the exact condition of important items, so if any major dents or defects occur in transit, you can show what it was like when you left.

4. If you're considering a full or partial self-move, look at moving dates in the midweek or midmonth when it is cheaper.

5. Ship your belongings thirty days before your move date to make sure your things have arrived when you do. Shawn Sironnen says she even sends the beds ahead of time. "I'd rather us sleep on air mattresses in the home we know, so we can have our own beds when we arrive at the home we don't know," Shawn says.

6. Pack a first night box: toilet paper, toiletries, sheets, blankets, some first-night kitchen items like microwave popcorn or microwavable soup, and maybe a pot to boil water.

7. There's a good chance that you will be in temporary housing before your belongings arrive. Go to the family center or community service center and make use of the Lending Closet, also called the Airmen's Attic in the air force. There you can borrow pots, pans, or anything else you may need to hold you over until your shipment arrives. And if you ship items before you physically move, you can also borrow whatever you need, complete a simple form, and return it when you're done.

Be Prepared for the Movers

When the movers are ready to come in, be prepared. They move quick (remember the story I told you about the pot of food that got packed up!). Make sure you are ready for them. If there is anything you don't want packed, move it out of the house or put it in a room with a locked door. Secure your personal belongings so that they travel with you. You won't find this advice in any official military handbook, but Pamela suggests having pizza or snacks and beverages available for the movers. In every instance, she has found that treating them nicely has a direct correlation to how nicely they handle your belongings.

PETS

You may consider your dog as part of your family, but unfortunately the government doesn't. Pets can be moved at your own expense, although the cost is tax deductible. When Pamela's family had a dog, they moved it themselves. To relocate your pet, you will usually need a recent health certificate stating that your pet is healthy and current with its vaccinations.

> **Pamela's Pick:**
> I remember trekking from Texas to Maryland with myself and my six-month-old son in one car, and my husband and the puppy in the other. I had to stop often to feed the baby and give him some attention, and we also had to give the dog a break. It made a long trip even longer. But I've learned that when you are dealing with kids and pets, you have to just go with the flow. Remember, patience is key.

If you're moving overseas, remember, most countries and the state of Hawaii have laws governing the entry of animals. Most require up-to-date rabies vaccinations for dogs and cats and may quarantine your pet for thirty days or more. Some overseas locations allow owners to reduce the number of days a pet spends in quarantine by following procedures on a checklist. If the pet meets all the requirements, it may be released directly, or after five days, to the owner. If the requirements are not met, the pet may be quarantined for up to 120 days. Talk to your relocation counselor at the Family Readiness Center for more details.

If you're traveling with a pet, be prepared to stop more often, and make sure your travel plans include hotels and motels that accept pets. Most don't.

Plan for After You Arrive

Sure, there's plenty of help to pack up, but when you get to your new place, you're on your own to put away the unpacked goods. That's when most spouses say the stress of moving really hits. The best advice we can offer in this regard is, the more organized you are on the front end, the easier things will be on the back end.

If you're moving on base, go to www.militaryonesource.com to view the floor plans for your new base housing. This can help you size up how much of your current furniture will fit, and you can start thinking about where you want to put what. To help make sure everything gets put down by the movers at or near the right location, try a color system. Designate a *color* for each room in the new home, such as yellow for kitchen, orange for dining room, and so on. Apply colored stickers on the box near the box number. In your new home, put a matching sticker on the door to each room. The movers will know where to put everything when they unpack. It's also helpful to post a big sign on the wall in the room where you want boxes stacked ("Boxes here, please") to keep them out of furniture and traffic areas.

When you begin to tackle unpacking, just take it one box at a time. Be resigned to find things when you get to it. If you start rummaging through boxes looking for one particular item, you will find yourself in a mess.

Get the Kids Involved

Moving is tough on the kids, too. The older they are, the more likely they have established relationships and routines, from karate to dance classes, that make it harder for them to move. Shawn Sironnen, a forty-two-year-old air force wife and service member, says she makes every effort to get the children involved and excited about the move. If possible, try to include vacation time in between your moves. If traveling by road, hit up a few fun spots or attractions along the way. Shawn's husband is a chief, so she moves every two years. With that kind of frequent relocation, she stays focused on helping her three children adjust. Shawn says one of the keys to easing the impact of the move on her children is to really be attuned to their personalities and needs. If your child is an extrovert who easily adapts, that's great. But if you have a child who needs to "warm up" to new places, be considerate of that and do as much as you can to help your child adjust, Shawn says. "When you move, you need to be able to go into that new school and fully explain your child's likes and dislikes. This helps the children feel more comfortable sooner rather than later," she says.

We've seen families on a waiting list for on-post housing or living in temporary housing for other reasons in one school district only to be moved on base or to other permanent accommodations in another school district just a few months later. That can be tough on a kid. Parents really have to help. (Get more parenting tips in Chapter 8.)

Another great tool is the Internet. You can research schools in your new area easily with SchoolQuest, a safe, secure online resource for military families. SchoolQuest (www.schoolquest.org) is organized so that you can access information that the Military Child Education Coalition has gathered to help you make decisions on future schools for your children. You'll be asked to answer basic questions about your family and each of your school-aged children. Based on the answers you provide, SchoolQuest will then present, at no cost, meaningful facts, resources, and transition advice to help you find out about the area schools that serve the military community you select. School-Quest also offers an online library that provides resources for families in transition.

After you've done your homework to select a school, you can still go one step further. Several moms said they go online and view pictures of the school, teachers, and the upcoming activities with their kids. "That helps whet their appetite for the next experience and they feel some sort of familiarity with where they are going," says Shawn. She also has her kids keep a moving diary to record memories from their old home and they get a disposable camera to take pictures of their favorite people and places.

It's also great to take as much as reasonably possible to re-create the same environment for the children. We know wives who will sacrifice weight in other places so the kids can have their comforters, sheets, and important toys with them. Sometimes they've done a partial move on their own just to accommodate the things they wanted to take for the children.

There's More to Do . . .

Packing up your belongings is one thing, dismantling and reorganizing your life is another. You have mail to forward, accounts to close, utilities to disconnect or connect. It's critical to update address and phone changes as quickly as possible. Credit cards and other bills that are delayed while the mail forwards may cost you in late fees and affect your credit records. If possible, arrange to manage these accounts with toll-free phone numbers during the move or online with e-mail reminders. Auto insurance premiums also may change with a new zip code, so be sure to update policies promptly.

Conveniently, the IRS has an address change form online at www.IRS.gov that can be printed and mailed so tax refund checks find their owners after a move. Many other important sources also have online forms or allow instant online address changes to save a few dollars in postage. Pamela finds it much easier to just put in a change of address form with the post office. If you don't know your new address, get a P.O. box in your new area. That quickly gets all of your mail forwarded, and then once you get settled on the other end, you will have more time to call creditors, banks, and the like. And every time you get a piece of mail with a big ole yellow sticker on it, you know it's forwarded mail from someone you haven't notified about your change of address. Not a bad system.

Should You Buy?

In some markets, it may seem more economical to buy a house rather than rent. If you've decided to purchase a home in your next relocation, be sure you start the process with the answers to the following questions:

- Can we qualify for a mortgage loan to buy a home?
- Is VA financing available if we qualify?
- Do we have the money readily available for a down payment and closing costs?
- How long is this military relocation assignment?
- Will we keep the home when the next military relocation comes along?
- Is the local real estate climate positive? Is there a strong rental potential? Do homes in the area resell quickly? Are real estate property values on the rise, declining, or stable?
- Before you purchase off-base real estate, consult a military tax adviser for details on tax benefits and restrictions of the BAH. For more details, visit the Department of Defense website's Defense Finance and Account Service page.

Moving In

Once you arrive at your destination, contact the PPSO and let them know; then expect to hang out in an empty house for a few days. You should have the cellphone number of the moving van driver and a number for the moving company anyway, so you can stay in touch to find out exactly when your belongings will arrive. In the meantime, you can start some basic cleaning and prep work, like lining shelves with contact paper or figuring out what goes where.

Do not let the moving company leave without unpacking your stuff. Many families make this mistake. The movers are paid to unpack. If the movers try to make excuses or tell you otherwise, stand your ground. Call the moving company. Call the PPSO immediately, or if it's after hours, contact the base inspector general.

Seasoned spouses say they can have nearly an entire household unpacked with pictures hanging in four days. Pamela's husband has a standing rule that the house is good to go in a week. You don't have to pressure yourself with these kinds of performances but know that it can be done by having a good system. As the movers systematically unpack room by room, someone should be right behind them picking up and putting away everything they unpack. Since you've had a chance to plan out your house on the night and days before, this should be fairly easy. Even if you have to rearrange things later, getting them put away somewhere is your first priority. If the movers start to run out of counter space or floor space while unpacking, this will be just the excuse they need to stop their work. Don't forget to buy them lunch, and it couldn't hurt to turn the radio on to their favorite station—not yours!

Any items on your inventory list that don't show up with your shipment or are damaged should be immediately recorded on DD Form 1840, which is the mover's paperwork for PPO. You are entitled to receive the pink copy. After you've signed the form noting any damages or losses, the mover will send a copy to PPO and you have seventy days to report any additional lost or damaged items and two years to file a completed claim.

And don't forget, the movers have to remove any empty boxes. They take up a lot of room, and many places have rules making them difficult to dispose of.

MOVING TERMS YOU SHOULD KNOW

You know the military has its own language for everything, and the moving and relocation process has its own gems. Here are a few key terms that you should know to make the process easier.

Accessorial Charges: A rate or charge stated in carrier tariff for extra services that is in addition to the line-haul rate.

Accessorial Service: A service apart from the line-haul transportation related to movement of personal property. This would include extra packing, crates, extra labor, or any special handling of the personal property.

Agent/Carrier: A bona fide agent of a government-approved carrier. A person or business who represents and acts for a motor carrier and works according to a preexisting agreement with the carrier and the government.

Area of Responsibility (AOR): A specifically defined geographic area where one military installation has been designated the responsibility for acquisition of storage, transportation, and related services.

Attempted Pickup or Delivery: The use of labor and/or vehicles to perform pickup or delivery to member's residence when ordered by the PPSO and service cannot be performed. This is usually due to the residence being not ready to pack, because of insects or the member/releasing agent not being at the residence. The "attempt" would be at the service member's expense. Costs range from $50 to $300 or more.

Command-Sponsored Dependent Entry Approval: This is required for overseas locations. The Personnel Support Detachment (PSD) handling the member's records will assist with obtaining a family member's entry approval, if required. Check with your local PSD if you are transferring overseas to see if this is needed.

Commuting Area: A distance designated by the military service from an origin or destination point (corporate limits of a city or town) that includes the majority of all shipments serviced. Usually within a thirty-mile radius of the military base AOR.

Crating: Items such as marble, large pieces of glass, or other unusual items that need special protection during transportation can be approved for crating by the PPSO or government inspector. A special crate can be made for such items. Crates are slatted and not solid containers. These crates are loaded into a truck, van, or solid shipping container for transportation.

Direct Procurement Method (DPM): A method of shipment in which the government manages the shipment throughout. Packing, containerization, local drayage, and storage services are obtained from a commercial firm under contractual arrangement. Usually small shipments with no furniture included.

Do It Yourself (DIY) Move: A move where you get all the services and equipment yourself, and perform all labor associated with the move. There are three types of DIY military moves.

- Rental Equipment: You rent a truck or trailer. You receive an advance operating allowance based on mileage authorized and estimated weight of shipment. Then you pack, load, drive, unload, and unpack the shipment on your own. Any necessary storage is at your expense with reimbursement.

- You Load, They Drive: You pack and load a commercial moving van/truck, the commercial moving company drives to the destination, and then you unload and unpack the van/truck. The commercial firm must give you the ICC number or state/federal regulation numbers. And you'll need weight tickets provided by the moving company.

- Privately Owned Vehicle (POV) DIY: There is no advance operating allowance for this type of move. This is where you use your own or a borrowed vehicle. And you must have written permission and current vehicle registration from the vehicle owner for all POV DIY moves. The POV must be a "cargo" type vehicle, not a vehicle that is designed for passenger transport.

Final Delivery Point: Place where carrier surrenders possession of property to the owner or owner's agent and no further transportation or services are required under the government bill of lading (GBL).

Household Goods (HHG): All personal property associated with the home and all personal effects belonging to the member and member's family on the effective date of the member's permanent change of station (PCS) or temporary duty (TEMDU/TDY) orders, which can be legally accepted and transported by a moving company.

Letter of Authorization: Allows the service member to designate a representative (agent) to act on his/her behalf. This letter is prepared by the service member and must be notarized or countersigned by a commissioned officer in the member's command. If no one is designated as an agent to release or receive the shipment, no one other than the member can accept the shipment or sign the shipment documents. (Even the spouse must be designated as a releasing/receiving agent.)

Nontemporary Storage (NTS): Generally considered long-term storage. This storage may be authorized for overseas, sea duty, temporary duty under construction, separation, or retirement. It is considered part of the member's weight allowance and is generally stored at point of origin for the length of the tour. Time limits vary depending on the type of orders (e.g., separation is 180 days while retirement is one year).

Per Diem: An allowance paid daily instead of actual expenses for lodging, meals, and related incidental expenses associated with orders.

Permanent Change of Station (PCS): PCS orders transfer a service member from one duty station to another. When a service member relocates from one area to another, his/her PCS orders provide the basis and authority for a shipment. In order to move, all orders must have appropriation data. Without this line of accounting, the PPSO cannot move a shipment. A member must have orders "in hand" before arranging for household goods/baggage shipments.

Personal Property Processing Office (PPPO): A PPPO prepares the documents for shipping and/or storage, then forwards these documents to the PPSO to book the shipment with a government-approved moving company or NTS company for storage. Other terms for PPSO/PPPO with other branches of the military are

- TMO (Traffic Management Office)
- TO (Transportation Office)
- JPPSO (Joint Personal Property Office)
- CPPSO (Consolidated Personal Property Office)

Personal Property Shipping Office (PPSO): A PPSO prepares and arranges for all areas of shipping HHGs and unaccompanied baggage (UB) and arranges for NTS. The PPSO actually books the shipment with a government-approved moving company.

Required Delivery Date (RDD): HHG or UB should arrive on or before the RDD. This is not a guaranteed date of delivery. It is important that you contact the destination PPSO as soon as you arrive, even if you do not have a delivery address at this time. You should provide the destination office with your work phone number(s), or any phone number by which you can be contacted.

Satisfactory Service: Performance that meets the moving, handling, and storage standards established by the government. Completing the customer service survey for both satisfactory and/or unsatisfactory service. This survey is one way in which the government quality control personnel rate the carriers' performance. Don't forget about positive feedback and try to be fair.

Shipment: Property made available by one shipper (member or agent) to the carrier for loading at one time, at one place or origin, for one consignee to one destination.

Temporary Storage (Storage In Transit . . . SIT): Storage in connection with a line-haul movement of personal property. Such storage is cumulative and may accrue at origin, en route, at destination, or any combination thereof. Storage is not to exceed ninety days, unless specifically requested and approved by the destination inbound section, before the ninety days' time limit. Storage beyond ninety days is not automatically granted.

The Mocha Mix
Real Talk on Mastering the Military Move

★ ★

The best thing I learned is not to be attached to personal items. I pack whatever I really need in my suitcases. Whatever else gets sent between usually two shipments. I always ship all my cooking utensils, linen, and towels in the first shipment. And I keep my moves very, very lean. I moved to Korea with family of five with only 3,000 pounds of goods.

—DIANE WIGGINS, ARMY WIFE OF SIXTEEN YEARS,
SEOUL, KOREA

I look at military moves like a Christmas present. It's almost always a surprise. Sometimes you like what you get, sometimes you don't. But there's always another Christmas coming.

—ALICIA WILLIAMS, ARMY WIFE,
SHAW AIR FORCE BASE, SOUTH CAROLINA

The army made it easy in that they would give you an inventory sheet. Those are very important. Have a great list beforehand and check off every single thing you own. I've lost things and things have gone "missing." With a good inventory list, you can file a claim and get your money back.

—HARRIETT STATEN, RETIRED SERVICE MEMBER
AND FORMER ARMY WIFE, ATLANTA, GA

My first move was traumatic. But I got the hang of getting organized beforehand, only moving completely necessary items, and learning to go with the flow.

—ELIZABETH WORTHINGTON, COLUMBUS, MS

We've been stationed at Fort Bragg for over ten years. My only moves have been from one base house to a larger base house, so things have been pretty easy. Clearing is rarely a problem for us.

—ANTOINETTE, ARMY WIFE

CHAPTER SIX

Working It!

Career and Education Planning
for the Military Spouse

You might not know where your next home will be or whether your military mate will be there to help around the house, but what you can be sure of is that overall, military folks are not any more financially well-off than civilians. Service members receive a set pay amount, at regular intervals, and typically are paid based on their skills, experience, education, and time on the job, just like civilians. And just like in many civilian families, sometimes it takes two incomes to make ends meet or reach a desired lifestyle for yourself and your children.

So what is it about the military that warrants a discussion about employment and education for military spouses? Well, let's start with frequent relocation and the rigid and often unexpected demands of our service members' lives. Many military bases are located in remote areas where skilled jobs are scarce, and good pay is even more rare. And it's hard to build a real career if you're moving every few years or to find an employer who will give you time off on short notice because your husband suddenly has to deploy or the twice-rescheduled homecoming is now, tomorrow! Not to mention that there can be long waits for child care on post and high costs off post. Or that if you're a licensed professional, you have the added burden of meeting different state standards or having to reapply for a license every time you relocate out of state. Yes, because of your lifestyle, long-term steady employment can be elusive for a military spouse. But not impossible. Navy wives may have a better chance at traditional career building, since many bases are located in large port cities with more job opportunities. Army and air force wives are more challenged.

Despite the challenges, about 74 percent of military wives do work, according to a report by RAND, a prominent think tank. That's a beefy number, but still far less than the 82 percent of civilian wives who work. And military wives earn as much as 60 percent less than their civilian counterparts, even though military wives tend to have higher education levels, the study found. Some of that may be attributed to fewer hours worked. Only 48 percent of military spouses work more than thirty-five hours per week compared with 59 percent of civilian wives working full-time.

Truth be told, as an MS you do get the short end of the career-building stick. After all, when you move to a new station, your husband will have a job, an established group of adults with whom to interact, a daily schedule, and someone to do all the settling in at home: you! On the other hand, you aren't so lucky. Sometimes you might feel that by the time you learn the neighborhood; find all the grocery stores, schools, and doctors; and settle in to the family schedules of military functions, schools, extracurricular activities, and everyone's social lives, there's no time or energy left for the job search. And that's if it's not almost time to pack up and move again. Not to mention that there's often an unspoken expectation that hubby's career comes first.

Savvy sisters who are married to the military and really want to work don't have to let the mobile military lifestyle put their careers on the back burner indefinitely. So take heart, you don't have to go for low-paying, unchallenging positions or completely give up working altogether.

Although it might not be possible to plan your whole career, since you will have little or no control over your life's geographical journey, you can position yourself to enjoy a life of getting paid to some degree, when and if it works for you. What you need, my friend, is a "portable" career track, and we can help you define and find one in this chapter.

But first, as usual, you need a little self-examination for you and your spouse.

To Work or Not Work?

Whether or not to work outside the home is a question military families should revisit over and over. Your decision to be a single- or dual-income family could change every few years based upon location, whether or not you have children, the ages and stages of your children, your financial needs, and more.

"I stopped working when I had three kids," said Diane, who has lived in Korea for six of the sixteen years she has been married to the military. "With one of us at work all day the other needs to be on standby for whatever comes up with the children. We made that conscious decision early on, and we talked about it before, during, and after they were born," she added.

Don't let runaway finances force you to work. "Whatever you do, live within your means because doing so will give you a choice about whether to work or not," advised Diane. "If you decide to return to work after being out for a while, keep your spending in check. If you didn't have it before you got a job, you probably don't need it after you get one."

Talk this over with your mate to decide what is best for you now and in the future, even considering his transition to the civilian world.

Is He Onboard?

Before you commit to building a career you need to make sure your man is with the program. Talk to him about it. Make sure he views your career aspirations as important as his own. Don't turn this conversation into an argument, though it's not known to be an easy discussion for many service members. Do not attack his career in the military or blame it for your own stunted career (after all, you willingly signed up for the military life). All you are asking is that he be supportive of your career goals and help you out emotionally or logistically during the inevitable career transitions as they come along. For example, when you move, is he willing to share in the relocation duties so that you both can devote time to career transition issues?

Now, as two seasoned women, we have to say that is equally important to listen to what your man says as to what he does. He may not want to sound all Cro-Magnon-like by declaring that, in reality, he'd rather you stay home and tend to the house. So, he may *say* he's supportive, but his actions tell you something completely different; that is, he does nothing regarding the moving and leaves you no time to deal with your career transition issues. Trust us, it's not that your man is being deceitful, but sometimes men aren't really aware of how they're feeling about a situation until they are in it and they have to do something (like more work or other sacrifices) to make it happen. This is where good communication will work wonderfully. Be up front and honest about the ways you need his support, and ask him to honestly commit to giving it to you, to the extent possible.

Getting to It: Creating a Portable Career

Now that you've figured out what's best for your family and have your man fully in sync, it's time to create a portable career. What is a portable career and where can a sister get one? It depends upon whom you ask. To some military spouses it means being able to earn money regardless of where they live. To others it might mean finding a job in their skill area or career field on a regular basis. For others still, it might mean being able to keep the same job regardless of where you or your employer is physically located. Or you may be able to identify national and international companies that need your skills and are willing to relocate you, let you telecommute, or open a satellite office. Believe it or not, the federal government is the ultimate portable employer. They've got jobs in everything from secretarial and administrative capacities to management positions, and every base employs government employees. No matter how you define a portable career, the bottom line is that you need to be able to pack up your skills and earning potential and take it with you wherever you go. Accounting is a really good example of a solid portable career because usually every military or civilian community needs accountants, and the licensing requirements are relatively minimal. Hairdressing, other service jobs, and some health-care professions are pretty good, too. And believe it or not, the roads have already been paved. All you need to do is be familiar with them and choose which one to travel.

TOP PORTABLE CAREERS

1. Freelance writing
2. Web design
3. Graphic design
4. Event planner
5. Home staging
6. Virtual assistance
7. Secretarial support
8. Transcriptionist
9. Information research

This section covers the following strategies to overcome the challenges of a mobile and unpredictable lifestyle:

- Work for a government contractor.
- Learn to work it: take advantage of employment programs designed for military spouses.
- Consider federal internship and employment programs.
- Use temporary work options.
- Be your own boss.
- Seek virtual success.
- Go back to school.

One thing I have learned from working with Pamela and talking to military wives is despite how advanced technology may be, never underestimate the power of the want ads of your local newspaper. Pamela found two pivotal jobs simply by checking the local paper. I won't age her by saying whether or not the Internet even existed beyond a government project at the time. But one was her first gig managing a job training program for at-risk youth. Then years later after a baby and two relocations, she went back to the local want ads and struck gold! She found a job listing for a career counselor for soldiers and family members who are leaving military service. It was right up her alley! Plus, the employer was a company that managed career centers all over the world on army installations, was military spouse friendly, and offered decent pay, education benefits, and paid vacation. Jackpot! By working for a government contractor she found an employer who understands a mobile lifestyle and wants to employ military spouses.

You can, too. The government saves a lot of money by hiring other companies to do jobs rather than having service members or federal employees do them. There are obviously a lot of advantages for them, but for you, it could mean being able to stay with the same employer and working in different locations and thereby being able to have a progressive career. Defense contractors like Boeing, Raytheon, and General Dynamics are known to do a lot of government work and typically have offices on or nearby most American military bases around the world. You can also look into large accounting, management consulting, or public relations firms.

To find government contractors in your area contact your local chamber of commerce, the trade organization for your profession, or a local business development office.

START YOUR OWN BUSINESS

One thing is for sure, the Internet has become the great equalizer. Small business owners can often compete with the big boys online by selling goods and services via websites. The beauty of a web-based business is that you can take it wherever you go.

In my book *The Mocha Manual to Turning Your Passion into Profit,* I advise women like you just how they can turn a skill, talent, or hobby into a moneymaking enterprise. There I propose a nine-step strategy, which includes reconnecting with your passion and life purpose, finding and researching the business side of any idea, learning how to successfully market and brand your business, and mastering some essential skills for entrepreneurial success. Those were some of the same steps I used to start www.mochamanual.com, an online magazine and community for black moms, and my consulting business. The site is now the Web's number one resource for black moms and a very successful online enterprise. Of course, I highly recommend that you pick up the book, but the point is that you can take control of your life, your career, and your income by becoming an entrepreneur—if you know how to do it correctly. It's not an easy life, but the long hours are worth it.

Other women have worked up a sizable "side hustle" doing everything from Passion Parties and Mary Kay to selling jewelry and handmade crafts and products. These may not fund that trip to Maui, but they can often make a solid contribution to the family income and finance your extracurricular shopping activities!

Sometimes the process of finding your own thing is by deliberate, step-by-step actions; other times a good gig comes from being attentive and proactive. After living in Panama all her life, Maritza married a military man and left her family and the computer graphic design studio and print shop business she co-owned for five years. Each time she and her husband moved, she had a hard time finding work, despite the fact that she had a bachelor's degree and six years of experience in her field. Maritza became very frustrated by the lack of jobs and by the abundance of employers who were biased against her because she was likely to move in a few years. There were also last-minute moves and her husband's multiple deployments.

As often is the case, Maritza made a way out of no way by creating her own opportunity. She noticed a local Hispanic bilingual newspaper that had bad translations and called to offer her help. She discovered that the company was very small and the owner was doing almost everything himself. He was impressed with the number of mistakes she found in the newspaper and offered her a job. She worked there for three years, after creating her own job.

While Maritza was successful landing in her new areas, she never fully mastered creating a portable career. Once she had a job as the creative director in a company's marketing department, but ended up having to move a whole year sooner than she planned. The employer asked her to stay for six months, even offering her a car and lodging—a very sweet deal. Although she really wanted to stay, again, like many spouses, she put her husband's career first. He had been in Kuwait for two years, so she opted to move with him to California. Her boss then worked out an Internet telecommuting arrangement, but it became too difficult to make it work. Two weeks later they had hired someone else for the job.

"I took some classes just to fill my time," said forty-five-year-old Maritza, who was accustomed to being an active member of many organizations in Panama. "I didn't know to expect all this when I married a soldier. I understand and accept it, but it has taken me some time."

Putting in the time and effort to start your own business or "side hustle" can help keep you fulfilled in between the big jobs or the no jobs and add some continuity to your earnings.

Get Help from Uncle Sam

For years, wives were seen only as necessary in supporting the soldier and furthering his career. Thankfully, Uncle Sam's attitude has changed. He now realizes that when Mama's happy, the family's happy.

Uncle Sam has "discovered" what wives have known all along: employment satisfaction impacts a family's overall satisfaction with military life, and service members and their families actually make decisions about whether to "stay in" based on that satisfaction. And now, the military powers-that-be have been fervently putting one and one together to help make two incomes within reach for military families by stepping up the level of spouse employment resources that already exist and establishing partnerships to create more.

Consider the following resources to assist in your job search or portable career building.

> **Pamela's Pick: Know the Law**
> Department of Defense Directive 1400.33 says that no one can hold it against you or your husband if you decide to work, go to school, or volunteer. His work performance evaluation should not in any way be impacted, and no one should give you grief about your activities unless your job creates a conflict of interest with his duties.

Work It: Special Employment and Education Programs for Military Spouses

All of the service branches provide free on-post help for spouses who want to work. Each of them offers job search skills workshops (such as résumé writing and interviewing), self-service tools (computer, Internet, fax, and printer access), a reference library, counseling, local job market information, and contacts. Getting help is as simple as walking in to your installation family services center and asking to sign up for the Army Employment Readiness Program, Navy Family Employment Assistance Program, Air Force Career Focus Program, Marine Corp Family Member Employment Assistance Program, or the Coast Guard Spouse Employment Assistance Program.

The Departments of Defense, Veterans Affairs, Transportation, and Labor joined forces to provide the Transition Assistance Program (TAP) to provide service members and their families with services to help the transition into the civilian workforce when they leave military service. Go to www.ta online.com/dependentspages/ for more information.

The military has also recognized that partnering with other entities to create employment opportunities multiplies the positive impact on military families. Following are some examples.

Army Spouse Employment Partnership (ASEP): The army has signed statements of support with thirty-first partners from the private sector and federal government. The partners have hired more than twenty-three thousand spouses. The ASEP also launched the Military Spouse Job Search (www.msjs.org) through the Department of Labor's America's Job Bank.

Department of Labor: Military Spouse Career Advancement Accounts (CAA): This program was developed to create portable career opportunities for military spouses. The CAA will pay for training and education that will give spouses the skills or credentials to compete in high-demand occupations (e.g., human resources and hospitality) and high-growth industries (e.g., education and health care). These accounts can be used to pay a maximum of $3,000 for one year, which is renewable for a second year. You must have a high school diploma or GED, and your service member must be assigned to one of the installations participating in the pilot program or is deployed or is stationed on an unaccompanied tour and has at least a year at the current assignment. For an up-to-date list of the pilot locations and the eligible courses of study, visit http://caa. milspouse.org/Portable/. If you are on post, go to your Education Center, Family Readiness Center, or Spouse Employment Program office.

Military Spouse Career Center: This website was created and developed by Monster.com and Military.com on behalf of the Department of Defense. You can apply for jobs, post your résumé, receive job alerts, research career fields, and get career advice. See www.military.com/spouse.

Milspouse.org: Jointly sponsored by the Department of Defense and the Department of Labor, this site is an online resource library for military spouses who are looking for information on employment, education, and relocation. It includes interactive locators from which you can glean location and contact information for the offices on an installation.

But the military can't do it all. There are numerous nonmilitary programs and organizations that create opportunities and resources specifically for military spouses, too.

Spouses to Teachers: At www.spousestoteachers.org, military spouses are helped to obtain the credentials to become a public school teacher. The site offers everything you need to get started, such as occupational information; job search, résumé, and interviewing help; and information on certification and licensure requirements for all states and agencies, required exams, reciprocity agreements, financial assistance, alternative certification, and distance learning programs.

Military Spouse Corporate Career Network (MSCCN): A nonprofit, this corporate direct hire program places job-ready candidates in virtual jobs with trusted corporate employers who support the military. The site, www.msccn.org, contains online forum discussions, a newsletter (*Military Spouse Employment Journal*), résumé posting, and countless other resources.

CONSIDER FEDERAL EMPLOYMENT AND EDUCATION

The government is *the* largest employer in the United States, offers federal internships, *and* has a military spouse preference program. So, for the patient military spouse who wants to maintain a career despite the frequent reassignment of her service member, a spouse could position herself well by seeking federal employment.

Be forewarned that the federal application process can be very complex and very long. To start, visit the official site of the federal government at www .usajobs.gov for job announcements, advice on how to build your résumé, job search tips, career exploration, and much more. Then be patient with the process and know that although the professional climb could be slow and intermittent, it can be rewarding in the end.

"During our travels with the military, my career often had to be put on hold. I am a civilian employee and I had to take jobs in whatever position was available, like a GS-4 Secretary and GS-5 File Clerk," said Claudine, an air force wife and contract specialist. (General Schedule refers to a pay scale for most civil service white-collar government personnel. Grades 1–7 are considered entry-level positions and pay.) "Some of the air force installations in Europe were very small and did not have many positions in my career field; therefore, it was a setback for me while overseas. But I am proud today to say that I have come a long way and am now at a comfortable pay grade, but aspiring to excel even further," she added.

Despite a late start, thirtysomething Nicole successfully worked her way through the federal employee system. For the first ten years of being married to the military, Nicole's work life consisted of working part-time and finding temporary jobs on post and through temp agencies. She and her husband didn't need the second income because they lived on post and had minimal expenses.

"I could do almost anything I wanted to do as long as we could afford it. I volunteered with Army Community Services, attended play groups with my children, saved a lot of money on child care, got my errands done when there were no crowds, and attended military wives' clubs meetings," recalled Nicole.

Nicole had always wanted to earn her bachelor's degree, but when she fell in love and got married midway through her completion of it, she got a little sidetracked because it became less of a priority. Besides that, she rarely lived in any one place long enough to finish it. After ten years of putting it off, Nicole decided to go back to school. "After my second child I had a strong desire to complete my degree, so I went to school at night for less than two years," she said.

Once she attained her bachelor's degree in general studies with a minor in business, Nicole started looking for a job and discovered something even better: the Department of the Army Material Command Fellows Program. This program was one of many civil service internship programs that offered growth and promotion potential in a short time, as well as graduate school. Nicole enrolled and was on her way to making up for lost time. This would be a perfect way to increase her marketability wherever her husband got stationed. All she had to do was complete four one-year job rotations and she'd be good to go.

"The internship program is built to be long term; however, the job rotations allow you to work within different professional areas, therefore familiarizing you with all the important aspects of a field, which is what you need when training for management," she said.

Upon acceptance, Nicole started as a GS-7 and had to move to Texas to attend six months of orientation and training for the program. Subsequently, she attended twelve months of graduate school while receiving full-time pay! The next phase of her internship required one-year rotations at various duty stations. Each year she received her promotion, but relocation came along with it. Nicole moved four times in five years. Nicole, her husband, and their children crisscrossed Virginia, Texas, Kentucky, New Jersey, and Georgia for a few years, rarely living together. When the stars finally aligned and both her and her husband's jobs were in the same state, they actually lived under the same roof for a whole year before separation came into play again. And that was when Nicole completed the program as a GS-13. The payoff: there can be as much as a \$40,000–\$60,000 annual pay increase between GS-7 and GS-13!

"This is when some wives begin to think it sucks to be married to the military. My husband was stationed in Atlanta and my permanent position turned out to be in New Jersey," she said. "I made the decision to resign my permanent-status civil service job instead of breaking up the family again."

The good news was that Nicole could be rehired as a temp employee for the same job. The bad news was that it would be for less pay. Once again, living up to the standard that we military wives have for making it work, Nicole took a temporary job for two years when her husband received orders to move again, this time to Arkansas. She won't have enough time to complete the two years of the temporary assignment (we told you how this goes!), but she continues to search online for a similar position near her new home. She is also willing to accept a job outside the federal arena. Showing true MS grit, Nicole takes it all in stride by looking on the bright side.

"This is a good move for my husband's career," she said. "I am ready for a change. I look forward to better schools for the children, and I will be able to be more involved with them. Hey, this might be the place we like enough to retire.

"As for my professional life, I am open to looking at whatever new opportunities present themselves," she added. "If I don't get federal employment, I may try again at our next duty station."

Either way, the skills and education Nicole has acquired are hers forever and will work for her one way or another.

If you are interested in pursuing the possibility of federal internships, visit www.opm.gov/careerintern. If you are enrolled in any school (high school, technical, vocational, college, graduate school, or professional school) or you have been accepted to an accredited institution, visit www.opm.gov/employ/students to learn about the Student Temporary Employment Program (STEP) and the Student Career Experience Program (SCEP). If you have a master's degree, law degree, or doctoral degree, check out the Presidential Management Fellows Program at www.pmf.opm.gov.

USE TEMPORARY WORK OPTIONS

Like Nicole, many military spouses have found permanent strategies to conquer temporary setbacks in their career and job goals due to frequent relocation.

One of the most common strategies is to seek temporary work, namely in substitute teaching and temporary placement agencies.

Temporary work, whether substitute teaching or assignments from temporary placement agencies, can put a halt to worrying about finding a job when you move and can solve a variety of employment woes. For example, such jobs can be used as a transitional means to enter the local workforce, a way to find a suitable workplace for the duration of your time in a particular location, a quick fix to a slow cash flow, a simple way to try something new, an excuse to get out of the house when needed, or the perfect way to balance a life at work and at home.

"When I was growing up, my mom, who was a teacher, stayed home until we all entered school. Having her there was very important to me and I wanted to do the same for my children," said Myra, who has been married to the military for twenty-one years. "Becoming a substitute teacher was the perfect situation for me. I didn't have to worry about child care or after-school care because my children were right there on the same schedule with me."

Myra substitute taught for two years in Hawaii and two years in Georgia. By the time she moved to Virginia, and her children were much older, she sought her licensure.

As for working full-time, "The challenges are all the same for all of us. It's difficult trying to give a job your all and doing the same for your kids. You have to find a balance between the two," she advised.

Temporary placement agencies can be another great find for military spouses. When Rhonda became frustrated by not being able to get a federal job on post, she went to a temporary placement agency off post.

"It was the best move ever. It gave me the opportunity to keep track of the workforce and technology, took away the added competition from other applicants, and I got to meet a variety of people at my own pace," she said. "This was one piece of advice I took with me everywhere we PCS'd (moved). I have passed it on to other ladies and they say it has really taken the pressure off having to anticipate what employers are looking for."

Look in the yellow pages under Employment Agencies to find some in your local area. Sign up with more than just one to increase your chances of finding continuous work.

Nicole also found multiple benefits in temporary work. When she married her husband and joined him to live in Hawaii, he had already been there for two years, so she knew her time there would be minimal and sought temporary employment. Once they moved to Maryland, she did the same.

"It is a quick opportunity to get work when you move to a new place. It keeps you busy, allows you to earn money, and helped me hone my interviewing skills," she said. "Besides, with temporary placements, I could work whenever I wanted to. Intermittent work was no big deal to me because that's what I wanted. If you do well as a temp, you can often be offered a permanent job, long-term work, or repeated callbacks," she added.

Sounds like a win-win-win situation to us.

Seek Virtual Success

The technological advances of the past few years have definitely created increased opportunities for military spouses to work. Today, not only can you take your career with you to your next duty station, but you can take the actual job with you, too! Taking advantage of technology can mean the difference between saying, "Oh no, we are moving again" and "Have job, will travel!"

High-speed Internet, laptops, cell phones, e-mail, and videoconferencing have become a viable way to get paid for your skills regardless of where you or your clients live or how often you move.

For more than a decade, Pamela has enjoyed a second career as a freelance writer, and she coauthored one other book, all made possible by advances in technology. Many military spouses are working all kinds of jobs online, and there are plenty of resources designed to support them. Chances are, you probably have access to free virtual career training right on post. Check it out.

For example, the Staffcentrix Portable Career and Virtual Assistant Training Program for Military Spouses uses a combination of onsite training (on post) and online support to help military spouses launch and maintain a successful virtual assistance business. For criteria, application process, locations, and more about becoming a Military Spouse Virtual Assistant (MSVA) visit http://www.msvas.com/entry.htm.

VSSCyberOffice (Virtual Support Services, LLC) was founded by an MS and army veteran. It provides online virtual business ownership training to help people learn how to "Start, grow, and manage their own virtual business in cyberspace." Military spouses who want to receive training to become self-employed at no cost should visit www.vsscyberoffice.com/vbo/.

If you think virtual jobs are limited, think again. Editors, graphics and web designers, research assistants, medical transcriptionists, translators, medical billing staff, online professors, and even lawyers are working on the Web, and many of them are military spouses. Two comprehensive websites that cover "everything virtual" for military spouses are www.military.com/spouse and www.milspouse.org/job/jobs/family. Another great resource is www.virtualvocations.com.

But is everyone suited for virtual work? Deb Kloeppel, president and CEO of Military Spouse Corporate Career Network (MSCCN), believes not. "A lot of people think they can work from home, but I think that only about 1 out of 100 people really can," she said. "If someone interviews for one of our corporate virtual jobs and cites wanting to spend more time home with children as a reason they want the job, that's usually not someone we think would be most suitable for the job."

The characteristics cited most by experts as those that contribute to success in the world of virtual work include:

- Strong communication skills—verbal, written, and of course, technological
- Self-motivation and the ability to be a good problem solver
- Self-discipline: able to create and adhere to personal boundaries while working
- Goal-directed: works toward completion of tasks, not toward a set time on the clock
- Strong work ethic: works until it is done correctly and with utmost professionalism
- Confidence in personal skills and expertise
- Possession of expertise over technology (and sense enough to know who to call when stuck)

If you decide to work from home, be sure to check local laws and base housing regulations and guidelines. You should also look into what is deductible as a home-based business operator to be sure you get all the proper deductions on your next tax filing.

Go Back to School

With all this talk about establishing and maintaining a career, we cannot overlook education, training, and certification. The Defense Manpower Data Center's 2006 Survey of Active Duty Spouses showed that the main reason military spouses were not in school was because of the cost. Additionally, the majority of spouses, between 78 and 95 percent of them, indicated that furthering their education was a goal.

To address this need, the Department of Defense partnered with the Department of Labor to put $35 million into the Military Spouse Career Advancement Initiative, a program to help military spouses with education, training, and licenses or credentials for portable careers. Refer back to the partnership section for details.

Pamela's Pick: School Daze

When I decided to go back to school for my master's degree, money wasn't the issue. Through my employer's benefits package, there was plenty of money to cover the community counseling degree I sought. Time was not a big issue, as I would be able to take the courses at night and my full-time job served as my practicum and internship. What turned out to be a potential problem was the untimely announcement that we were moving again. I thought it would be no big deal because I would transfer my credits back to the school I started at, but I learned that for graduate studies there was a limit of *two* courses that would be accepted into the program.

Once again, "adapt and overcome" had to become my mantra. And so, I bid a temporary farewell to my hubby so I could "do the damned thing." We rented out our home to another family, and he headed to Virginia from North Carolina to rent a new home for us. Meanwhile, my four-year-old son and I stayed back in North Carolina and rented out a furnished apartment. I continued to work all day and attend school at night while being a temporary single parent until I completed all but two courses of my requirements. We were paying rent on two homes *and* a mortgage on a third until

I joined my husband in Virginia, so I guess you never know when keeping good personal finances will come in handy. I immediately completed those two courses in Virginia, transferred them back to North Carolina, and returned to North Carolina six months later to walk across the stage on Mother's Day. I was seven months pregnant with my second child. Come hell or high water, I was going to finish what I started, and I thank God that my husband was so supportive.

DEGREE COMPLETION AND SPOUSE EDUCATION PROGRAMS

Money isn't the only factor in spouses not completing education. As you might guess, relocation plays a big part in this area, too. Credits may not transfer or you have to leave midsemester; as you're learning, anything can happen.

Now, there are programs that facilitate degree completion by military spouses. The Servicemembers Opportunity Colleges (SOC) is a consortium of more than eighteen hundred colleges and universities that offer associate and bachelor's degrees on or near army, navy, Marine Corps, and Coast Guard installations worldwide. This network of colleges, universities, and technical institutes has agreed to accept credits from each other, thereby helping soldiers and family members save time and money by not having to lose credits each time they move. They also offer distance learning courses for those who live in isolated areas. Visit www.soc.aascu.org or call 202-667-0079 for more information.

AER Overseas Spouse Education Assistance Program (OSEAP) of the Army Emergency Relief Fund offers educational assistance to spouses who are living with service members overseas. Visit www.aerhq.org/education_spouse_Overseas .asp to apply. They also offer need-based financial help through the Stateside Spouse Scholarship Assistance Program. Visit www.aerhq.org/education_ spouseeducation_StateSide.asp. For information on either overseas or stateside assistance, call 866-878-6378.

The Air Force Aid Society offers the Spouse Tuition Assistance Program (STAP) to spouses who will attend college while living overseas with the service member who is assigned there. Visit www.afas.org/Education/body_stap.cfm.

The Navy Marine Corps Relief Society offers the Spouse Tuition Assistance Program (STAP) to spouses who will attend college while living overseas with the service member who is assigned there. Visit www.nmcrs.org/stap.html. They also offer needs-based loans.

The Coast Guard Mutual Assistance program offers supplemental grants for expenses other than tuition to any family member as well as offers spouses the opportunity to take select tests, such as CLEP (College Level Examination Program) and DANTES (Defense Activity for Non-Traditional Education Support) at no cost. The program can also cover study guides such as SAT (SAT Reasoning Test) and ASVAB (Armed Forces Vocational Aptitude Battery). Finally, it offers various scholarships and numerous resources at www.uscg.mil/spouses.

The National Military Family Association provides countless scholarships and other resources to military spouses. In 2008, nearly 400 spouses received the Joanne Holbrook Patton Military Spouse Scholarship. About 180 spouses of service members who were injured or killed during the global war on terror also received scholarships through various programs. Visit the Education and Employment Resource Center at www.nmfa.org for additional information and to find out how to access the Military Spouse Education Resource Guide.

The Montgomery GI Bill is extended to family members. The MGIB was enacted by Congress in 1944 as an education benefits package to attract quality men and women into the armed forces. It's been one of the biggest recruitment drivers, especially in our community, for years. With the rising costs of higher education, who can resist a free education on Uncle Sam's dime? The package gave financial assistance to those on active duty who wanted to pursue education and training. For as long as I can remember, service members have asked: Why can't I share my Montgomery GI Bill benefits with my dependent family members? It made perfect sense. The spouses and children share the burdens of being a military family; namely, the negative impact of military life on education and professional progression. Why then should they not share in the benefit of receiving education and training that will lessen the impact? Now, sixty-five years after the original law was created to entice people into the military, the new GI Bill (also called the Post 9/11 GI Bill) will go into effect August 2009 and likely be used to entice personnel to stay in the military. Service members will finally be able to use their MGIB to pay for their dependents' tuition. Visit the Department of Veterans Affairs at www.gibill.va.gov for updates, eligibility requirements, and information. Or call 888-GIBILL-1 and pack a lot of patience as this is a popular topic. According to the Armed Forces Press Service, this benefit may be worth an average of $80,000!

FOURTEEN STEPS TO JOB SEARCH SUCCESS

Following is a compilation of strategies military wives have found to be helpful in overcoming whatever challenges come your way when it is time to look for a job.

1. Determine why you want to work to help set clearer and more specific goals.
2. Narrow down the type of work you want to do and stay focused on it. Don't fall into the trap of applying for anything and everything. Your résumé and other documents will be much stronger if you tailor them to a certain type of work. You will also be more likely to find a job you love if you are not all "over the place" when it comes to looking for vacancies.
3. Decide on an acceptable pay range. First, do your homework to learn the going rate for your skills in that location. Then look at your financial situation. Make sure your pay range will be such that you don't later regret taking less than what you are worth or less than what you can afford.
4. Gather and update all your professional documents. If you don't already have a portfolio that contains your résumés, a master application, contact information for your references, cover letters, samples of your work, letters of recommendation, past evaluations, and transcripts, degree, and certificates, get it together now. Different employers want different documents in the application process. You can be best prepared by having all your professional documentation on hand. There is nothing worse than catching a vacancy the day before the deadline and having to create from scratch what is needed to apply for it. By using this strategy, you can save yourself a lot of stress by simply having to slightly modify what you have already prepared.
5. Network. For as long as I can remember, networking has been the most successful job search strategy around and I don't think anything else will bump it from the top of the list. Don't wait until you

get to your new location, though. Start calling and e-mailing people you know who live or have lived in that location. Also reach out to the HR department of your current employer, if they have offices in your new city. When Pamela moved from Hawaii to Georgia she started networking about nine months in advance. And it paid off. She had a poolside interview in Hawaii on New Year's Eve, with a prospective employer who happened to be in town on business and expected to have a position available by the time she relocated that summer. About six months after she arrived in Georgia, it was a done deal.

6. Visit the spouse employment program on post to get help with career planning. Many of these programs offer workshops on job search skills, job vacancy announcements from local employers, job fairs, access to office equipment, and career counseling.

7. Locate your backup resources. If you have just relocated, find out where you can get access to a fax machine, copier, scanner, and other office equipment, since yours may not be available if your household goods have not yet arrived. Even if you do have your equipment, technology has a way of "bugging out" when you need it most. How many times have you lost Internet reception, run out of ink, been unable to download a document, not been able to access e-mail, or had any other crazy mishaps when your deadline is looming? Have a plan B.

8. Explore your child-care options. There is likely to be a waiting list for child care on post, so you will need to have other alternatives. Ask the child development center staff for a list of family child-care providers. These caregivers must be certified by the installation, so they are a choice you can be comfortable with. Also request information for school-age services if your older children require before- and after-school care, and be sure to check the regulations concerning child supervision guidelines for children being left at home and the appropriate age for babysitting siblings.

9. Purchase all the office supplies you will need to submit applications. For example, buy résumé paper and matching envelopes. Make sure you have fresh ink cartridges in your printer and fax machine.

10. Set a schedule to find a job and use a variety of sources for vacancy announcements. Vacancy announcements are not around forever, so make sure that you select a group of sources and rotate among them each week. That way, you can catch all the new announcements in each of them.

11. Practice your interviewing skills. Admittedly, no one knows you better than you, right? So why do we often get tongue-tied when asked, "Tell me about yourself"? Or when we can't think of the name of an award we received, the accomplishments that put us in the best light, or why we think we are a match for this job? Even worse, why don't we recognize and avoid the pitfalls of interviewers who will try to evaluate us on whether we are suited for the job based on how long we will live in our current location? Because we did not take the time to review the announcement, review our résumé, anticipate the questions, make and review notes, and practice our answers.

12. When interviewing, be prepared to use being a military spouse to your advantage. (For example, say you have flexibility; are able to work in any setting and fit in; have experience with many different people, races, levels, etc.; and are able to hit the ground running.)

13. Prepare your interviewing wardrobe before you ever start getting calls. Gather three interview outfits and all the accessories, interchangeable pieces, shoes, purse, pantyhose, jewelry, and so on. Try it all on to make sure you have everything in order and hang the outfits in your closet. On the night before the interview, select the outfit that makes you feel powerful and confident. If you are relocating, be sure to hand carry a few coordinating pieces to mix and match in case you get a job before your household goods arrive.

Pamela's Pick: **Be prepared.**

Once I got off the plane from Hawaii at about 6:00 A.M. and by 10:00 A.M. I was called for an interview on the very next day. Luckily, I had brought a couple of interview outfits with me, so I was all prepared to interview. But I was asked to start work the next day and didn't have enough business attire to do so. The shipment of our household goods wouldn't arrive for weeks. I left the interview and rushed straight to Stein Mart and T.J. Maxx. It was a great excuse to shop, but it's not nearly as fun when you *have to* do it with relocation and house-hunting stress hanging over your head.

14. Make sure you are more marketable when you leave a location than you were when you arrived. You may not be able to build seniority in a specific company, but you can build upon your professional experience and give competitors in any location a run for their money.

Pamela's Pick:

In my coauthored book, *Work It, Girl! The Black Woman's Guide to Professional Success,* Lorraine Morris Cole and I provide a blueprint that will empower you to define success on your own terms, discover your passion, and *Work It, Girl*! As military spouses and female service members you will especially benefit from this read because it applies to all stages and phases of your career. Plus, this book can be used to reinvent yourself again and again as you move around from place to place with your military man. For example, it discusses having it all, how to make working from home work for you, turning your hobby into a career, and working for more than just money.

A Word to the Working Girls!

If you're among the over 70 percent of working military spouses, big ups to you! Being married to the military is a challenge on its own, but throw in full-time employment and you really deserve some kudos. To make the most of your working-girl status, use your power to choose from two benefits plans. Since the military is known for its strong benefits package, most wives default to their man's military plans and overlook the benefits their own employer provides. That's a mistake. You may be able to take advantage of benefits the military *doesn't* offer or double up on valuable incentives and tax savings.

If you're eligible for benefits at your job, take a look at these key areas to make sure you're getting the best bang for your hard-earned bucks:

RETIREMENT PLAN

Your spouse may contribute to the military's Thrift Savings Plan (TSP), but that shouldn't stop you from signing up for your employer's 401(k) or similar plan—*especially* if your company offers matching funds, which the TSP does not. Contribute at least up to the amount matched by the company. Otherwise, it's like turning down free money. Check out retirement savings calculators to make sure both you and your spouse are saving enough to meet your goals.

FLEXIBLE SPENDING ACCOUNTS

These plans allow you to pay for health-care or dependent-care expenses with pretax dollars. If you spend a significant amount of money each year on medicines, doctor visits, day care, and other eligible expenses, "flex accounts" could save you hundreds in taxes. The military doesn't offer these plans, so be sure to take your employer up on the deal if they do.

HEALTH INSURANCE

It's hard to compete with TRICARE's free offers, but review any plans offered by your employer to find out which plan best suits your family's needs. You may find something by comparing co-pay amounts, deductibles, and the convenience of physicians in the plan. Or you may be able to mix and match certain elements, such as dental from one plan and prescription drug coverage from the other.

LIFE AND DISABILITY INSURANCE

If your family counts on two incomes, then life insurance for you and your spouse becomes even more important. Servicemembers Group Life Insurance (SGLI) from the military is a great bargain, but it may not be enough to fully protect your family. Similarly, disability insurance may be necessary to continue your income if you were to suffer a debilitating injury or disease. For either scenario, your employer may offer insurance options that are of lower cost to you than the military plans. If your employer doesn't offer this type of coverage, shop around. Term life insurance is reasonably priced and easy to find.

The Mocha Mix
Real Talk on Careers, Higher Education, and the Hubby Factor

★ ★

I worked for extra money for travel and to put something aside for retirement.

—Juanita, Air Force wife, Germany

With three children I needed to work for extra income and wanted to get away from being just a mom and wife.

—Nicole, Army wife, North Carolina

When the moving truck left, it was time to get a job or I would be bored to death. Staying home is not for me.

—Kezia, South Carolina

I haven't worked since my third child was born six years ago due to the fact that day care would end up costing more than I make.

—Michelle, Air Force wife, Alaska

We are a relatively young couple. A second income helps us to achieve short-term and long-term goals.

—Summer, Army wife, Texas

I work because I like to shop.

—Karen, Army wife, Pennsylvania

The Hubby Factor
We always agree because my husband knows I cannot get a job because we move. If I want to work, he agrees. If I don't want to work, he agrees.

Why? Because I support him 100%; therefore he should do the same for me.

> —LaTanya, Air Force wife, South Carolina

My husband knew I wanted to be with each of our children full-time until they were in school.

> —Nicole, Army wife, Texas

My husband is extremely supportive and admires my work choices and ethics. The only advice he has always given me was that I was not being paid enough for my knowledge and experience.

> —Roshelle, Air Force wife, Maryland

We respected each other's career choices. We had our careers before we had each other.

> —Patricia, Army wife, Virginia

Sometimes we would have conflicts about who would do what and when.

> —Coyea, Army, Georgia

I have been working full-time for only about six years. He understands my need to have a career and my love for money.

> —Nicole, Army, Georgia

Certain careers relocate well in military environments and some just don't. Be prepared to learn new things in case you are unable to find a job doing what you like or what you are used to doing.

> —Von, twenty-year Army wife

Higher Learning

My education was put on hold many times due to moving around with the military. I am still grateful because I was able to take classes wherever we were stationed and completed my bachelor's and master's degrees.

—ARMY WIFE

I received my associate in child development, technical certificate in child development, and certification in administration of child care programs. And I've almost completed my bachelor's degree in education.

—MICHELLE, AIR FORCE, GERMANY

I got my master's degree by going to school on weekends, taking my two-year-old son to class and having supportive sorority sisters to help me get my master's in educational computing.

—JUANITA, AIR FORCE, GERMANY

I am currently in ABD (All But Dissertation) status for a doctoral degree.

—SUMMER, ARMY, TEXAS

Career Strategies for Service Members
Always pick your battles and don't burn any bridges.

—JACQUELINE, ARMY

Make a plan and every day work toward your very own sense of success—be sure it is *your* goal therefore tapping into intrinsic motivation.

—MICHELE, ARMY RESERVE MAJOR

Stand your ground and get your point across without being the stereotypical angry person to where people won't listen to you. Always get along with your boss. Understand what your boss's needs are and work to achieve them. Keep it all in perspective even if you have to work twice as hard. Don't take everything so seriously.

—SAKENNA, TWENTY-FIVE YEARS IN THE AIR FORCE

Mrs. Jean Ellis

Balancing family and career goals as a military spouse can be tricky, but not impossible. Mrs. Jean Ellis, wife of Army General (Ret.) Larry R. Ellis, shares her story and advice on family, career, and education based upon having moved more than twenty times in almost thirty-four years as a military spouse.

The Early Days

When my husband and I married in my senior year at Morgan State University, I didn't know anything about military life; it was all unchartered territory. When he talked about travel, I envisioned Paris, London, and Madrid, not Fayetteville, Columbus, and Bloomington. We got married in August and by January he was on his way to Vietnam. With the moving I really wasn't thinking so much of what would be my career, because we hadn't settled in one location and I hadn't grasped this whole concept of the moving. And then we started a family right away. That put me in the thought process of trying to understand this balance between family and community and career.

Back to School

As a military spouse, you have to look at your family goals and your career goals because each impacts the other, and you have to be ready for whatever comes your way. We moved a lot, so again, I wasn't concentrating on my career. But when my husband was given the opportunity to be on the faculty at West Point I realized that it could also be my time to get a graduate degree, which would make me competitive for employment since I had not done anything since I had graduated.

Then, the question became how I would fund graduate school with child care and other living expenses. I decided it would not be realistic to try at the time, but once we moved there, that changed. One thing I really learned as a military spouse is that you really have to take advantage of opportunities when they are presented to you. Once we arrived at our new station, I was able to get a job at the academy. Then, since I was earning money, I could afford to go to graduate school. I worked during the day and together we balanced the family, community support, and church activities, and I went to graduate school in the evening.

Making the decision about what to study took some strategizing. I went to the Army Education Center and got information on the kinds of master's programs being offered. Then I looked at how much time we had at West Point because that certainly impacted what kind of degree I would get. I had enough time before we were supposed to move to complete a master's in counseling. I was not going to be there long enough to get an MBA. I pursued the master's in counseling because I wanted to complete my degree before we moved again.

After that, since I did not have a lot of employment experience behind me, I was able to use education and volunteerism with many brief work experiences to be more competitive for the jobs I sought. At our next duty station I worked as a high school counselor. I went to apply for substitute teaching and the school had just received notice from one of its counselors that she would not be able to return for the school year. I had just gotten my master's in counseling, and I was there, and it was an opportunity. I applied and was hired. So that helped me to form a career pattern, but with the military it was time to move again after a year.

Life in Germany

After getting the family settled in Germany I was able to get a job working for the army in Equal Employment Opportunity for about a year and a half and then work as a personnel staffing specialist in civilian personnel. I considered this to be a critical point in my employment because years ago it was very difficult for spouses to gain civil service employment because of the way the laws were structured. At the time I was in Germany, the Spouse Employment Program started. If you worked twenty-four months overseas and returned to the United States, you could compete for a position as if you had competitive service.

When we moved to Fort Polk, Louisiana, I said to my husband, "I thought you said you were doing okay in your career, why are we going to Fort Polk?" Fort Polk was in the development stage so I had heard a lot of negative stories about it. The lesson I learned there is, it's not the location, it's the people. That turned out to be a wonderful assignment for us.

Family Versus Career

That was a pivotal point for me because I worked exactly twenty-four months overseas and was able to use my Spouse Preference to get a position at Fort Polk. I therefore continued to work as a federal employee as we continued to move. So again, it was really a matter of taking advantage of the opportunity as it was presented. I never once made the choice to stay at a location for a promotion, because my commitment was to my family and my relationship and I believed the employment opportunities would present themselves along the way. And they did.

Serving the Community

I have always said, as a military spouse, the military installation is our community, and we need to contribute to our community no matter where it is. I see that as volunteerism and support of unit activities and any other activities to make your community better.

While at Fort Polk, we had lots of field rotations and military training and there were not enough service member volunteers to coach the number of children who wanted to play soccer, so several of us spouses took on the teams. Now that meant going to the library to learn about soccer, but we do what we have to do to support the community.

Another time, a group of spouses got together and ran a summer school program on the installation. We looked at all the skills we had among fifteen or twenty spouses and offered courses based on that because there was not much else going on there. We offered a Shakespeare course, a calligraphy course, and many others. We all pitched in to make it happen. As spouses, if there's a need, we fulfill it.

These are the kinds of things that eventually evolved into the Family Readiness Groups we have today and other family-related programs like Army Family Action Plan, and child-care services. It all comes from spouses just providing support to the community.

The reality is that when you have children and a spouse in the military, someone has to take on those responsibilities when the other person is not there. The military is very demanding. You have to understand the balance between your family and your career goals. You have to be available to do what it takes, because the parenting role is not something you can pass on to someone else.

The most important thing is to really understand how your career goals can balance out with your family goals and your family structure. When your goals are not in balance, it can be very frustrating.

Just remember that to make the most of your military life: embrace your lifestyle, balance family and career, and always communicate with your spouse.

CHAPTER SEVEN

Military Money Matters

Don't Let Your Money Get Funny

Nothing causes more stress than financial problems. It's the number one relationship killer and can put undue strain on a military family. Money troubles at home can affect a service member's performance and often take the biggest toll on the wife and children.

To master your military lifestyle you must get control of your finances. And the earlier, the better. This is especially true for members of the reserves or National Guard, who are often called suddenly to active duty and frequently are the primary wage earners in the home. When they leave, the family and children are typically not financially prepared for such an absence. It's one thing to be prepared for deployment from a professional standpoint, but it's a completely different matter to be financially prepared. You need both areas covered!

Getting a grasp on money can be even more challenging for us. As black people we aren't typically socialized to be powerful about money. We tend to be raised in homes where stock market performance and money management tips are not common dinnertime conversation. Instead, for many of us, our association with money when we were growing up was conversations about "making ends meet."

Depending on your life circumstances, you or your hubby may have joined the armed forces for better job opportunities or as the only way to afford higher education. Your husband's military pay could represent more money and more stability than you ever thought possible for your life. If so, all the more reason to do your part to manage it and master it properly. Let's face it, we don't have a strong legacy of wealth building. As a people, we love to spend on depreciating assets like cars, rims, clothes, and televisions, instead of investing in appreciating assets like real estate. But you can use your military life as a tool to reverse the tide, to change the pattern in your family, starting right now with you. No, the military won't make you rich, but if you have the strength, courage, intelligence, and ability to earn your MS (military spouse) degree, you have all the tools to help your family become financially strong. By following the suggestions in this chapter, you'll be off to a solid start.

If you want to have fit military finances, you need to tackle two key categories: one is everyday savings and money management, and the other is future planning. Covering both areas puts you in good stead for long-term financial strength.

Understand Your Money Flow

To get your day-to-day budget under control, you need to first have a basic understanding of how military pay works. Like most working folks, service members get paid every two weeks. But understanding how pay increases and fluctuates based on life and work circumstances can help with your financial planning.

It's a lesson Sherice Rodgers learned the hard way ten years ago as a new army wife. About a month after she married her husband, Devin, he was deployed to Korea. As you will learn in a few minutes, being deployed overseas or in "hardship" areas can mean big bucks added to your husband's paycheck. The few extra hundred dollars for hazardous pay and the extra $1,000 for a cost-of-living adjustment made for a fat paycheck by Sherice's standards. "I thought, this is great! And I was so busy buying things and taking on credit card debt in the name of 'setting up house' or getting things ready for Devin's return, I had no idea how his pay would abruptly drop when he returned." After a fifteen-month deployment and Sherice's spending sprees, there wasn't enough savings to cover the new expenses and bills with Devin's postdeployment salary. It's a common financial reality for military wives. Don't let this happen to you. First you need to understand exactly how military pay works so you will know exactly what your husband will be getting, not getting and when. Let's get started.

Basic Pay: This is based on his pay grade, such as E-6 or O-1, and is all taxable income. This pay increases based on years in service or a promotion and is not affected by marriage or children.

Basic Allowance for Housing (BAH): This component goes to active-duty members who live off base to help offset the costs of living off post. The BAH, which is nontaxable income, is mostly determined by the cost of living in your area, so large metropolitan areas and overseas locations will have a larger BAH than less expensive rural states. Marriage or family status can increase the BAH, but don't expect the kind of big jump that house renovations and shopping sprees are made of! Sometimes the difference can be as little as $50 or $100 more per month.

Basic Allowance for Subsistence (BAS): This money covers feeding your husband, not you. This one is tricky, because the BAS can disappear in a flash when a service member deploys and the military is now feeding him. Many families are caught off guard by the reduction in pay. BAS is a flat rate. In 2009, it was $223.04 per month for officers and $323.87 per month for enlisted members.

Those are the basics of military pay. But a service member can earn more by increasing his training and skills or working in more difficult or dangerous circumstances. Those pay components include the following.

Family Separation Allowance (FSA): If your man is away from you for thirty consecutive days, you are entitled to $100 per month. But it has to be thirty days. If he goes away for twenty-eight days and comes home for the weekend, you won't get the FSA.

Hazardous Duty and Imminent Danger/Hostile Fire Pay: You gotta admit, the military really spells things out for you. This one is exactly what it says. Being assigned to a dangerous situation has value—about $150 extra per month.

Hardship Duty Pay: Well, there's hazardous and there's hardship. Hardship is serving in difficult areas, either on deployments or in remote locations, and for that you'll get $150 per month.

Military pay can also increase because of a specialty; that is, the job skills or job situation of your spouse. Some of the key areas of specialty pay include the COLA allowance.

Overseas and CONUS Cost-of-Living Allowance (COLA): Living overseas can be pretty lucrative in the military. If you move overseas or to Alaska or Hawaii, you can see a big increase of up to $1,000 a month or more. This is particularly true for less popular or high cost-of-living locations like Japan.

Other pay bonuses include the following allowances.

Uniform Allowance: This is a once-a-year stipend of between $200 and $400 for enlisted to cover the cost of uniforms and similar purchases. Officers only get this allowance once at the start of their careers, and then they have to cover this expense for themselves.

Dislocation Allowance (DLA): This money helps cover the costs of relocating to your new permanent duty station. This can be up to several thousand dollars, and given the high costs of moving house, you should make sure you know exactly how much DLA you're receiving so you can budget properly.

Remember, military pay can change as often as every month depending on your man's circumstances. Normal military activities like training, deployment, relocating, and hardship duty can affect your income for the better or worse. So understanding the pay system and keeping track of how much he should receive (overpayments and underpayments are common military blunders) will go a long way in mastering your finances.

Pamela's Pick:

Write down this website, ladies, www.dfas.mil, and then bookmark it. This is the online home of the Defense Finance and Accounting Service. You'll need this site to check your spouse's monthly Leave and Earnings Statements, predict next month's pay, and deal with any pay-related problems.

Save, Save, Save

Now that we've already covered how to understand military pay and your new military pay guru status, you are now prepared to get your family on sound financial footing. And in order to be financially strong, you must start building an emergency savings account. An unexpected expense can quickly derail even the best-laid money plan. An emergency savings account should have at least $500 cash sitting in a high-interest savings account like those offered by INGDirect or HSBC.com.

Direct Deposit

Every good financial plan for military families should involve direct deposit. I know there are still mistrusting, money-in-the-shoebox, money-orders-only women out there, but direct deposit is a lifesaver. Some of the special pays and bonuses we discussed earlier, particularly those related to relocation, temporary duty, and deployment are often paid at the last minute. When things are happening quickly, you don't want to be worrying about a check arriving in the mail and then making the trip to deposit it. Direct deposit makes sure your money goes directly into your checking account as soon as possible.

Everyday Money Management

Once you understand your pay and have it coming straight into your bank account, it's now time to manage it wisely. There are lots of things you can do to trim your budget every day and help keep your spending down. Reducing your spending gives you more money to put toward savings and your emergency fund. To start getting good control of your spending, keep a spending journal for at least two weeks. Get a notebook and write down every penny and nickel spent from lattes to lollipops and from groceries to gizmos. After doing this exercise, countless women are surprised to find out their true spending patterns. There's always an "I didn't know I spent that much on *that*!" at the end of the tracking period. If this happens to you, no worries. The key is to act on your new information. Now that you know your spending holes, it's time to plug them up. Find ways to cut back and find more money to save. After you've tracked your spending, and plugged up your spending holes, try these money saving tips:

1. **Make good use of the commissary.** Many service members, especially unmarried members, overlook the value of the local commissary. You'll find many items at a deep discount, which means more money in your pocket. Single service members save an average of $1,000 each year, while a family of four tallies at least $3,000 in annual savings just by shopping at the commissary, according to

some military reports. To get even more bang for your buck, use coupons at the commissary.

Don't live near an installation? The Defense Commissary Agency (DeCA) can still help you save. Its "Virtual Commissary" offers a variety of gift items shipped directly to the recipient. DeCA is working to expand its product selection to include other nonperishable items that could be shipped directly to patrons. Through special sale events, DeCA also is reaching out to under-served communities by taking the commissary benefit on the road. Through coordination with local reserve commands, DeCA also holds special sale events. To learn more, visit the commissary website at www.commissaries.com.

2. **Take advantage of travel and recreation discounts.** Explore Morale, Welfare and Recreation (MWR) and Marine Corps Community Services (MCCS). Service members, retirees, and military families can save big on quality recreation programs and venues across the country. From armed forces recreation centers in places like Hawaii, Florida, Germany, and Korea, to swimming pools and hobby shops, recreational opportunities abound at your local installation. Visit the Tickets and Tours Office for discount admission to dozens of local and national theme parks and recreation venues. Make sure you compare prices, though. Sometimes the "military discount" is not the lowest price available. For example, on a recent trip to Disney World, Pamela and her family found that the resort where they stayed offered a better deal on park tickets than Shades of Green, the army resort they almost drove to just to get "the deal." Better yet, they found that the park itself had an even better rate available to anyone at the gate with a military ID. On the other hand, whenever Pamela purchases tickets for shows from the army's Tickets and Tours Office, she almost always found a better price for great seats. Bottom line: do your comparison shopping. Some installations even rent travel trailers and beach cottages! These services are provided at significant savings over comparable services outside the installation. In addition, you may be entitled to free access to some of the world's best-equipped fitness facilities.

3. **Don't forget your Exchange.** Installation retail stores offer a tremendous variety of products at very competitive prices. And once you get used to paying those prices, it's hard to stop. "My husband retired after twenty-two years in the navy and even now, years later, I still have to get my groove on and go to the commissary and Exchange," said Trina from Atlanta. Exchanges offer price matching within the local market. If you find an identical product advertised locally at a better price, take the ad to your local Exchange and it will match that price. The ideal time for this price checking is during holidays that traditionally have deep discounts, like during the Christmas holidays. Plus, Exchange purchases are sales tax exempt, so you save even more. Profits from retail sales are reinvested in MWR and MCCS programs, so it keeps benefiting military families. If you live off base, you can still shop the Exchange online or through the printed catalog for the same savings found in stores.

4. **Traveling? Don't overlook Space-Available, or "Space-A," travel opportunities.** If you have an adventurous spirit and a flexible schedule, then Space-A travel may be for you. Once you arrive, low-cost lodging may be available at the local temporary lodging facility (TLF). You can also save money by using temporary military lodging, whether you are stateside or traveling around the world, if you have a valid U.S. military ID card, including active and retired personnel, guard and reserve, and 100 percent DAVs (Disabled American Veterans).

5. **Check out the child development center (CDC).** Child care often is one of the most expensive recurring items in a military family's budget. Military CDCs offer good care at reasonable prices, providing quality programs for children from infancy through grade school. Some installations even have summer camp programs for school-age children. Fees are based on income so everyone can access quality child care. But again, it helps to do your research. Depending upon what state you live in, the local going rate may very well be comparable to on-post care. This is usually the case in places with a low cost of living. When Pamela lived in

North Carolina, the day-care center in her subdivision several miles from post was less expensive, had wonderful services, and was obviously more convenient.

Each year, the National Association of Child Care Resources and Referral Agencies (NACCRRA) releases a report card for child-care programs in each state. Many DoD day-care centers consistently rank among the best in the state in many areas. Families located away from an installation or waiting for space at a CDC can utilize programs developed through a partnership between DoD and NACCRRA. Military Child Care in Your Neighborhood provides placement assistance and a monthly subsidy payment to families on a wait list for child care in an installation center or located in an area not served by an installation CDC. Operation Military Child Care provides placement and fee assistance to activated or deployed guard and reserve families. To find out more go online to www.naccrra.org/militaryprograms/index .php or call Operation Military Child Care at (703) 341-4100.

6. **Consider your housing benefit.** If you haven't thought about using military housing, you may want to think about it. Thankfully, military family housing and service member housing for singles has improved greatly over the years. Privatization and an increased focus on quality-of-life issues have transformed government housing into an exceptional benefit. Being close to work and having recreation amenities and medical and shopping facilities nearby can also curb gas spending and wear and tear on your car—more money saved!

Talk about getting fiscally fit while getting physically fit. Living on post can also create much sought after free time for general wellness and fitness. Pamela has only lived on post twice in her nineteen years of army wifedom, but both times allowed her to fit exercise into her life with no problem—and without wasting money on a little-used gym membership. At Aberdeen Proving Ground, in Maryland, the fitness center was across the street from her job and one mile from home. In Hawaii, she worked across the street from the pool and down the street from the fitness center. She

spent many days swimming laps during lunch or immediately after work, under the most beautiful Hawaiian skies. Free access to
all this, plus being fit, toned, and stress-free: priceless.

7. **Understand your medical benefit.** TRICARE Prime beneficia-
    ries can eliminate out-of-pocket medical expenses simply by en-
    suring that all care is initiated through their assigned primary
    care manager. TRICARE Standard beneficiaries can reduce med-
    ical expenses by using TRICARE providers.

    Prescriptions are filled at the local medical treatment facility
    at no cost to the patient. Maintenance medications can be ordered
    through the TRICARE Mail Order Pharmacy (TMOP), which is
    much cheaper than the retail pharmacy. TMOP beneficiaries can
    get a ninety-day supply of medication for the same cost as a thirty-
    day supply at a retail pharmacy. TMOP prescriptions are even de-
    livered right to your home. And if you don't live near a military
    base, the benefit extends to your community by allowing you to
    obtain prescriptions at deeply discounted prices right in retail
    stores like Wal-Mart.

8. **Reduce deployment-related expenses.** Mobilization or deploy-
    ment can create a variety of unexpected expenses, like shipping
    and communication costs. The U.S. Postal Service offers dis-
    counted postage to FPO and APO addresses. The new Priority
    Mail Flat Rate Box can be sent domestically.

    Communication expenses can add up quickly, so consider
    e-mail rather than phone calls. When an e-mail simply won't do,
    try a VoIP (voice over Internet protocol) service such as Skype to
    avoid costly international long-distance calls. Check out at www
    .skype.com to download the service onto your computer.

9. **Check your withholdings.** All service members complete a W-4
    when entering the military. Over time, changes to your family size
    and circumstances may warrant a change in withholding. Increasing
    the number of exemptions on your W-4 will result in more money in
    your pocket from paycheck to paycheck because less federal tax will

be withheld from your pay. The Internal Revenue Service (IRS) provides a withholding calculator on its website to help you decide how many exemptions to claim and whether or not to withhold additional money. To access the calculator, visit www.irs.gov/individuals/page/0,,id=14806,00.html. Service members may electronically update their W-4s by logging into their MyPay account online.

10. **Contribute to the TSP.** Time goes by quickly. And retirement will be here before you know it. Get prepared now. The Thrift Savings Plan (TSP) allows service members to contribute a portion of their pay to a tax-deferred retirement account. It works something like a 401(k). Every year, your husband can put away a percentage of his pay, up to 7 percent of basic pay and 100 percent of special and bonus pay, in a specified mutual fund monitored by the TSP administrators. This contribution reduces your taxable income dollar for dollar today while building a retirement nest egg for the future. The money is taxable upon withdrawal at retirement, but you likely will be in a lower tax bracket. For complete information on the TSP, visit www.tsp.gov or ask one of the financial counselors on post.

The TSP ain't perfect, however. It doesn't allow spouses to participate, and the government does not match contributions. Meanwhile, the future of the government money backing the retirement accounts is in question. So if you or your spouse has an employer-sponsored retirement savings plan that matches your contributions, use that plan, too, as a backup—and so that you don't miss out on this "free money."

Another smart strategy for many military families is to establish a Roth IRA. While contributions to a Roth are made with after-tax dollars, the principal can be withdrawn at any time without penalty, and the earnings are tax-free and penalty-free once you reach age $59^{1}/_{2}$ and have had the account for at least five years.

The TSP can be a good tool to augment the Roth IRA or a spouse's 401(k). Beyond the plan's limits for contributions from basic pay, participants can contribute up to 100 percent of incentive pay or special pay, including tax-exempt pay earned while serving in a combat zone.

Of course, all the suggestions for managing your military pay and planning for the future are useless unless you create a budget and stick to it. Once you determine where your money is going, you can take steps to reduce unnecessary expenses. Military aid societies and personal finance managers at local installations can help you set up a budget that works for you.

11. **Avoid payday loans and high-interest-rate products.** All of these money-saving ideas won't matter much if you've got high-interest payments on credit cards or short-term loans. Although the Military Lending Act (MLA) has curbed some predatory products targeting service members, many unscrupulous lenders have introduced slightly modified products to avoid falling under MLA protection. If you do find yourself short on funds, seek out assistance from your local aid society or your installation's bank or credit union first before considering a high-interest loan product. That particularly includes payday lenders.

Payday loans are short-term, small loans that typically range from $100 to $500. They are marketed as great tools to hold you over until payday, but they are dangerously deceptive. Here's how they work: To get one, you write a postdated check for the amount desired, plus a fee. The check casher or payday lender holds the check until you get paid. The typical loan period is two weeks. On payday, you take cash to the lender and exchange it for your postdated check, or you allow the lender to deposit the check. If you do not show up with cash, the lender cashes the check.

The real problems with payday loans begin if you cannot pay back the loan at the end of the two-week period. If you ask the lender to hold the loan for another pay period, you'll pay the fee a second time and the loan rolls over. A typical borrower of payday loans pays $15 for every $100 borrowed in a two-week loan. That ends up being about a 400 percent annual percentage rate. If you are charged a $20 finance charge on $100, your annual percentage rate is 521 percent.

For years, payday lenders and other loan-shark lenders have taken advantage of military families, luring borrowers into these high-fee and high-cost loans with empty promises of "easy money." One study of military installations found that most had upward of twenty—and sometimes as many as forty—payday lenders within just a few miles of the base gates. Military families caught off guard by pay changes or whose pay is delayed by bureaucratic red tape often use these loans as a short-term fix. All too often, well-intentioned spouses find themselves swallowed up in a dangerous spiral of debt—harming their families, threatening careers, and weakening military readiness.

The Military Lending Act combats abusive lending practices targeted at military families and places certain requirements and limitations on loans to service members and their dependents. It targets three specific products that are particularly dangerous: payday loans, vehicle title loans, and tax refund anticipation loans (RALs).

For these types of products, the military annual percentage rate (MAPR) for loans to "covered borrowers"—members of the armed forces or dependents of such members—cannot exceed a maximum of 36 percent, inclusive of interest, fees, credit service or renewal charges, credit insurance premiums, and other fees for ancillary products sold in connection with the loan. The new law also says the lender "can't hold on to the service member's personal check or have electronic access to their bank account as collateral for this type of loan. The threat of the lender depositing the borrower's check, which would often not clear the bank, has been a key way to trap borrowers in loans they end up paying back many times over in interest."

Excluded from coverage under the new rule are mortgage loans and refinancings, home equity loans and lines of credit, purchase money vehicle loans, secured personal property loans, loans secured by qualified retirement accounts, and credit that is not subject to current truth-in-lending disclosures. Additionally, credit cards are not covered by the new rule.

The bottom line: get help. See a financial professional, especially if your family is going to see a significant cut in income after your spouse's deployment or if you have any of the above-mentioned loan products. Some insurance policies will allow you to suspend paying premiums while your spouse is serving and then pick them back up when your spouse returns. Retirement accounts and education savings accounts are also costs you can suspend on a "temporary" basis.

Although family finances are the last things many families want to consider when a loved one is being shipped across the country or to foreign lands, it's a necessary planning step.

Rapid Deployment

One thing is for sure with military families—anything is possible. Deployment can come with a few months' or a few days' notice. In the case of a rapid deployment, there may not be time for all the recommended planning that typically needs to happen. Things need to happen quickly! It's time to prioritize.

In rapid-deployment cases, with only a few days before reporting, quickly handle the following chores first:

1. Make sure that you or a trusted friend or relative has been assigned power of attorney. This allows you to act on your spouse's behalf when dealing with banks, insurance companies, creditors, utilities, and other financial institutions. It also helps to have someone making health-care decisions. There are different kinds of POAs so learn what they are now, before you need them.

2. Set up automatic payment plans for all bills. You've got a lot more on your plate. Put your bill payment on autopilot. You don't want important insurance coverage, utilities, or credit cards to go unpaid while your spouse is away. You may even want to look at cutting coverage for one of your automobiles, if it's going to be in storage, or cutting off your service member's cell phone if he's not taking it with him.

3. Make sure your landlord, insurance companies, banks, credit card companies, and utilities know how to get in touch with you.

4. Send a copy of the power of attorney with contact information to all of these companies to make sure they understand that you are now authorized to handle all affairs.

Just one warning in this high-tech age: don't rely on communicating by e-mail to make important money decisions. Depending on the state of combat, communications devices can be reserved solely for the war effort rather than personal communication.

Maintain Your Credit

Good credit is no longer a luxury. It's a life necessity. If there's one thing I learned during my time as the personal finance editor of *Essence* magazine, it's that black folks and credit have a tricky relationship. Comedians love to joke about us putting bills in our baby's name because our credit is jacked up, but it's definitely related to poor spending choices. Improving matters starts simply with paying your bills on time (see the box "Understanding Your FICO Score").

If you're experiencing financial hardships while your husband is deployed, one of the best things you can do is notify your creditors about your situation. There are federal or corporate programs to assist military family members during deployment.

One help for military families is the Soliders' and Sailors' Civil Relief Act, first passed in 1918. It suspends many civil legal proceedings—including bankruptcy, divorce cases, and civil suits—until a service person returns home. It also allows for a temporary 6 percent interest rate on credit cards, auto loans, mortgages, equity lines, and other installment loans. This only covers accounts carried jointly, not debt held separately by a spouse. And the lower rate is only good for charges before your call-up, not during active duty. Ask a finance professional for further information.

The Servicemembers Civil Relief Act (SCRA) protects the civil rights of military personnel, including reservists and members of the National Guard, while they are on active duty. Among its various protections, the SCRA temporarily reduces the financial obligations of individuals who can't repay as a result of going on active military duty. While your spouse is on active duty, creditors are limited in their ability to start legal proceedings against him to collect payments for any debt you incurred prior to his active duty.

Your husband's military orders will designate the type of duty being performed. Active duty includes certain training activities, such as initial active duty (boot camp). You must provide proof of active-duty status to the creditor.

The SCRA provides for a maximum annual interest rate of 6 percent during the time of active duty on obligations incurred *before* active service. To receive the reduction, you must provide written notice to the creditor of your request for the rate reduction and a copy of the military orders. You have up to 180 days after the termination or release from active military service to claim a rate reduction. The creditor must reamortize the debt and lower the payments. Creditors may not keep the payment amount the same and shorten the maturity of the loan. The 6 percent limitation is effective from the date active duty begins, not the date that you notify the creditor. Remember, the interest rate provision of the act applies only to debts incurred *prior* to his active duty in the military. Debts incurred after entering active service (including loan extensions and advances, e.g., credit card purchases you make during active duty) may not be subject to the protections of SCRA. So don't run up honey's credit card while he's away and expect a payment break. Creditors are not required to adjust the interest rates in every situation, even when the debt is incurred prior to active duty. For more detailed information, please contact the personnel office at your military base.

UNDERSTANDING YOUR FICO SCORE

If you don't know your FICO score or haven't seen your credit report lately, it's time to get with the program. These days everyone from insurance companies to apartment leasing companies check credit scores before approving applicants. Start with getting your credit report. You are entitled to one free credit report annually by going to https.annualcreditreport.com. Check your report for any errors. Then, get to know your FICO. You will have to pay one price to get your score from the three major credit bureaus. You can do this at www.myfico.com, and it is well worth the nominal fee.

What Is FICO?

Well, it's a complicated credit scoring system created by Fair Isaac Corporation. FICO scores range from 300 to 850. The best number to have is 720 or above. If your score is 720, there's really no need to try and raise it because lenders lump you in the same category as folks with a score of say 800 or 820. At 720, you are viewed as a safe risk and typically receive a loan without problem and at a low interest rate. However, if your number is below 700, it's definitely worth your time to try and pump it up.

Here's what makes up your FICO score:

- **35 percent/Payment history**: If you have a history of missed or late payments on credit accounts, this is going to put a big dent in your score.
- **30 percent/Amount owed**: This measures the amount you owe relative to the total amount of credit available. Someone closer to maxing out all their credit limits is deemed to be a higher risk of late payments in the future and this can lower their credit score. So if you have a $500 limit credit card with a $400 balance, this is adversely affecting your score. You should try to pay down credit card balances to about 30 percent of the credit limit.
- **15 percent/Length of credit history**: In general, a credit report containing a list of accounts opened for a long time will help your credit score. The score considers your oldest account and the average age of all accounts. Closing old accounts is not always a good thing for your credit score, especially if you've had it for some time. Better to cut up the card so you don't use it, and let the zero balance stay on your report.
- **10 percent/New credit**: Opening several new credit accounts in a short period of time can lower your credit score. Multiple credit report inquiries also can represent a greater risk, but this does *not* include any requests made by you, an employer, or by a lender who does so when sending you an unsolicited, "preapproved" credit offer. Also, to compensate for rate shopping, the score counts multiple inquiries in any fourteen-day period as just one inquiry.

- **10 percent/Types of credit in use**: Your mix of credit cards, retail accounts, finance company loans, and mortgage loans is considered. Having all store cards is not a good mix of credit.

Fixing Your FICO

First of all, there is no quick fix for a poor credit score. Although you can't raise your score overnight, you can do so fairly quickly. The scoring formula gives more weight to recent activity. So, even six months of "good behavior" will have an impact, demonstrating that you have cleaned up your act. Please don't spend your hard-earned money on so-called credit repair companies promising to boost your credit in no time. You can improve your own score yourself with a little time, effort, and commitment to new habits. Here's how:

1. Pay bills on time. Consider online or automatic debits to make sure your payments arrive on time.

2. Pay down credit card balances. Pay more than the minimum payment; you'll never put a dent in your balance just paying the minimum. Remember, FICO scores reward people who use a smaller percentage of their available credit.

3. Don't go credit card crazy. Avoid opening a lot of new accounts at once—this makes lenders queasy—particularly if you don't have a long credit history. Many recommend not having more than five credit cards.

4. Rotate and use all of your cards—a dormant credit account will not help your score. If you do have a late payment, it's worth a call to the lender to see if they will remove this information from your records in a "goodwill adjustment." You can also choose to dispute the late payment report. While it's in dispute, the item will stay on your credit report but not factor into your FICO score.

Getting to know your FICO score and regularly checking your credit report for errors and inaccuracies can help you and your spouse have a solid financial future.

Identity Theft

Military families are not immune to the fast-growing crime of identity theft. In fact, military families are often more susceptible since social security numbers are used so commonly throughout the military to identify its members.

Identity theft can take years and a lot of time to clear up. The military has taken several steps that you should know about to protect its members and their families from identity thieves.

The Defense Finance and Accounting Service dropped the first five digits of each person's social security number from all hard-copy leave and earnings statements and checks to guard against identity theft.

The Defense Department put into place measures in the E-Government Act of 2001 that control what personal information gets posted on government websites.

The department teamed up with the Federal Trade Commission to launch Military Sentinel (www.consumer.gov/military). This online complaint network enables military members and DoD civilian employees to report identity theft and other consumer frauds.

Meanwhile, the services have launched far-reaching education campaigns that include fraud alerts and reading materials posted on various military websites. The bottom line is to use caution in giving out personal identifying information. If your spouse becomes a victim of identity theft, report it as quickly as possible to his chain of command, legal assistance office, and Military Sentinel.

Before Deployment

Before your spouse ships off, there are things to get financially prepared for what lies ahead.

1. All accounts should be in both spouses' names with "or" between the names so only one name is required to cash or deposit checks.

2. Savings and checking accounts should be maintained either in the hometown or at each permanent station, so checks can be cashed.

3. The truth is, survivor benefits for widows and dependants are a relative pittance compared with the cost of living. Make sure you purchase life insurance of your own. Term life insurance is cheaper, easy to get, and should cover all your needs.

Cash Crunch? Where to Get Help

Try to have an emergency savings fund—it's the most critical element of a financial plan. Most emergencies can be handled with $500 in savings.

You can also get a grant and no-interest loan from military aid societies. The DoD has worked with the Federal Direct Insurance Corporation (FDIC) to encourage banks and credit unions to develop small, low-interest loans for service members and their families if they are caught in a financial bind. These funds are provided for emergencies and essentials, such as rent, food, and utilities. Currently, there are financial institutions on about fifty-one installations providing these types of loans, and more are considering doing so.

You can also get personalized help from financial management courses and financial management specialists—often known by their initials "PFMs"— at military installations. In the army, these services are located at the Army Community Service Office; in the navy and marine corps, you'll find these services and experts at the Fleet and Family Support Office; in the air force, they are located at the Airman and Family Readiness Center.

Pamela's Pick:

Money troubles? Military OneSource offers free, confidential financial planners and counselors available toll-free 24/7 at 800-342-9647. Military Homefront (www.militaryhomefront .dod.mil) is the official DoD website for reliable quality-of-life information to help service members and their families.

If you are considering a one-income lifestyle because of limited job prospects or to stay home with your kids, these six steps can help you reach your goals:

1. **Assess your current income.** On a sheet of paper, make three columns. In the first column, list all monthly income sources, such as salaries, dividends, and interest. The second column will contain the dollar amounts you bring in for each. If you earn a salary of $1,200 a month, for example, you'll list it in the second column. In the third column, under the heading, "Variable, Yes/ No," indicate if each income source varies from month to month (commissions, tips, or other income that isn't consistent). Add everything in the second column to come up with your total current income.

2. **Calculate current monthly expenses.** This is similar to planning a budget. Use these categories (along with the recommended percentages):
    *   Housing/utilities (30 percent)
    *   Food (10 percent)
    *   Savings/investments (10 percent)
    *   Taxes/charitable contributions (10 percent)
    *   Transportation/car loan/gas (10 percent)
    *   Recreation/vacation/gifts/Christmas (6 percent)
    *   Clothing/dry cleaning (5 percent)
    *   Debts (5 percent)
    *   Education/miscellaneous (5 percent)
    *   Insurance (5 percent)
    *   Medical/dental (4 percent)

3. **Determine current assets.** Once you gain a clearer idea of your assets, consider items you may be able to sell or liquidate to reach your goal of one-income living. You may be able to downsize your life by moving to a less expensive home or selling a car to pay cash for an older vehicle. Do your homework to obtain accurate numbers. For example, you may have more equity in your home than expected; review your latest mortgage statement, then go to a website such as www.zillow.com to find a rough idea of the fair market value of your home. Do the same for car loans, via www.edmunds.com or www .kbb.com, to determine the "private party" value of your vehicles.

Then list each asset: home, checking account, savings account, retirement plan, stocks/bonds, mutual funds, other funds, cars, boat/RV/luxury items, furniture, household items, jewelry, antiques. Next to the asset, list the amount owed (if applicable), the equity or actual cash value, and whether you can sell or liquidate it.

4. **List current liabilities.** Determine your debts and decide what must be paid down before living on one income. Next to each liability or loan, list three things: total balance due, minimum monthly payment, and months until paid off. List each liability: home, cars, furniture/computers, student loans, boat/RV/luxury items, outstanding taxes, store credit (list each separately), credit cards (list each separately). Add your totals in each column.

5. **Project your one-income numbers.** Basically, you'll deduct any second income and include your primary income and investment earnings. Use the total amount of this adjusted income as a basis to determine goals for projected expenses that allow for one-income living.

    Take out your sheet from step two that lists all current expenses and break down your projected numbers, just as you did for the current numbers, by applying the percentages given in each expense category. The new numbers are your projected expenses. For example, if the new projected income is $40,000, then according to the percentages, the monthly "housing/utilities" expense would be: $40,000×30 percent, 12 months=$1,000. Next, subtract each "projected expense" number from the respective "current expense" number and list that amount as "difference." These numbers show how far you'll need to go in making the jump from two incomes to one.

6. **Think about other sources of savings.** Compare projected income with expense goals and see how they match up. If projected income doesn't jibe with the expense goal numbers, then tweak the numbers to fit your unique situation and establish realistic expense goals.

There are other things that may help you reach your one-income goal. For example, some expenses may decline when you're on one income—child care, your work wardrobe, commuting expenses, meals eaten out, and so on—thus lowering your overall cost of living. Remember, too, that you are not required to stick to the exact recommended expense percentages. If you live in base housing and you don't need 30 percent for "housing/utilities," then adjust it accordingly and shift funds to another category. Are you willing to part with any assets to meet your one-income goal? It's all about making sacrifices for the end goal. Consider what you and your spouse are willing to give up in order to build the savings account safety net you need.

Tax Time

Filing your taxes ranks on the joy-meter somewhere around a root canal. And since your hubby is already giving his life to this country, you don't want to give Uncle Sam any more money than you have to. Fortunately, the Internal Revenue Service (IRS) has some tax deductions and allowances to help you and your family.

Most families, however, don't take full advantage of the various opportunities available. Out of confusion or hastiness, they often end up paying more to Uncle Sam than they actually owe. Not good! Don't let this happen to you. As a savvy military spouse, you've got to get tax smart.

A really good starting point is reviewing the IRS Armed Forces' Tax Guide (Publication 3), which is available online at www.irs.gov. The publication explains the many tax rules that apply specifically to service members.

Even if you can decipher the IRS instructions on your own, making decisions about tax strategies can still be a daunting task. Here are a few tax tips that should help ease the tax time stress.

Tax extensions: Citizens or residents posted outside the United States and Puerto Rico are allowed an automatic two-month extension until June 15 to file their returns and pay any federal income tax. However, if you pay your taxes after the regular April 15 tax deadline, then interest will be charged until the taxes are paid.

For individuals and their families serving in a combat zone, the deadline for filing, paying taxes, or filing a claim for refund is automatically extended for 180 days. For purposes of the automatic extensions, the IRS definition of "combat zone" includes the following areas:

- Persian Gulf area
- Qualified hazardous duty area of Bosnia and Herzegovina, Croatia, and Macedonia
- Qualified hazardous duty area of the Federal Republic of Yugoslavia, Albania, the Adriatic Sea, and the Ion Sea north of the 39th parallel
- Afghanistan

Moving expenses: Let's face it, moving is a way of life in the military. There may be a tax benefit in it. Individuals on active duty who move because of a permanent change of station can deduct unreimbursed moving expenses and don't have to meet the distance test. Learn more about military moves in Chapter 5.

Uniforms: Your spouse generally cannot deduct the cost of uniforms if he is on full-time active duty. However, in the case of a member of the reserves, the unreimbursed cost of uniforms may be deducted if military regulations restrict wear except while on duty as a reservist. In figuring the deduction, the cost is reduced by any nontaxable allowance received for expenses.

Travel expenses: A member of a reserve component of the armed forces who travels more than a hundred miles away from home in connection with the performance of services can deduct travel expenses as an adjustment to gross income rather than as a miscellaneous itemized deduction. The amount of deductible expenses is limited to the regular federal per diem rate and the standard mileage rate, plus any parking fees, ferry fees, and tolls.

Mind over MAGI: Perhaps the most important figure you calculate in filing tax returns is your modified adjusted gross income (MAGI). MAGI is the amount that determines whether you qualify for certain tax credits and deductions, and it plays a big role in your overall tax liability.

For active duty military personnel, gross income generally includes only basic pay, incentive pay, and some special pay and bonuses. Allowances for housing, moving, travel, and a host of other items are not taxable and are therefore not included in your gross income. Depending on the service member's rank, certain pay received while serving in a combat zone or hazardous duty area is also excluded from gross income and is tax free.

The government automatically subtracts exempt pay from your taxable income, but understanding how the figures are calculated can give you a more complete picture of your tax situation.

Families may also qualify for the nonrefundable Retirement Savings Contribution Credit, designed to help offset the costs of contributing to a retirement plan such as the military's Thrift Savings Plan (TSP), a 401(k), or an IRA. Depending on your MAGI and your filing status, you could receive a tax credit equal to 10, 20, or 50 percent of your first $2,000 in contributions.

Home relief: The Military Family Tax Relief Act of 2003 can help ease the tax burden on families dealing with some common hardships of military life. Perhaps the most popular element of the plan is the part that offers some tax savings to military families required to sell their homes and relocate. Here's how it works: when any taxpayer sells a primary residence, the law allows up to $250,000 ($500,000 for a married couple filing jointly) of capital gains to be kept tax free, provided they owned and lived in the house for at least two of the previous five years. But because military families move frequently, many haven't been able to qualify for this exemption—until now. The new law creates a special exception to the "two-of-five" rule for military personnel called to "qualified official extended duty," allowing them to suspend the rule for up to ten years for one property.

Know where to file: Filing a tax return in the correct state may seem obvious for some, but it's often a point of confusion for service members stationed away from their permanent home address. As a general rule of thumb, file your return with the state you claim as your home of record. So if you're stationed in Maine but California is your home of record, you would generally be subject to California state income taxes.

There are too many tax laws and bylaws to cover here (and this book isn't meant to be a sleep-inducing aid), so let a tax professional help you. Getting your finances in shape is worth the time and effort to get your house in order. After some initial hard work, you'll be well on your way to fit finances and a fabulous military life.

The Mocha Mix
Real Talk on Keeping Your Money Right

★ ★

I try to manage our finances with the assumption that my husband's pay will be messed up. Inevitably this will happen, and I've seen families really caught out there because of it. Plan like it will happen so when it does, you'll be okay.

—CAMILLE, ARMY WIFE, FORT BRAGG

My best advice is to live within your means. All the time.

—JOYCE, NAVY WIFE

I've definitely seen wives get excited and start overspending when they receive extra money, for example, hostile combat zone pay, but when hubby comes home and that pay disappears, they find themselves in an awful hole.

—EVELYN, ARMY WIFE

Make sure your financial paperwork is in order. Surprisingly, my husband was more comfortable doing the will, life insurance, and other financial documents than I was—even though it is for my and the children's benefit. Even if it feels awkward to discuss those things and sign those papers, you must do it.

—REBECCA, ARMY WIFE

Once my husband's pay got messed up and we had to do one of the payday advance loans. It was a very bad experience with so much fine print that they never mentioned. We were too embarrassed to tell anyone we needed the loan, let alone ask for help to get out of it, and I vowed to never put my family in that situation again.

—ANONYMOUS, ARMY WIFE

CHAPTER EIGHT

Parenting

Raising Children in the Military Lifestyle

If you are reading this chapter, then we will assume you are a parent or primary caregiver to a military child. And yes, we know what they say about assuming, but we're going to throw out another assumption anyway: you're going to really appreciate the structure of this chapter. It is geared toward helping busy parents learn a lot of strategies in a little time that will enhance their military children's lives. Most of the topics here, such as deployment and relocation, will be addressed in other areas of the book, but in this chapter those topics are discussed only as they relate to children. Of course, we think military kids are some of the best kids in the world—they're more traveled and more confident, and they have had more exposure than most other kids. But there are some challenges. We'll take you through the down and dirty, nitty-gritty of what will help you raise a vibrant child! So let's get started.

Children need stability in their lives, and military children are no exception. Children also need solid social interaction, good coping mechanisms, and honest communication. This is even more important for military parents.

Yet, with frequent relocation, children's lives might seem anything but stable. Every few years, there's a new house, new friends, new school, and other big changes they have to deal with. What's more, their military parents are on an endless cycle of living in the home one minute, being gone the next, and back again; and they may be so far away from other family members that the relationships just aren't as close as they could be. So can a military child really have stability? Absolutely! All they need are adults in their lives who help make each and every transition as smooth as possible, usually by having a positive attitude, making the children a part of the process, and maintaining consistency in the "how" rather than focus on the "where."

Pamela's Pick:

There are brats, and then there are military brats. Civilians don't like to be called brats because it almost always means a child who is rude, unruly, and otherwise undesirable to be around. However, children who grow up in the military don't have a problem with being called a brat as long as it is preceded by the word *military*. In our community there is nothing wrong or derogatory about being called a military brat, because all it means is someone who shared our lifestyle because he or she had an active-duty parent while growing up. Many military kids even refer to themselves as military brats and are so proud of it that they will wear the T-shirt to prove it. What's more, military brats who are all grown up will often continue to refer to themselves as military brats, and they will instantly strike up a conversation with other adult military brats no matter where they meet them.

Creating Stability in Relocation

Moving often is a way of life. It's something folks in the outside world just don't get. Whenever Pamela introduces herself as a military spouse, she almost always gets a "Girl, don't you get tired of moving?" or "What about your kids, how do they handle it?" in return. Well, the truth is, so far, she hasn't grown tired of it; and her two kids have handled it just fine. Thankfully, Pamela's kids are still young, and we know that as children get older moving creates more and more havoc in the house. (And we believe almost anything when it comes to teenagers.) But we also know and have seen how a parent's perspective can make all the difference. Even though unexpected moves can happen at any time, most of the time military families will have an idea of when they can expect to receive orders to move based on when they arrived at the current assignment. That means there can be some front-end prep work with the kids before the move. Even before you receive orders you can start mentioning the possibility to give your children a heads-up instead of letting it come as a surprise.

Of course, in some cases, they might be able to tell you when it's time to leave again, like the daughter of Lieutenant General and Mrs. Teresa Rice. "We started moving when our children were very young so they got used to it. Once, after living somewhere for ten months, my daughter came to us and asked where we were going next. My husband told her we were not going any-where right then. She replied, 'We always do. We move every summer.' The next thing you know, he had a job interview and got the job, so we were going to move after all. All my daughter had to say was, 'I told you so.'"

THE ANNOUNCEMENT

Once your husband gets orders, there is sure to be grief if the announcement goes something like this: "I have bad news. We have to pick up and move again. The new city is too hot/too cold. The cost of living there is too high. I have heard that the schools are low performing and unruly. I will never find a job there. And by the way, we have to leave next month." If I were a kid, I would probably respond similarly. "I hate moving. I love my friends and don't want new ones. This is not fair!" Can you blame them? So what's a sister to do? Get them involved in the moving process.

DISCOVER THE UNKNOWN

The first thing kids always want to know is: what's it like there? It's your job to become the public relations manager for the move. You need to sell it! Show the children the benefits of each move. One thing I've learned in business that is also true with children is that everyone listens to WII-FM—that is, "What's In It for Me?" When you tune into your kids' WII-FM station, you'll be able to sell them on the move. If your daughter listens to the soccer "station," then research teams and programs in the area and let her know what's coming.

If there aren't any sports or hobbies of interest, play up other benefits. For example, when Pamela moved to Virginia, she sold the fact that they would be much closer to her family in the Northeast, and just minutes away from the nation's capital. In Rhode Island, they were less than one hour from her childhood neighborhood and close relatives. That mean the children would get to hang with their favorite cousins. There wasn't much selling required for the Hawaii move, that one was a no-brainer even for the children.

Next, make the actual move an adventure. Plan some fun activities for the transitional period between leaving the old house and moving into the new one. One year Pamela's family started saving coins in a big glass water bottle to raise funds for a trip to Disney. By the time they cashed in the jar, they had hundreds of dollars and they couldn't wait to get there! Karene Millner, a navy mom, always checks out attractions on the road trip route and plans for many fun stops as they travel to their new home.

FINDING A NEW HOME

If you're finding your own accommodations, Pamela is a big fan of making the children a part of finding a new home as soon as they are old enough to do so. "When my son Tré was about five years old, we were moving from North Carolina to northern Virginia. We loaded him and his best friend in the car and made the six-hour drive to go house hunting. What a difference it made for him to have someone his own age. First, the car ride was a breeze. They really kept each other occupied enough for my husband and me to carry on conversations! Second, what an adventure northern Virginia turned out to be. The snow was a big hit. Living in the south meant that they hadn't seen much snow. And since most of the houses were empty, they were able to explore just the way little boys love to: without keeping their hands to themselves. A kiddie traveling companion was a big hit—for all of us!," she says.

Now sometimes the move isn't simply a car ride away, that's where good use of the Internet and help from other military families can go a long way.

"When we moved to Hawaii, my husband did a lot of research online early on about our new location. By the time he schooled all three of us on everything there was to know, we picked our top three counties and located a real estate agent who helped us find exactly what we wanted. Every week or so the agent sent us listings via e-mail and we gathered around the computer as a family, reading descriptions, looking at pictures, and even taking virtual tours. We narrowed our options. And the excitement was growing," Pamela says.

Either way, including your children as much as possible in the process can help them feel better about where they are going.

Mrs. Jean Ellis, wife of Army General (Ret.) Larry R. Ellis

Children learn from us and we learn from them through the military experience. My girls are adults now and they remind me that although I thought their transitions were easy, they sometimes were not. For example, they shared with me a time when they went to school in the South and we did not live on post. They were being teased the first few weeks of school because they talked funny. They didn't have a southern accent. And the other kids assumed my kids, being African American, would speak a certain way and they didn't. Acclimating to life in certain locations was a little more difficult for them. They didn't share it at the time, they just handled it. I learned that we have to be sensitive that as children, in certain environments, their peers may perceive them differently.

PREPARING THEM TO MOVE

The military does alleviate some of the moving stress by providing packers to do all the hard work. But there is still plenty to do, and you should definitely share the load with the kids. Have them go through their rooms and sort out what goes and what stays. Plan a yard sale together and use the proceeds to fund activities during the transition. This would be a great time to get back online and find the fun things to do in the new city or along the way if you plan to drive.

MOVING INTO THE NEW HOME

Pamela has always sought to ensure that no matter where they found themselves serving, it was important to quickly turn the house or quarters into the "McBride home." "We work very hard to quickly get our house or quarters unpacked and looking like a home. This is important for the psyche of both parents and children alike. Quickly turning these empty rooms into familiar sanctuaries are vital to transition," says Doug, Pamela's husband.

Another moving strategy is to have traditions. For example, Nicole told us that their grandmother has a tradition that the first thing to be brought into every new house is a broom, mop, dust pan, and bucket. The kids help pick out Grandma's "cleaning items of the home" and each one of them carries in an item.

CHANGING SCHOOLS

For some military kids it seems that just when they have gotten used to a new school, it is time to move again. According to the Department of Defense, about 1.5 million military children attend schools other than those sponsored by the Defense Department, and military families move about three times more than their civilian counterpart. Sometimes changing schools can impact academics, especially for high school students. But recently, the Department of Defense has partnered with the Council of State Governments and education experts to develop the Compact on Education Transition for Military Children to alleviate some of the problems that result from frequent relocation and deployment. Participating states have agreed to uniform standards of such things as transferring school records, course placement, graduation requirements, testing inconsistencies, and other issues. As of July 11, 2008, ten states have signed the compact: Arizona, Colorado, Connecticut, Delaware,

Florida, Kansas, Kentucky, Michigan, Missouri, and Oklahoma. To find out if your state has adopted the compact since the writing of this book, go to www.defenselink.mil and search for education compact. At long last, something to potentially cut through the BS (bureaucratic stuff, that is) by allowing the use of temporary transcripts until the official ones are received and allowing a grace period of enrollment for families to get their children vaccinated in compliance with local requirements.

If you live on or near post, there is probably a school liaison who can help you sort out the local details about school transitions and work out any problems that arise. Check with your post Child and Youth Services Office for contacts. You should work with this staff at your current location to obtain advice and information about the next location. Many times they can help with schools that are outside the gate, too.

Frequent relocations affect your child's social life at school, too. But Nicole, mother of three, orchestrated a wonderful way for her children to transition into a new school midyear.

"A third-grade teacher and I worked out a pen pal system. The students who would be in the same class wrote and sent brief introductions of themselves to my child and my child wrote and sent a brief introduction to them. By the time we arrived in Texas, all the children were really anticipating 'the new student' and the 'new student' couldn't wait to meet them. In fact, it was a great feeling for both my child and me for the children to recognize each other from the pictures."

If possible, try to choose a school where there will be other military children. Our informal panel of military kids tells us showing up as the only kid who hasn't known everyone since kindergarten is particularly stressful. And here's something else they say, moms: first impressions do matter, so do splurge if possible on the first-day-of-school outfit.

OTHER TIPS FOR SCHOOL TRANSITION

- Hand-carry any documents that you will need to register your child for school.
- If your child is involved in sports or other activities, contact those coaches and teachers to get information about them and set up a day to introduce your child to them. Ask if they can assign a peer buddy to your child.

- If your child has no extracurricular activities, check out the school website to see what it has to offer and pick one or two to try out. Make contact with the teacher as listed above. Again, ask for a peer buddy.
- Get a copy of *Military Students on the Move: A Toolkit for Military Parents* (http://www.militarystudent.dod.mil/ParentsToolkit_0406.pdf).
- Check the school calendar online for key dates like the first day of school, open house, orientation, or special events.
- Frequently communicate with teachers during the first few weeks to monitor adjustment and classroom performance. It may be rocky at first, so give things time to settle in before you jump too soon to resolve issues.
- Talk to your children every day about school, even if it's like pulling teeth, so you can monitor if they feel like they are fitting in. Ask how the day went, whether they made any new friends, what was the highlight of the day, and whether there were any difficulties.
- Get feedback about the school from military neighbors.
- Get involved at school. Younger children love parents to volunteer, visit, and have lunch with them during the school day. If you are not employed early in the transition, you may have time to do so. Older kids are another story. They may not be as receptive to parental appearances at school, so check out the PTO or other parent-based group.
- Let them take the school bus or walk with neighbors instead of driving them to school so that they have the chance to connect with other kids.

ONLINE SCHOOL TRANSITION RESOURCES

- Department of Defense, www.militarystudent.dod.mil
- Department of Education, www.ed.gov/parents
- Military Child Education Coalition, www.militarychild.org
- National Military Family Association, www.nmfa.org
- Military Impacted Schools Association (MISA), www.militaryimpactedschoolsassociation.org

- Specialized Training of Military Parents, www.stompproject.org (Special Education or health needs)
- Yellow Pages for Kids with Disabilities, www.yellowpagesforkids.com

HOMESCHOOLING

Thinking of homeschooling? Homeschooling used to seem a little, well, hokey. But now the trend is on the rise. According to the National Center for Education Statistics, approximately 1.1 million students are being home-schooled in the United States, up from about 850,000 just a few years ago. Military parents looking for the stability and continuity of learning that is often at risk with a mobile military lifestyle are also considering homeschooling more and more. About 1.3 percent of all black children are homeschooled, compared with 2.7 percent of white children.

It ain't mainstream yet, but reports show that homeschooling works. Parents and students who take learning seriously and provide the proper conditions for learning can excel, and those children can compete with their traditional school counterparts. It's important to consider that resources for families who are stationed overseas may be limited, and in locations where community resources are not available, families may have to purchase them online or from catalogs.

Note: The Department of Defense Education Activity (DoDEA) neither encourages nor discourages DoD sponsors from homeschooling their minor dependents.

ADVANTAGES

1. Educational continuity is created for military children despite their mobile lifestyle.
2. Teaching parents and student siblings experience a unique family bonding.

3. Resources to support families are available online, in public libraries, in community networks, in youth-serving organizations, and sometimes in the public school system.
4. Scheduling is flexible and can be tailored to children's individual learning styles, interests, and extracurricular activities.
5. Some schools will offer use of library, loaned textbooks, and participation in music or art classes.

DISADVANTAGES

1. There is *potential* for isolation and therefore lack of socialization.
2. Resources for families who are stationed overseas may be limited.
3. In locations where community resources are not available, families may have to purchase them online or from catalogs.
4. Children switching to homeschooling may find it difficult to learn on their own or learn from a parent.
5. Children switching to traditional schooling may need more attention from the teacher and be accustomed to spending as much time as needed on a particular topic.
6. If your child is dead-set against the idea, there may be resentment and difficulty.

MAKING HOMESCHOOLING A SUCCESS

If you decide homeschooling is for you, follow these tips for optimal results:

- Read everything you can get your hands on.
- Talk to other homeschooling parents *and* children.
- Look for homeschooling resources both inside the gate and outside of it.

- Talk to your children about expectations and get them involved in the planning process.
- Get organized. Create a plan for how you will approach homeschooling, and gather all the materials and supplies you need to get started.
- Decide on whether you will purchase or create your lessons and your teaching approaches.
- Create a weekly, biweekly, or monthly schedule. Too much flexibility can lead to ineffective learning.
- Maintain good recordkeeping practices. At a minimum, keep a three-ring binder with dividers for each child's work and a file system of the curricula, testing results, and other pertinent documentation.
- Go one step further by creating a portfolio with samples of each child's work.
- Give yourself and your children time to evolve into strategies, schedules, and activities that work for you.
- Praise your children on their work.
- Make learning fun. Learn by interacting, using art and music, going on field trips and get-togethers with other homeschool families to share in the learning.
- Check installation bulletin boards for homeschool family announcements or put up your own.
- Check post newspapers for homeschool announcements.
- Sign up your kids for community activities to meet other homeschool families.
- Visit your post Child and Youth Services Office for school liaison staff.
- Contact your Family Readiness Center at your new post for laws, testing, documentation, and support services.
- Also, visit the following websites:
  Home School Legal Defense Association, www.hslda.org
  National Home Education Research Institute, www.nheri.org
  National Home Education Network, www.nhen.org

- Homeschooling Resources:
  Home School Internet Resource Center (www.rsts.net)
  National African American Homeschooling Alliance, a resource for
  homeschooling and a social network called the Black Homeschoolers
  Club.

HELP CHILDREN ESTABLISH AND MAINTAIN FRIENDSHIPS

Help your child meet new friends as soon as possible. Being a hermit for a few weeks won't help anybody. If you live on base, there's plenty of help. Most installations are very similar in the services and programs you will find there, and you can count on having access to a variety of things for your kids. Most installations will have child development centers, recreation centers, teen centers, arts and crafts, bowling alleys, movie theaters, swimming pools, and more. If you move during the summer, the pool is a great place to meet kids. "My child has enjoyed the benefits of military family life—church, youth activities, PX and commissary privileges," said one army wife and mom. As soon as you arrive at your new location find out where youth services and programs are and visit them briefly to help your children feel more familiar with their surroundings and possibly meet new people, something they're probably pretty good at, being military kids and all.

Also, visit the neighborhoods on post and check out where the schools are located. Then, venture outside the gates to find those same things in the community. Hopefully, you will discover other things of interest to them, like miniature golf, their favorite eateries, and the local malls. Visit the playground often or find a playgroup. Sites like www.meetup.com or www .playgroupsusa.com can help.

ENROLL YOUR CHILD IN SPORTS AND ACTIVITIES

If there was any one thing that moms said created stability for their kids, it would be their involvement in sports and other activities. The frequent interaction is bound to forge a friendship somewhere along the way. No matter where Pamela has lived, she always called ahead or did online research to find out about the sports programs. (In some cases you can sign up for the base sports programs, the county recreation programs, and eventually, even school sports.) Not only could her kids count on another ready-made group of people to meet (school mates was the first group), but they could participate in activities they loved and were good at.

"Both of my kids were very active in sports and cheerleading. This always gave them that extra assistance with integrating into any community," says Doug, Pamela's husband, who has served for nineteen years. "Sports and other team-oriented activities expedite the integration process by enabling them to form close bonds early in the PCS (permanent change of station) move, which made the transition that much smoother. Church is an outlet as well."

STAY CLOSE TO EXTENDED FAMILY

Cousins, grandparents, and other extended family members are great connectors for your kids. Here are some ways for grandparents and other extended family members of military children to stay in touch:

- Maintain consistent telephone communication.
- Visit as often as feasible, and make sure you spend alone time with the kids and not just the parents.
- Attend a grandparent-grandchild summer camp. Or send the kids to camp with their cousins.
- Babysit the children when the parents go on vacation.
- Have them visit you during school vacation.
- Join them on a family vacation.
- Exchange photos by mail.
- Use technology. If you don't have a computer, use one at the public library to e-mail them or to send them a handwritten fax.
- Set yourself up to use a webcam (or use someone else's) to chat with them face-to-face.
- Encourage their efforts, too. Ask them to fax report cards. Or they can send videos of them dancing, singing, and tumbling via e-mail. "Grandma, look at me!"
- Send notes by snail mail. Kids love to receive "real mail" addressed to them.
- Send younger children recordings of you reading them bedtime stories.

- Be there to celebrate important life events when you can or call when they happen to let them know you wish you were there and want to hear all about it.

Encourage your child to keep in touch with old pals—e-mail and some social networking sites (with your supervision) are good ways for children to keep in touch.

CREATE FAMILY TRADITIONS

Having family traditions from Friday taco nights to eating out the night before school can help the kids have a routine and familiarity no matter where they are. It also promotes family bonding and creates a sense of commitment.

ENCOURAGE THEM TO EXPRESS THEMSELVES

It's never a good idea for children to keep their feelings bottled up. This is particularly true for military kids, who have a lot more going on in their lives—from deployment to news reports of war; it's important to keep the lines of communication wide open. When they do share, try to respond with encouraging and positive feedback.

Pamela's Pick: **How to Teach Kids About Rank**
Certain parenting matters are unique to military parents. One area is understanding rank. The military is a very structured environment where everybody knows your name and rank if you are wearing a uniform. Rank does matter, but children need to understand the proper context of it all.

When it comes to teaching kids about military rank, most parents agree on two things: first, that the amount of information you give your children about rank is on a need-to-know basis and two, it's not as simple as black and white.

Teaching kids about military rank doesn't have to be much different from teaching kids about noncivilian workplace hierarchies. As a military spouse who works in corporate America, I do not explain to my children in great detail anything associated with the stature of the people I work with unless it is necessary in order to put something in context. And when it comes to Doug's military chains of command, we haven't found it necessary to elaborate on it in that case, either.

We teach our children that all adults are to be respected, period.

We don't teach them the difference between officers and enlisted, or who outranks whom. We explain in general what a workplace environment is like in any case. Everyone has a job to do and must do it well regardless of what it is. Everyone has someone else they have to report to, just like in school. Maybe you get to be in charge of gathering the homework folders in your class and someone else is responsible for handing them out at the end of the day. The teacher assigns the duties and is the manager of her class. The teachers report to the principal, who is the manager of the school. The principal reports to the superintendent, and so on.

Doug and I also use phrases that describe relationships rather than emphasize rank. We might say, so-and-so works with Daddy, so-and-so is Daddy's boss, or Daddy is so-and-so's boss.

We do use rank to introduce our children to someone because it is proper to do so, but it is for the same reason we might use Mr. or Ms. when we introduce them to civilians.

Having asked several military wives this same question about whether teaching rank is important, we received answers that ranged from "not at all" to "very much so." Here are some of the responses we received:

Rank means nothing to my children, and it shouldn't unless they serve. In the military you have to respect the rank, but as civilians, they can respect the man or woman, not the rank on their arm.

—Michelle Moore, Air Force, Alaska

Children should be somewhat aware so that they can be proud of what their parent has achieved. However, [they should know] that rank doesn't make a child more or less important than others; it should not be used to segregate and bully children.

—Michelle Schofield, Air Force, Germany

Our children are not soldiers. What difference does it make? They should be taught to respect all adults.

—Kateria Reddick, retired Army, Maryland

It's good for them to have a broad knowledge, but not to the point where they think rank matters.

—LaKrisha Lindo, Army, Illinois

I think children should not have to worry about if they can be friends with someone because their parent outranks you.

—Felecia Pritchett, Army, California

Depending on their age, I think they should concentrate on basic courtesies: yes, ma'am, no, sir.

—Maxine Wheeler, retired Air Force, Alabama

I think it serves more as a discriminatory tool than anything else. . . . Children, like spouses, tend to "wear" the ranks of their service member, when doing so is inappropriate.

—Juanita, Army, Georgia

Parenting Through Separation, Deployment, Injury, and Death

Any type of long-term parental separation can be difficult for children, but separation due to deployment is particularly so. There have been more than 1.5 million troops deployed since the war in Iraq began through May 2008, and it is estimated that 700,000 children have at least one parent deployed. If your child(ren) is among them, we highly recommend that you read the chapter on separation and deployment for a detailed account of the emotional cycles you and your family will experience and learn strategies for getting through them. In this chapter, however, we focus solely on your child's experience.

PREPARING YOUR CHILDREN FOR DEPLOYMENT

1. Be open and honest with them by providing an age-appropriate explanation about what is going to happen and how it will impact them. For example, your man may introduce the topic to your four-year-old by saying, "Daddy has a new job and I have to live in a different place to do it even though I will miss you very much. I will come back home to live with you and Mommy after your next birthday. I will call you as much as I can." To a fifteen-year-old he might say, "I have gotten notified that I have to leave for Iraq in six months and I will be there for a year. I will be safe because I am well trained for what I have to do. I am really going to miss you." Allow them to ask any questions they have, and answer them all as best you can.

2. Tell them as much as possible about your new job and new location. In Pamela and Doug's house this became a learning experience. "The kids would do the research and locate my deployment destination on a map or globe," says army dad Doug. "They see how far it was away from home and what other countries were in close proximity. They read about the culture and what is available at the location. This is critical as far as them having somewhat of an understanding of the lifestyle that Dad would be living. We discussed R&R leave and what that entailed. This assured them that although the deployment was long . . . they would see Dad at some point during the deployment."

3. In all cases help them understand that as important as it is for you to do your job, they have an important one, too: keeping up their grades, helping around the house, calling Daddy if possible, and sending him letters and pictures.

4. Tell your child's teachers, school counselors, coaches, and other caregivers about the impending deployment or separation. It will be helpful to have others who can spot behavior changes. Let the children know that those people are aware of the situation and that if they need to talk about their feelings when Mom is not there, it is okay to talk to them.

5. Talk to your child about behavior expectations and discipline. First,

review the house rules that will stay the same and those that may change. Children need to know that sometimes when they are feeling sad or missing Daddy, they might not feel like behaving, but that Mommy and Daddy will need them to cooperate.

6. Encourage Dad to give each of the kids one special gift that they can hold when they are missing him. The kids could also do the same for him.

DURING DEPLOYMENT AND SEPARATION

While a parent is away, it is still important for a child to have structure and predictability in order to cope. Therefore, don't be too lenient about rules and routines. Bedtimes, chores, extracurricular activities, and even celebrations of special occasions need to stay the same.

The separation is likely to bring about some stress in their lives. Be aware that it often manifests itself through physical ailments. When children complain of headaches or stomachaches, or show moodiness and irritability, it may be a sign of stress. Sleeping more than usual or inability to sleep, as well as noticeable increases or decreases in appetite, may also signal stress. Be available for children to express themselves about what's bothering them. They may simply need a hug and your reassurance that Daddy will be home soon and that you both love them very much. Don't avoid talking about Daddy often; your children need to feel that he is still a part of their lives as much as possible. If you are doubtful about whether these symptoms are stress related or not, seek medical advice.

Sometimes, younger children revert to behaviors that they had moved beyond or develop new habits, such as bed-wetting or thumb sucking. Don't make a big deal about them. Again, talk to your child or seek medical advice when you are unsure of how to handle it. Of course if your child is displaying serious behaviors such as violence, extreme anger, tantrums, and very poor school performance, seek help from your doctor, school counselor, or pastor; or visit www.militaryonesource.com to identify other resources in your community.

Some parents have found it helpful to limit their child's exposure to media, especially those with military or violent content, whether it be news broadcasts, movies, or video games. If your kids are older, you may allow them to watch TV news under your supervision so you can answer any questions. Either way, try to keep them busy and spend more time interacting with them and planning outings and fun activities at home.

WHAT TO DO WHEN THEY ARE MISSING DADDY *RIGHT NOW!*

There will be times when kids just want their daddy and no one else will do—not even you! Don't take it personally or get discouraged when what you are doing to comfort them is not working. Give them time and space to go through it. Let them experience the very real emotions and let them know it is okay to be upset or angry or whatever they are feeling. If they want a hug, give them one. If they want to be left alone, leave them and just check in on them periodically. This might be a great time to remind them about the special gift Daddy left for them, to listen to a prerecorded message or story from him or, as one parent told me, to spray one of his work T-shirts with the cologne or aftershave he uses and let them cuddle with it. If they want to talk, stop what you are doing and listen to them.

SINGLE-PARENT SURVIVAL SKILLS

Let's face it, an MS is technically a single parent most of the time. Try these strategies to keep your sanity and your family running smooth during these times:

- Make household chores a family affair.
- Limit the number of weekly activities each child participates in.
- Ask for help from family and friends.
- Post chore lists and schedules to make things easier.
- Set rules and enforce them by following through with consequences.
- Praise children for doing well.
- Prepare school clothes on the weekend for the following week.
- Cook enough for more than one night.
- Take time out for yourself.
- Let loose and have fun with the kids regularly.

Don't Overload Your Children with Responsibility

We all need help from time to time, especially when our partner is away. And we want our kids to grow up knowing how to clean, cook, and handle other household chores. But when Daddy's away, be careful not to overdo it.

"Too many times parents expect their child to be more mature than she should be," said a former family child-care provider for military children. "I believe a child should be a child. It saddened me to see that parents put so much on them than necessary when their life is already so difficult."

Give children chores that are appropriate for their age. If you need help with bigger or more difficult ones, give them a valuable lesson in teamwork by all doing them together so it's not too much on any one of you, and make it a fun way to sneak in some quality time.

Don't Overload Your Children with Activities

It is a good idea to keep them busy as a way to keep their mind off the deployment, but be careful about doing too much, and therefore creating more havoc than anything else. Take cues from them about what's fun because their definition just might differ from yours. Also take the cues about when enough is enough. If their shoulders drop at the mention of another activity, that might be a sign you need to give them some free time.

Stay in Communication with the Deployed Parent

Boy, oh boy, have times changed. When Pamela's husband was sent to war for Desert Shield/Desert Storm in 1990, communication was extremely limited. There was a lot of old-fashioned letter writing back then, just like in the movies. Cell phones weren't the craze, so phone calls were limited, too. If your man was lucky to get to a phone to call you, you were lucky if you happened to catch the call. If you came home and found a message on the answering machine, you had mixed emotions. You were happy that he was doing well, but disappointed, sad, and even angry at times, that you missed his call. You never knew when the next one would be and if you would miss it again. "When I missed Doug's calls, I would play the message over and over. We both had tape recorders and plenty of cassette tapes. Wow, that was ages ago. Today, my kids barely know what a cassette tape is," says Pamela.

The advent of technology has created more modern ways to stay in touch. In preparing this book, we met parents who make video or CD recordings of them reading their child's favorite stories so their kids can listen to them whenever they just want to hear Daddy's voice.

The Browns, who also call themselves the webcam family, have become experts in staying connected to their army husband and dad. Now living in Texas, the Brown family has had two deployments to Iraq and are preparing for their third, but Mom has become an expert in "hooking them up" to Dad.

"I set up a webcam in my bedroom, and Gregory set up one over there. When we had something to tell him, we would send him an instant message and hang out in there waiting for him to come to work. It was always fun to see who would be the first to yell, 'Daddy's home' and they'd have their daddy time almost as if he was right there."

The most creative and touching way Pamela used technology to connect with Doug was when he sent photos showing some of his unit's humanitarian work. The very next time he was able to call, Pamela had the laptop set up on the kitchen counter programmed to run the photos in slide show mode and put on the speaker phone. He described what was going on in the photos, the kids asked question after question, and he answered every single one of them. As soon as her daughter, Taylor, saw other kids in the photos she wanted to know if they were there then, why couldn't she be there. "I held my breath," Pamela says. "How was he going to handle that one?" Her husband gently explained that they lived there, and Daddy and his workers were helping trying to provide things they very much needed. "Whew. A picture is worth a thousand words, but those that connect families separated by thousands of miles are priceless," says Pamela.

Pamela's Pick: Keeping Dad in the Picture

I always encourage my kids to send letters, cards, homework, and artwork as often as possible and not just on special occasions. This can be very easy to do if you plan ahead. Set aside a place at home to store items you accumulate for care packages. This includes priority boxes, customs forms and labels from the post office, packing tape, permanent markers, and whatever else needed to prevent you from having to run around every time you are ready to send a package. We purchased all kinds of cards to have on hand, picked up postcards everywhere we went, and bought things like his favorite snacks, T-shirts that reminded us of him, and other items whenever we were out and about.

Technology also allows deployed parents to keep up with what's going on with the family. Many schools now post grades online. Many wives scan and e-mail report cards, tests, and papers. Pamela often CCs her husband on any e-mail correspondence with teachers just to keep him in the loop. "My son fills him in after every game, and my daughter fills him in after competitions. He also likes to read the football, basketball, and cheerleading newsletters from the coaches as well as the one we receive from our neighborhood and any articles I publish while he is gone," Pamela says.

Just remember that technology is not perfect. "One year, my husband deployed right before Father's Day and we knew the package might not make it to him on time so we also sent him e-cards with music and animation from each of us and sent it to arrive in his inbox on Father's Day. We were disappointed to learn that due to security limitations, he was unable to open the cards online. But, as any military family would do, we adjusted and composed a plain text e-mail from each of us expressing our greetings and describing our cards. He loved it!" Pamela recalls. You too can make fond memories even when you're miles or continents apart.

If you do mail stuff, remember that timing is important, so explain to your children that depending on where their dad is stationed, it may be necessary to mail holiday and special occasion packages a month ahead of time. On the day before Thanksgiving, before Pamela even starts cleaning the greens, she and the kids are on the living room floor wrapping Daddy's Christmas gifts and packing them to be shipped. Nothing happens in the McBride household on that day until the trip to the post office is complete. It might also help to mark a calendar with all the special occasions and note the dates the packages need to be in the mail. Whether it's his birthday, Valentine's Day, St. Patrick's Day, Easter, Father's Day, Fourth of July, or Ground Hog Day, the kids may really get a kick out of creating themed boxes for their dad that contain little gifts, store-bought and handmade; his favorite snacks; cards; and letters. They should also know that sometimes Dad's mail to them may not always arrive in time for birthdays or special occasions even if mailed on time and it's not his fault. One year Pamela received her Mother's Day card on July 7, despite its being mailed way in advance!

Pamela's Pick:

We also purchased a bag full of inexpensive, but colorful photos albums and took photos all the time. We filled the albums and sometimes even added little notes or labels so he could follow along with what had been going on at home. And he did the same for us, but by using technology to get them to us instead of snail mail.

Pamela's Pick: **Keeping Your Family Safe**

I am a chicken. A scaredy-cat. A wimp. Or whatever you want to call it. But I am somewhat paranoid about everyone knowing my husband is away. Since we usually live off post, it just feels safer to keep it to myself. Don't get me wrong, living on post is not a 100 percent guarantee of safety; there are bad people everywhere. Now of course a few neighbors know about it and my children's friends' parents, but I make it a practice of limiting the information to those who need to know. Here's what I do and don't do:

I don't put out a yellow ribbon or other "Support Our Troops" paraphernalia if it wasn't up before my husband left.

I make sure that my husband's car is parked in the driveway and in different spots.

I keep his voice on the outgoing message on the answering machine.

My children are not allowed to say, "My dad is deployed" when someone calls. "He's not here right now, but my mom is here" is their response.

I usually have my dad or a friend sit for repairmen or at least be there with me.

When I go away on a business trip, my dad stays at my house with the kids. When I go on vacation and leave the dog home, our friends come over to feed, walk, and play with her and bring in the mail.

I generally keep lights on outside and inside when we are not in the house.

My children and I are programmed to lock the door every

time we come in. Sometimes we even get a good laugh when we accidentally lock each other out because of this, but hey, it's not a bad habit to have.

My son and I both check every door in the house before going to bed.

I keep my eye out for any suspicious or sudden activity around my home and will call the police if I think *anything* seems out of order.

LOOKING AFTER YOU

Finally, as the at-home parent you need to take care of yourself also. Eat healthy and get enough sleep, exercise, and fun to help manage your stress, too. Arrange for playdates so you can have a break. Visit a spa. If money is an issue, look for local schools that provide training for cosmetology, massage therapy, and the like for more affordable options. Say yes when others offer to assist. Seek help when you need it, and be specific about what you need. Check the Child and Youth Services Office to determine whether respite care is offered on post or near it when you just need to breathe.

REUNION AND REINTEGRATION

Reunion and reintegration refers to the deployed parent's homecoming and fitting back into the family. And although the family will be overjoyed initially, having Dad enter into the family equation again could be bumpy at first. Sometimes the issues will be minor ones.

"The challenging aspect was getting used to having to share the bathroom and his leaving dishes on the counter," said Kateria Reddick, wife of a retired soldier. "It's so much easier teaching this to your children than your spouse."

Other challenges are a lot more serious.

"I had to relinquish the role of head of the household and learn how to transition back slowly rather than jump back into the way things used to be," says Kateria. "This was absolutely the hardest part for my son."

No matter how big or small, though, these issues could lead to big arguments.

"We fought about everything that happened in our two-year separation during the first week he was home," said Adrienne, an army wife from Hubbard, Texas. "After that, we were fine."

Unit Ministry Teams provide reunion and reintegration training for service members, and, often, family members can also receive training on post. This helps both sides know what to expect and provides strategies for the family to work together to adjust to the changes that have occurred during separation. Depending on their age, the changes could be huge.

If you've been out of touch during the deployment, then soldiers returning to much older or more mature children may find it difficult to treat them the age they are now instead of the age they were when Dad left. Whatever difficulties you experience, all change is best handled through communication and compromise whether it is between the adults or involves the child.

Expect that children will act out if they think they are not getting enough attention. Both parents should be aware of their interactions with all family members and ensure that no one is being too standoffish or monopolizing all the attention to the point where anyone feels neglected or less important. Reactions from both children and adults can range from detached to clingy. Truth be told, this balancing act can be even trickier for the adults, who may also sacrifice their interactions with each other for the sake of the children. One way to help the situation is for everyone to spend individual time with each of the other family members as well as spending time all together.

Reintegration takes time. There is no shortcut back to "normal," but there are cues that indicate when you or your loved ones might need help. The Operation READY Post-Deployment Battlemind Training for spouses lists the following things that can signal help is needed.

Cues Children Might Need Help

Look for changes in how your child normally behaves and problems that persist:

- Irritability, problems controlling his/her temper
- Getting into fights, hitting, biting, and/or kicking
- Having problems paying attention or sitting still
- Withdrawing from friends, becoming a loner at school or at home
- Being unhappy, sad, or depressed
- Academic problems
- School personnel, friends, or others tell you that your child needs help

CUES SPOUSES MIGHT NEED HELP

If any of the following are severe and are persistent or interfere with your daily life, seek help:

- Feeling depressed and down
- Repeated crying episodes
- Feeling angry, tense, irritable, hopeless, and/or resentful
- Difficulty sleeping or sleeping too much
- Significant appetite changes
- Not finding fun in things previously enjoyed
- Using medications, illegal drugs, or alcohol to cope
- Taking out frustrations on others
- Suicidal or homicidal thinking, intent, or actions
- Isolating yourself or withdrawing from important relationships
- Family, co-workers, or friends tell you that you need help

CUES SOLDIERS MIGHT NEED HELP

If any of the following are severe and persist or interfere with your daily life, seek help:

- Strong memories, nightmares, or sleeping problems
- Easily startled
- Conflict, arguing, anger and hostility
- Excessive use of alcohol or other substances
- Performance problems at work or home
- Distant from spouse or children; talking of a divorce or separation unwanted by spouse
- Aggressive driving
- Feeling down or not able to enjoy life; not making future plans
- Family members, NCOs, or friends tell you that you need help
- Suicidal or homicidal thinking, intent, or actions

If you realize that anyone in your family needs help, reach out to the chaplains, your medical doctors, MilitaryOneSource.com, or your service's family service center.

Help Your Child Deal with Injury or Loss

It is estimated that about twelve thousand military children have injured parents. How will yours react when Dad comes home injured? There will be mixed feelings in that she will be thrilled he has returned, but she will still feel a sense of loss, because he is not her "old" dad. Maybe he used to run around playing tag or hide and seek and now with his physical limitations or losses, he simply can't. Depending upon your child's age, he may think he will hurt you by playing and be less inclined to do so. Some children even fear leaving the parent alone, believing that something could happen and no one will be there to help. Certain children may never stop worrying about his getting better and begin to display extreme signs of stress.

Your child is not the only one who will have a hard time adjusting. Your honey may experience a variety of negative emotions as he deals with the loss personally. Extreme sadness or anger may come into play. And because other mental health issues may be present, like depression, posttraumatic stress disorder (PTSD), or traumatic brain injury (TBI), the problems will only get more complex. The chapter on tragedy and loss provides a detailed description of all these conditions.

Understanding a Child's Reaction to Death

Children react to grief in accordance with their age.

Babies (birth to two years old) may become more irritable and need to be cuddled more frequently. They can retain memories of the lost parent, and some of them may emerge as they become older.

Children ages three to five see death as sleep. They may become insecure and fearful that the safety of their world is threatened. Play that involves physical contact, large muscle movement, and creativity are helpful.

Youngsters ages five to nine see death as something that happens to others, and nine- to ten-year-olds are concerned with biological functions of the deceased. Both groups tend to want to talk about the details continually. They may become distracted from schoolwork and feel guilt, failure, or anger and regress to earlier behaviors; they also may not sleep well and suffer physical manifestations of the grief. Involve them in group discussions and creative activities in reading and writing.

Adolescents rely heavily on peer support. They want family and friends to know they understand death, yet need confirmation that their feelings are appropriate. They can revert to earlier behaviors and indulge in risky behaviors. They can benefit from opportunities to share their thoughts and feelings.

TIPS FOR TALKING WITH CHILDREN ABOUT DEATH

- Listen to what they have to say and accept their feelings; don't correct them. If they take on blame or guilt, help children understand that they could not have prevented the death.
- Allow them to participate in the family activities that relate to celebrating the life of the deceased.
- Answer their questions briefly and honestly even if they keep asking the same ones.
- Talk with your child's teachers, counselors, and coaches about the best ways to help. The school may offer group discussions to help children during difficult times.
- Make sure they understand that death is a normal part of life, but we all work to keep ourselves safe.
- Don't rush them through the grieving process. They need to go through the stages at their own pace just like adults.
- Arrange to have a relative or friend who the children are close to be with your family to help. You may find that you are so emotionally distraught at times that you are unable to care for your children. It is helpful to have a backup plan. Having the right person to care for the kids lessens the possibility and severity of additional acting out due to resentment that you are not paying enough attention to them.

The Mocha Mix

★ ★

The Good: What sisters said about the positive impacts of raising kids in the military life

Being raised in New York City, growing up in tough streets, I am so glad my children will never have to grow that way. The military lifestyle has given my children the opportunity to grow up in a safe and caring environment.

—LaTanya, Air Force wife, South Carolina

Despite moving around, I believe my son has a very mature outlook on life and the world because of his travels.

—Liz, Army, Germany

My son has learned to accept people regardless of race, rank, or purse strings.

—Kateria, Army wife, Virginia

They have had the opportunity to travel and explore cultures and activities in overseas DoDs Schools.

—Juanita, Air Force, Germany

My family defines my children's life, be it the military or a civilian job.

—Toshanika, Army, North Carolina

My fifteen-year-old daughter knows how to take care of herself and is very independent.

—Felecia, Army, California

The Bad and Ugly: What sisters said about the negative side of raising kids in the military life

The education. Military children are exposed to curriculums that are great and the not-so-great. Some states lag behind, which puts military children at a disadvantage. In addition, they must often pay out-of-state tuition to attend college in most states because of their parents' military obligation.

—KATERIA, ARMY, VIRGINIA

Separation anxiety is a big challenge in parenting. Kids fear Mommy or Daddy will leave again to go back to the war and never come home.

—CARLA, ARMY, MARYLAND

I'm often away from home or every time some family event comes up I am at drill.

—LISA, ARMY RESERVE, NEW YORK

Not really having a place to call home.

—CHERYL, ARMY, GEORGIA

It's difficult being away from my children and having my parents to raise them in my absence due to deployments. I converse with them daily, but it's not the same as being there to guide them in each daily situation or give them the affection that they deserve from me. My son is four years old and I have yet to spend an Easter, Mother's Day, Valentine's Day, or any holiday events that occur between the months of February and June.

—KENNA, ARMY, GEORGIA

A Soldier's Story: Dealing with Deployment and Daddy Duty

I have always remained committed to being involved in everything my children do. If it is important to them, then it is important to Dad. I have always made a conscious effort and commitment to ensuring balance in our lives between performing my military duties and being a complete husband and father.

It is very easy to become [so] consumed in our jobs upon PCS (permanent change of station) that we fail to acknowledge that our children's lives have been temporarily disrupted and may need some focus and attention up front. We as professional soldiers have our jobs, unit camaraderie, and previous relationships to carry us through the transition. Our children don't have it as easy.

There is no substitute for spending quality time with your children. You must commit and dedicate yourself to "being there" for your children. Broken promises can be devastating to a military child who is already dealing with new beginnings.

—Doug, Army officer, Pamela's husband and father of two

CHAPTER NINE

Double Duty

Life as a Dual-Military-Career Couple

Being married to the military is tough enough, but what if you're in the military and married to the military? Well, you've got a unique set of challenges, my dear. Believe it or not, dual-military-career couples are on the rise. Call it the romantic air of training camps or the "uniform syndrome" in hyperdrive, but there are more than eighty-four thousand military-married-to-military couples in the armed forces, and about thirty-six thousand of these couples have children.

Turns out, prior to 9/11 and Desert Storm, dual military couples were a mostly forgotten phenomenon. But when Desert Shield/Desert Storm came fast and furious with its rapid and frequent deployments, the unique plight of finding child care for the children of dual military couples poised for deployment became a massive government problem. Several dual military couples frantically scrambled to find adequate child care, and many had their deployments delayed for lack of it. Prior to 9/11, dual military couples found it much easier to juggle marriage and children because military life was so much more predictable. But post 9/11, military life with its longer deployments caused some government debate over whether dual military couples would even be allowed to continue in the military service. Thankfully, they didn't go there. But the challenges remain.

Even when there are no children, two married soldiers are still considered a family. And if child care is not the issue, keeping that family of two intact certainly is. Although branches of the service, most notably, the army, are investing big chunks of money and time into resources to help strengthen marriages, there is very little support for dual military couples, who are often on different deployment and work schedules or at different locations. It's very hard for these couples to attend retreats or group meetings or utilize other resources that are now in place to help families cope. By some accounts, dual military couples are the forgotten families.

Some veterans of the military lifestyle say the government wrongly assumed that dual military couples didn't need the same support services as traditional military couples (where one spouse is a civilian) since each partner "understood" what the other was going through. But we spoke to more than our fair share of divorced dual military couples. And we heard about countless more—enough to make a real government case for some serious intervention.

If you're a service member married to a service member, the first step is to acknowledge that you are in a very unique situation. Your situation redefines the term nontraditional family. With the ongoing "war on terror," the dual military family is under more stress and making even greater sacrifices than ever before. The increased deployment schedule means that some couples barely have time to hand over the car keys or the kids before the other one is off again, let alone having quality "dwell time" together at home. Even when couples are domiciled together, their schedules may make them not more than two strange ships passing in the night—literally! You're under a lot of strain on a daily basis, and recognizing that allows you to deal with your unique situation, well, uniquely. That means that there may not be a cookie-cutter answer for your challenges, so expect a lot of trial and error; and be flexible to make adjustments when plans don't work out.

Pamela's Pick:

Here's an interesting tidbit: across all services, the biggest number of dual marriages are among enlisted soldiers. And the largest percentage of dual military marriages occurs in the air force. Dual marriages in the army have not increased since the war on terror began.

Dual-Edged Sword?

Of course, there are distinct advantages to being married to a soldier. Nobody can understand the plight of a service member better than another service member. And for some military folks, having that understanding from their spouse is something worth the challenges of the dual-military-career life. There's a special bond between them that comes from a shared commitment to military service, advancing their military careers, and keeping their family strong.

"The best part is mutual understanding," says Keisha Odom, an air force service member and spouse of six years. "I have someone who understands how hard I work for my accomplishments on the job and off. I have someone I can complain to about midshifts. I have someone who can check my uniform and physical appearance and understands why all of my friends are guys," she says. "And when I was TDY, he was there being Mr. Mom to our four-month-old for six weeks."

On the other hand, during times of deployment, your stress is doubled worrying about your spouse being in a combat zone. Of course, you are soldiers first, then spouses. But most male soldiers say they would be a lot happier if their wife was at home or working in a noncombat zone.

Couples with children have to call on friends and family members to help out and make sacrifices to support their military service. Asking children to make sacrifices and accepting help from extended family and friends can sometimes become a source of guilt and a cause for conflict in dual-military-career relationships. Some family and friends may even be critical of you if you have children. We met many female service members who were told that they should not have a family—that their children "didn't ask for this life." This kind of stuff can be stressful.

Staying Together

Even though 81 percent of the more than twenty-one thousand dual-military-career couples in the army have joint domicile assignments, that doesn't mean they are buffered from the hardships and marital difficulties of military life.

And to have some women tell it, those difficulties are doubled, even tripled, when the service members are in different branches of the forces. The stresses of keeping a marriage and family together while being a soldier are compounded with dual military couples. In the military, duty always trumps family, and that's a difficult maxim to live by.

"My husband and I are both active-duty air force members and it is truly a challenge," says Tomeka Wright, a twentysomething spouse who was stationed in Germany when we spoke to her. "For instance, there were several times when we were on different schedules and when I came home from work, he was just waking up and getting ready to leave. We would see each other maybe an hour or two each day. Fortunately, these periods didn't last longer than three or four months at a time, but it is definitely difficult," she says.

Katrina Wilkerson, a thirtysomething spouse and service member, lives a similar experience. "For years, he worked nights and I worked days. Most of the time, I'd pass him on his way home and when I was dropping our daughter off to day care on my way to work. Other times he was TDY and I was working twelve- to fifteen-hour days. Our marriage and our lives had some tough times, but fourteen years and counting, we are still seeing them through," Katrina says.

One way to strengthen marital bonds for dual couples is the Married Army Couples Program, established in August 1983. The military also has a Joint Domicile Program. Both are designed to ensure soldiers married to other soldiers are together whenever possible, even though together could be fifty miles apart. The program is also open to army service members who are married to soldiers in other branches. Of course, managing joint assignments in two branches of the armed forces is an even greater challenge. But hey, it does happen. And although the program has some successes, it doesn't necessarily guarantee you will be assigned together. And sometimes it takes couples years to finally be together.

To enroll in the Married Army Couples Program (MCAP), married couples need to submit a Department of the Army Form 4187, Request for Personnel Action, to their local military personnel office. The personnel office will then process the information and enroll the soldiers. If the soldiers are currently assigned to separate duty stations, each of them must submit a DA Form 4187 to his or her respective office.

There are a few things that can make it difficult for MACP to station a couple together and, of course, the army has other military priorities besides keeping you with your boo. For example, if two soldiers have the same low-density military occupational specialty (MOS) or job title, they may be more difficult to station together. Or perhaps a soldier has a job title (MOS), like a translator, in which most available assignments are outside the continental United States. And although MACP applies to soldiers married to members of other services or to U.S. Army Reserve or National Guard soldiers, it is even more difficult for station managers to station them together. Besides being from different career fields, there are also problems assigning couples together when they volunteer for special duty.

Here's the fine print on how the program works. Married, regular army couples desiring assignments to establish a common household may request enrollment in the MACP. When one member of the couple is not an active army soldier, he or she may not enroll in the program but may request reassignment to join his or her spouse if married to a member of another U.S. military service or to a member of the reserve components who is called to active duty for one year or more.

Married army couples must be enrolled on the HQDA Total Army Personnel Data Base (TAPDB) to be considered for joint assignment. Under the MACP, both soldiers will be considered for a joint assignment at the point when either of the two is nominated by Total Officer Personnel Management System (TOPMIS) or the Enlisted Distribution Assignment System (EDAS). If the assignment is from the continental United States to overseas, PERSCOM will coordinate the two requirements with the appropriate overseas command or liaison office. Both soldiers will receive their assignments/pinpoint assignments in the same TOPMIS/EDAS cycle, or the special instructions in the assignment instructions will state that a married army couple assignment was considered but could not be accommodated.

Enrollment is a simple process of verifying that two soldiers are married to each other and having this information transmitted from the servicing military personnel division/personnel service battalion to the TAPDB. A separate standard installation/division personnel system transaction is required for each spouse's social security number and component (i.e., commissioned, warrant, or enlisted) to be entered on the master files of both soldiers. Once enrolled, both soldiers will be continuously considered for joint assignments. Enrollment in the MACP guarantees that both soldiers will be considered for a joint assignment. Although readiness is the number one priority, the

Enlisted Personnel Management Directorate strives to accommodate joint domiciles whenever possible.

For some couples the program has really worked. We spoke to another woman, currently deployed in Iraq, who was dealing with the very first separation from her husband in eight years of marriage.

Creating Your Own Destiny

There's asking the government to keep you with your honey, and then there's taking matters into your own hands. Some couples say the key is being proactive and managing your career. For example, one married service member who served in Bosnia and Afghanistan without his spouse says when he was up for an assignment outside of the continental United States, he volunteered for duty in Korea with the hope that his wife would be able to follow. When his wife was being moved to West Point, New York, he called his branch manager to find out what was available to him at the same location.

Another couple says they decided to decline appointments to command sergeant majors for five years because as command sergeants major it would have been harder for them to be stationed together.

Managing Work Assignments

There's no doubt about it, dual military couples have to work even harder to make their marriage work. It's true that civilian wives make career and other sacrifices in the military lifestyle, but these can occur more frequently and deeply for dual-military-career couples. Most will have to make serious trade-offs between career and family. The best thing is to really get to know what it takes to advance each other's careers. One may pass up a career-enhancing move in order to stay together, or one may accept a less desirable job so the spouse can advance. Of course, as married service members move up the ranks, these decisions become more difficult—and more delicate.

Meet the Robinsons. When Michael and Dianna first met as fresh air force recruits during technical school, they never planned on taking things all the way to the altar. But fate had a different plan for them. After an initial breakup, they ended up being stationed again together in Georgia. That's when they took it as a sign. Now he is a chief master sergeant, and she is a senior master sergeant. Both have had solid careers while maintaining their twenty-year marriage. But not without some sacrifices and flexibility. Originally Chief Robinson was a lab technician in the same career field as his wife, but he decided a change in career fields would be more suitable to the married life they envisioned for themselves. "When we first got married the opportunity arose for me to go into a new career field and become an air traffic controller," Michael says. "This was a great opportunity for me, but also better for our relationship so that we could have more assignments available to us." They have been separated often, even missing wedding anniversaries several times because of deployments. But Michael offers this advice: "My advice is to volunteer for deployments and remotes if you want to really keep your relationship going. That may sound like weird advice, but if you don't volunteer, you might end up spending even more time apart."

And even though the Robinsons have spent a total of five years apart due to deployments and remotes, they both say those separations made their relationship stronger. "We really needed to rely on each other throughout all of our separations and really learn how to communicate in a different way," says Dianna.

Your Children

Now, to the very important little people in the mix. In most cases, the children of military service members are the ones most affected by deployment. The government recognizes that the children of dual military couples make sacrifices for their country, too. And while the military services has always had regulations that require single parents and dual military couples with children to have plans concerning the care of their dependents in the event of deployment, these weren't strictly enforced until Desert Shield/Desert Storm. As I mentioned, the Desert Storm incident taught the military the importance of having contingency plans in place should both parents be deployed simultaneously. So the military instituted mandatory family care plans (FCPs) to be completed by all dual couples and single parents. And the DoD is not playing games. This is how it goes down: dual military couples have thirty days after arriving at their new duty station to create a family care plan, which among other things, includes naming both a short-term and long-term care provider. Each branch of service has its own FCP plan. Failure to complete the FCP in time can lead to separation (that means termination to us civilians) from the service. As we heard it from many couples, finding a responsible person can be a real challenge early on in your career, when you're unlikely to know anybody at your new duty station, or you're very far away from your own family, let alone finding someone you trust enough and is willing to sign up for responsibility of your kids. The bottom line is that you must have an FCP. Here's how it works.

Family Care Plans

Family care plans have three basic requirements: short-term care providers, long-term care providers, and care provision details.

Short-Term Care Providers: Single parents and military couples with children must designate a nonmilitary person who will agree, in writing, to accept care of the member's children at any time, twenty-four hours per day, seven days per week, in the event the military member is called to duty or deployed with no notice. Although this person cannot be another military member, the person can be a military spouse. The short-term care provider must live in the local area where the military member(s) are stationed/located. The short-term care provider must sign the FCP, indicating that he or she understands the responsibilities that are being entrusted.

Long-Term Care Providers: In addition to the short-term care provider, the military member(s) must also designate a nonmilitary person who will agree, in writing, to provide long-term care for their children in the event the military member(s) are deployed for a significant period, or in the event they are selected for an unaccompanied overseas tour, or are assigned to a ship at sea. The long-term care provider does not have to live in the local area, but the FCP must contain provisions to transfer the child(ren) from the short-term care provider to the long-term care provider (finances, airline tickets, etc.), in the event a no-notice deployment turns into a long-term deployment. Long-term care providers must sign the FCP, indicating that they understand the responsibilities that are being entrusted to them.

Care Provision Details: After you've got your short-term and long-term care providers lined up, the FCP must include detailed plans for the care and support of the children. Family care plans must include provisions for what is called logistical movement of the family or caregiver. Logistical arrangements include, but are not limited to, arrangements to relocate, if necessary, the caregiver or family to a new location and the financial, medical, and legal support necessary, so care can continue to support family members during the movement. Logistical arrangements must provide for financial support necessary to transport the family or caregiver to a designated location. If your family members include infants, children, elderly, and disabled adults, you must also include arrangements for a nonmilitary escort.

Show them the money: Family care plans must also include arrangements for the financial well-being of family members covered by the FCP during short- and long-term separations. Arrangements for financial care should include power(s) of attorney, allotments, or other appropriate means to ensure the self-sufficiency and financial security of family members.

Each of the services have special provisions in place that allow designated care providers to have access to military base facilities (commissary, BX/PX, medical) in order to ensure the care of the military dependents when the FCP is actually in effect (i.e., care has been transferred from the military member to the care provider).

COMMANDER REVIEW

After you've completed the FCP, it must be reviewed for workability and completeness by the commander or a designated representative. The "designated representative" is usually the executive officer or first sergeant. After the initial review, the plans have to be updated and reviewed at least once a year.

TIME FRAMES AND DEADLINES

When a military member first becomes a single parent or military couple with children, he/she must notify his or her commander, supervisor, or the commander's designated representative immediately but no later than thirty days of the occurrence of change in family circumstances or personal status (sixty days for guard/reserve members). After that, the military member(s) have sixty days (ninety days for guard/reserve members) to submit a completed FCP. If mitigating circumstances are involved, the commander or supervisor concerned may grant the member an additional thirty days to submit an acceptable FCP. Further extensions are not authorized. The same sixty-day rule applies for active-duty military members who move from one military base to another. They have sixty days to find a short-term care provider who lives in the local area.

Penalties: Like we said, Uncle Sam is serious about this one. Failure to produce the required FCP within the time periods required can result in involuntary separation from the military for enlisted members and officers by reason of parenthood. Reservists who fail to produce the required FCP can be discharged or transferred to an inactive or retired status.

Staying Together: Look into Other Alternatives

Did you know that a soldier at one army installation can agree to "swap" assignments with a soldier at another installation, as long as it doesn't cost the government any money? It's true, and it is part of a little-known and little-used program for exchanging assignments, unofficially known as the "SWAPS" Program.

Every month (or so) the *Army Times* publishes a list of soldiers who wish to locate others of the same rank, MOS, and basic qualifications, stationed at installation(s) they desire to be assigned at. Soldiers can use this listing to contact these soldiers desiring to SWAP, and make an informal agreement. One of the soldiers then initiates the SWAP request, using DA Form 4187.

The soldier initiating the SWAP includes the following statement on the DA Form 4187:

> I have read and understand the provisions of AR 614–200, and hereby waive any and all claims against the U.S. Government for transportation for myself, my family members, my household goods, and my personal property incident to travel and shipment resulting from reassignment from (current station) Fort (enter name and state), to (new location) Fort (enter name and state), as requested by me. I further agree to waive any and all claims against the U.S. Government for mileage allowances and/or per diem allowance both for myself and my family.

The initiating soldier also includes the following statement on the form, from the soldier he/she has agreed to SWAP with:

> I agree to an exchange assignment with FOX, Guy S., 000–00–0000, SGT 11B20 presently stationed at Fort Defense, VA. If this request is approved, I understand that all expenses (including transportation of family members and household goods) incident to this

reassignment will be borne by me. I further understand that any time used as travel time between duty stations will be charged against me as ordinary leave. The following personal data are submitted: Name: WOLF, John S. Grade: SGT, E5 MOS: 11B Unit and station: Co A, 2d BN, 4th Inf, 86th Inf Division, Fort Service, NY 01122.

Of course, there are terms and conditions. Here are a few of them. Get fully briefed by your personnel office:

- Both soldiers must agree to the SWAP, must be of the same rank, same MOS (job), and be similarly qualified.
- Exchanges must be CONUS (continental United States) to CONUS or OCONUS (Overseas) within their same OCONUS command.
- The commanders of both soldiers concerned must concur in the proposed exchange assignment and agree on the date of assignment.
- Soldiers must serve at least twelve months at current duty station and have at least twelve months time remaining in service upon arrival at the gaining installation.
- Soldiers will pay all costs incurred in relocation, and all travel time will be charged as ordinary leave.
- Eligibility for foreign service does not change, and no stabilization period is authorized for either soldier.
- Soldiers in receipt of AIs, or in a deployed status, are not eligible.
- If a married army couple currently occupying a common household is separated because one soldier is granted an exchange assignment, the other soldier may not apply for reassignment to the same installation to reestablish a joint residence.

Dealing with Child Care Issues

Creating a family care plan requires tackling some tough issues. One of the biggest issues is child care during deployment. If you aren't fortunate enough to have a family member who can look after your children, you may have to look into hiring a nanny or other in-home care provider. Please note: the costs of child care during deployment are not covered, so even if you're paying a caregiver or family member to uproot their life and support yours, you have to financially prepare for this additional expense. Here are some other key points to remember:

- Dual military couples usually get priority placements at the local child-care centers on post.
- If family is far away, consider a military spouse on base who may have a child your age. Or a childless spouse who may be interested in "playing mommy" for several months.
- Some dual military couples who live on base have hired nannies and au pairs who are under the watchful eye of nearby friends and neighbors (see the box "Twenty Questions").
- Make sure your care provider shares similar parenting styles and values and that your child is comfortable with this person.
- Have a written financial agreement with your care provider, even if it's your mama.
- And although Big Mama may seem like an easy choice, does she have the energy to keep up with the activities a child of deployed parents needs?
- Your provider should have an agent letter so he/she can use base amenities like the commissary.
- Although your family care plan is submitted to your commander, have copies made for key people in your life. The more people who know about the plan, the better.

Finding someone you trust with the care of your children is no easy task. If you don't have family, or other military families you feel comfortable with, you might consider hiring a nanny or au pair to move into your home. Whether you use a nanny agency, referral from a friend, or your own resources, make sure you are thorough in your selection process. Use these resources for child-care assistance:

Army Families Online
(800) 833-6622
http://www.armyfamiliesonline.org

Army Families Online staffs the Army Information Line from 8:00 A.M. to 4:30 P.M. EST. It offers information and referral services for army soldiers, civilians, retirees, veterans, and families and addresses all issues and concerns. For mental health services, it refers to One-Source or for active-duty soldiers, it can connect soldiers to their chaplain or someone in their chain of command.

National Association of Child Care Resource and Referral Agencies
(800) 793-0324 ext. 341
www.naccrra.org/MilitaryPrograms

NACCRRA works with the Department of Defense (DoD) to help those who serve in the military find and afford child care that suits their unique needs. For help finding a child-care provider, contact Child Care Aware at (800) 424-2246 or at childcareaware.org. To reach the Military Subsidy Department, call the number listed above.

TWENTY QUESTIONS

When it comes to who's taking care of your children, you can never ask too many questions. In fact, the more thorough you are, the more likely you are to find the right fit. Having your questions prepared ahead of time helps ensure you cover all your bases. Use the following questions as a starting point for the best interview.

∽ AU PAIR AND NANNY INTERVIEW QUESTIONS ∽

- What do you like most about yourself? What would you like to improve about yourself?
- Describe your most recent child-care experience and why it ended. What were the ages of the children you cared for?
- What was the worst child-care experience you had and how did you handle it?
- As a child, how were you disciplined? What would, or do, you do differently with your own children?

- What do you feel is the most challenging or interesting thing about working with children?
- Have you ever been in an emergency situation? How did you handle it?
- Tell me a little about your own childhood and your relationship with your family.
- What types of things do you like to do in your free time?
- What are your favorite television shows?
- How would your closest friends describe you?

ADDITIONAL INTERVIEW QUESTIONS TO USE IF YOUR CHILD IS UNDER TWO YEARS OF AGE

- How do you handle a crying baby? How do you feel at the time?
- What do you think is your primary responsibility to a child of this age?
- When you last cared for a baby or toddler, what types of activities did you engage the child in?

ADDITIONAL INTERVIEW QUESTIONS TO USE IF YOUR CHILD IS TWO TO THREE YEARS OF AGE

- If you were in a grocery store and the child had a temper tantrum, how would you handle it? How would you handle it in the home?
- How do you approach toilet training? Did it work?
- Where does outdoor play and interaction with peers fit into a child's day?
- What educational activities would you do with a child this age?
- What indoor activities would you do with a child this age?

ADDITIONAL INTERVIEW QUESTIONS TO USE IF YOUR CHILD IS THREE TO FIVE YEARS OF AGE

- How would you set limits for or discipline a child of this age? Give me an example of how it has worked in the past.

- What television shows are appropriate for a child of this age? What would you be doing if the child was watching television?
- Would you be willing to supervise play time with other children in our home? Would you be willing to take our child to activities or play groups and participate if necessary?

✎ ADDITIONAL INTERVIEW QUESTIONS TO USE IF YOUR CHILD IS FIVE OR OLDER ✎

- What are your thoughts on outdoor play without direct supervision? For example, if you were in the house with another sibling.
- Are you comfortable assisting with homework? Reviewing homework?
- Are you comfortable supervising friends of your children during a playdate while you are in charge?

Make notes during the interview process so you can confirm answers later. When you call references, and you *must* call references, ask about events or claims that the potential caregiver brought up during the interview. For instance, if the candidate shared with you that she cared for a child from the age of two years until the child was six years of age, verify that with the reference. The questions are easy to ask and can quickly uncover critical inconsistencies. The time and effort you put into this process will show in the quality of care you secure for your child.

CHILD MALTREATMENT

Using data from the Army Central Registry and the Army Family Advocacy Program, researcher Deborah Gibbs of RTI International studied 1,771 families of enlisted U.S. Army soldiers who experienced at least one combat-related deployment between September 2001 and December

2004. Records indicated that at least one substantiated incident of child maltreatment, defined as the neglect, physical abuse, emotional abuse, or sexual abuse of a child, had occurred in these families during this time. For 90 percent of families, the maltreatment was an isolated incident, while an additional 9 percent had documented cases of maltreatment on two or more days.

Gibbs found that the rate of child maltreatment in these families increased 42 percent during times in which the soldier-parent was deployed, with nearly tripled rates of abuse or neglect among female civilians. Among deployed soldiers, rates of abuse by Caucasian males home on leave also increased. About two-thirds of child maltreatment cases involved child neglect, which tripled during deployment. Meanwhile, there was no significant change in mild cases of child maltreatment; moderate to severe cases further increased 60 percent during deployment. Interestingly, child maltreatment rates did not increase among male civilian parents.

As the report suggests, these "findings confirm the need for supportive and preventive services for Army families during times of deployment." The army has responded by reportedly hiring an additional one thousand family readiness support assistants, increasing funding to its respite child-care program (designed to give parents a short-term break from child care), and raising the number of home visits to parents at bases with the highest rates of child neglect.

Triple Duty: Soldier, Mother, and Wife

Being a soldier is tough, but being a mom is even tougher. As the number of women on active duty reaches 200,000, of a total of 1.4 million, it means that more mothers are discovering what it really means to balance job and family under extreme circumstances. For soldier moms, the commute is really hell, the "business trip" can last six months to a year, and the note for the babysitter also includes your power of attorney and a will. And if you're leaving your husband in charge, you find yourself conducting a crash course in braids, baths, and bedtimes. Military service is certainly acceptable work for a man, but being a soldier still lands very high on the list of raised-eyebrow careers for a mom.

Pamela's Pick:

Military mothers of newborns receive a four-month deferment from duty away from the home station for the period immediately following the birth of a child. This provision is to assist the member in developing family care plans and to establish a pattern of child care. Single members or one member of a military couple who adopt receive a four-month deferment from the date the child is placed in the home as part of the formal adoption process. Similarly, reserve component members receive a four-month deferment from involuntary recall to active duty.

And despite what even the most self-evolved man will tell you, dual-career couples, civilian or military, face challenges in their marriage. Even the most self-proclaimed Renaissance man still holds on to some of society's expectations of a man's role and a woman's role in a household. And when deployment strikes a dual-career couple, a man may have to find himself doing things he thought was "woman's work" (see "Dads on Duty" section that follows). Sometimes this creates an irreparable rift, if not handled properly. A recent study by RAND found that female service members have more than twice the divorce rate of their male peers.

Needless to say, when you put together two of the world's most demanding jobs and throw in some traditional wifey expectations, you've got a volatile cocktail. Yet thousands of soldier moms make that extreme sacrifice every day. Some pay a very high price, from strained relationships with their children to failed marriages.

"I've had five major separations in about nineteen years of marriage and sixteen years of motherhood, including the nine months my husband kept our then four-year-old daughter and three-year-old son while I went to flight school in Alabama. During all those separations, we blew a lot of money on plane tickets and making AT&T rich. But when it comes to my children, I always talked to them every day, even when they couldn't talk back. I read bedtime stories and sang songs at night or made cassette tapes of me singing that my husband would play for them at night. When my children were a little older, I would mail them something every day. Nothing extravagant, just something simple, like a balloon, sticker, piece of gum, anything I could send with a small note or postcard. As a family we always tried to see one another and be together every four to six weeks or so. By working together, my husband made my deployments easier for me. We both stuck it out to retirement," says one soldier.

Inside the military or not, working mothers struggle with the same issues of balancing career and family, the ever-present guilty mom syndrome, and wondering how much sacrifice is too much. In civilian careers and military services, for some mothers the price of a demanding career path becomes too much to bear. "I love the military and I'd love to stay in it, but the separations are becoming too hard, especially my current one because I have no idea when I'm going back home," says Regina, a female service member we spoke to while deployed in Iraq. "I'd like to be around to raise my two kids." After this assignment, she will be ending her military career after only eight years.

Other women have struggled with similar issues when balancing their duty to their country and their duty to their children. Autumn Morrison was part of a dual-career couple in the air force with her husband of seven years. She had a successful career full of high marks in her performance evaluations, she became an officer, and she was so highly regarded that she had an opportunity to interview for a military personnel job at the White House. But the price of duty became too dear when her daughter was about three years old. While completing a war exercise, Autumn and her husband received word that someone in their daughter's day-care class had contracted chicken pox. "I hadn't taken any vacation, sick leave, or personal time in over a year and when I immediately notified my superiors of the situation, they told me I had to find someone to watch my child while she had the chicken pox. My husband was also denied time off," she says. "I typically work seventeen-hour days, so to find someone to provide that kind of care for a week for a sick child was impossible or felt so. It really was a turning point for me and my military service." Thankfully, her daughter didn't catch chicken pox. But Autumn left the air force soon after anyway. "That day I realized that my priorities had changed, and what was really important to me was my daughter, not my career. I want a life where my children come first, and I'm glad that I no longer have someone telling me when I can care for my sick child. I'm just no longer up for that level of sacrifice," she says.

Although some moms have positive experiences of daily webcam "visits" and bedtime stories during deployment, there are also tales of sleepless nights with pictures tucked in pillowcases, and nightmares of their children being harmed or in pain and they can't do anything to help. Other mothers felt their children slip away. Sometimes absence makes the heart grow fonder, sometimes it doesn't. "My three-year-old daughter would cry in the background that she didn't want to talk to me," said Richelle, a soldier mom, of her six-month-turned-18-month deployment in Iraq. "It would kill me," she says. "It got harder to talk to them. I think they resented me being away so long."

If you're a military mom, make the most of the resources and advice for helping kids deal with deployment. Your FRG has DVDs, pamphlets, and more on great things you can do to help your child better understand deployment. Visit Internet sites like www.deploymentkids.com for kid-friendly activities and exercises to do before, during, and after deployment. Like any mom with a career she values, you want it all—family, career, and hubby. By recognizing the challenges, arming yourself with the best resources and support, and communicating with your mate, you can certainly have it.

Of course, there's another integral piece to this puzzle—your spouse. Understanding what he's going through will go a long way to keeping your marriage intact.

Dads on Duty: When Mom Goes to War and Dad Stays Behind

With record numbers of women joining the armed forces, many dads are being left at home while Mommy goes to fight the war. Greg, an army recruiter whose biochemical specialist wife was deployed for over a year, admits that the role switch was difficult at first. "Well, it certainly deepened my appreciation for all my wife does to keep our house running smoothly. There were many nights when I said, 'I can't do this.' But I support my wife's career, and I'm proud of her. I'm here to do what I have to do so she can focus on completing her mission and getting home safely."

Other military men said they experienced pangs of jealousy, knowing their wife is in the middle of the action. "I can see it now, my grandchildren asking what we did during the war and me telling them that I stayed home with the kids. Grandma will have all the war stories and pictures," one navy dad said.

But he knows his wife has been in his shoes before. She stayed home with the children several times while he was at sea. And it was even harder for her, he said, because the family was living in Japan and everything was unfamiliar. "This has given me a whole new respect for the military spouses," he said.

And that's exactly the right attitude, experts say. Dad's attitude can make all the difference in how the children cope. Even Richelle admits that her relationship with her army recruiter husband had become strained as he stayed behind to play Mr. Mom. She thinks his terse tone whenever she called set the tone for the kids, who knew Daddy was not happy. Richelle's husband, a former football player, was more a traditional guy, who was used to her keeping the house and managing the kids. But when the roles were reversed, he, like many men, found himself in an unusual and often uncomfortable situation.

If you're a dad on duty while wifey is deployed, use the time to strengthen your bonds with your children. Take advantage of family services like money management programs, child-care help, and other support services on base. Don't be too proud to ask for help or accept offers of help from neighbors and friends. Join a support group to get advice on the practicalities of being a single parent and to share concerns about having your wife deployed.

Pamela's Pick: A Special Word to Female Service Members Married to Civilians

We already said the female service members have a divorce rate nearly twice that of their male peers, and the highest rate in that group is among civilian men married to women in the military. Now there are a lot of theories out there as to why this is so, but one really good reason could be that most of the family support programs are traditionally geared toward women, making it harder for men to create a strong support network.

Recently I was reading a newspaper article and was struck by a story written by a civilian dad who had sent his wife off for a deployment. He wasn't too worried about her safety because luckily she was in a noncombat zone. Even though he knew she missed the family terribly, her assignment gave her time to take yoga classes, work out daily, and relax with her buddies at the base cantina. Meanwhile, he was back home dealing with exploding diapers, nightly bedtime battles, piles of laundry, and longing for some adult interaction. In time, jealousy and resentment began to build. He developed insomnia, lost a lot of weight, and even became paranoid of her male colleagues.

Ladies, the point is, don't forget about your man at home. A man is still a man, even when he's fulfilling your old roles. And a black man . . . well, we don't even have to go there. Experts say men deal with grief when their wife is gone and may feel isolated and overwhelmed by anxiety and exhaustion. And yes, I know, we as women deal with this all day, every day, but we both know men aren't built of the same stuff we are. So there needs to be some understanding on both sides. It's not easy for you being deployed, working long hours, and being away from the family. And it's not easy for him, working and holding down the home front. Getting involved with spoken or unspoken games of "who's got it worse" won't serve you, your relationship, or your children any good.

Instead, encourage your man to be more like a woman in one key area—build a support network and learn to ask for help when he needs it; that's something military wives know is essential to keep families together. In the end, periods of deployment can help you communicate better and build more trust and mutual understanding in your marriage. And when all else fails, you can always find another dad dealing with more kids or less support than your man is. Gently remind him that other families have it even worse.

A House Divided: Career Competition, Professional Jealousy, and . . . the Black Man

Career competition is very real. Ever since women stepped into the workforce and dual-career couples became more commonplace, everyone from scientists to psychologists have been debating the impact of a modern career woman on the institution of marriage. In our community, and in our debate forums like barbershops, hair salons, and church socials, the essential discussion has centered around one loaded question: Can a black man deal with a black woman who earns more?

According to Jim and Jane Carter, in their book *He Works, She Works* (1995), the number one conflict faced by women in dual-career families is role conflict. Actually, women are used to multiple roles. Taking on multiple responsibilities in connection with others traditionally gave us our power and our feeling of self-worth. However, women are so often in a situation of giving precedence to one role, either wife or mother or their career, that it causes a lot of stress. Those who study this sort of thing call it role conflict, which results in role overload.

In contrast, married men may be given more leniency by society in their gender socialization to identify with work and family roles without trading one off against the other. In their book, the authors argue that the number one conflict among male clients in dual-career marriages is the lack of nurturing that they receive from their wife or significant other because their partner is not fulfilling the "feminine" part of their marriage or couples contract. There are expectations of intimacy (and I would add, homemaking) that were supposed to continue after work and children. Here is the crux of the situation. Dual-career couples have been proven to be among the most financially successful marriages, yet also have the highest rate of divorce in the United States. Houston, we have a problem.

In military couples, the dynamics may play out to an even greater degree. After all, the military is all about rank. Rank equals respect. Rank equals self-worth. Rank equals pay. And pay is closely linked to manhood. Relationship experts say the "I am my money" syndrome and the male versus female cash-flow competition is a lingering by-product of long-held societal roles that distinguish men as providers and woman as nurturers.

In our community, black women outearning men is not news. For several years and counting, black women have outnumbered our brothers on college campuses and then outearned them in corporate America. But that was corporate America and this is military service—the bastion of male-dominated, physically intensive, pee-in-a-cup, sleep-in-your-boots, and don't-shower-for-days manliness. This is a man's domain.

Now, it needs to be said that some competition between spouses is healthy. Many women in dual-military-career marriages whom we spoke to said there was a good competitive spirit between them and their spouse that kept them on their toes and helped them succeed. But others say, it went too far.

Harriet Staten is a retired service member who served twenty-two years in active duty in the army and two years in the reserves, who looks back on her years of military service with mostly fondness. She had an enviable career, making it to the position of full colonel and becoming the first black female selected as an executive officer of the deputy commanding general of an army reserve command (CK). For ten of her twenty-four service years, she was in a dual military marriage. After striking out with civilian men, whom Harriett says thought she was too independent, she thought a military man would really understand her. And for several years of her marriage, Harriett says she felt really blessed. They were mostly stationed in Fort Bragg, and eventually she had children. But over time, the fact that Harriett had more years of service and therefore a higher rank and pay became a problem in the marriage, she says. "My husband felt he was competing with me in our military careers, and I never thought about things like that," Harriett says, speaking from her home in Georgia. "I came into service before him so I was up for promotions before him. That's just the way it is. When I was promoted to captain, he was still a first lieutenant. So at formal dining events, I was wearing my captain's uniform and he would get teased by some of his guys that his wife outranked him. I noticed that things were becoming more distant between us. One day he just blurted out, 'You know, I outrank you by virtue of position.' He said this because he was an executive officer and I was a platoon leader, but I was shocked. I had no idea these things were going on inside his head. My paycheck went into the same account as his and as far as I was concerned, we were a team. In the end, my husband cheated on me with wives of lesser-ranked military members who looked up to his rank of service. My advice to all dual military couples is to separate your work from your home. Communicate, communicate, and communicate about the things you are going through instead of taking it out on your spouse."

While doing months of research for this book, I came across a *Time* magazine cover story profiling a husband and wife team of army rising stars, both lieutenant colonels, likely to be the first married battalion commanders ever to fly into battle together. As they were off to pilot Black Hawks and Apaches in Iraq, they were leaving their fourteen-year-old daughter anxiously waiting and living with friends. But what struck me most about this story were the comments of the husband, Jim, about his wife's, Laura's, success. The story reads: Jim credits their mutual success to friendly competition. "The reason she is moving up so fast is that she got to see all of my mistakes and has been able to avoid them," he says with a smile. He has four years of seniority over her and insists that she will never outrank him, since he will retire before that ever happens. Jim also vows that he will never let his wife beat him in any physical-training event, a hard promise to keep: when they were in Korea, Laura's unit had a yearly Iron Man Contest, and "after 5-ft, 4-in Laura beat dozens of men to win the contest, the event was renamed the Iron Person Contest," the article said. It was clear that staying above his wife in rank and physical strength was really important to Jim. I almost felt sad for the poor guy.

One thing is clear, dual-career competition remains a taboo topic. But it's definitely there. Women can't have the conversation without some sort of conflict, and men just don't want to compete with women, especially their spouses. One way to counter competition is to ignore it, experts say. A good sense of humor can help, too.

And when it comes to dealing with a black man, experts say the issue is often not money, but power. Traditionally, money has been equated with power in relationships. Men equate money with power and self-esteem. They are all intertwined together for them. It's a blow to their ego when they don't earn as much as their mate, because they feel like they are not being a "man." It's ingrained in their DNA that they should be the breadwinner, and the ego-charged nature of our black male culture only adds fuel to that fire.

The worst part about a man who feels insecure about his wife's higher rank or pay grade is that he could begin to feel inadequate, which could lead to problems in the marriage. Psychiatrists say it is common for a man in that situation to be resentful, to develop self-doubt, and possibly even resort to verbal, psychological, or physical attack of his mate to feel better. If you see this happening in your marriage, talk to your mate about what is really going on with him as soon as possible. Don't let it linger. If possible, get counseling or speak to another trusted couple in a similar situation.

Ladies, there may be more you can do. In a *Black Enterprise* article, Kevin Cohee, the no-holds-barred chairman and CEO of One United Bank, one of the nation's largest black-owned financial institutions, said that today's black man is not intimidated by a sister's cash flow; he's more concerned with her control issues, namely, how she makes him feel when they're together. "In to-day's society, men fully recognize the benefits of having a high-quality part-ner," Cohee argues. "If you make a bunch of money but are unable to make that man feel cared for, or if you don't know how to comfort that man, he will draw the conclusions that you can't be warm or intimate, and that you can't ac-cept his love.

"A man wants to know that he can trust you to accept his love and care for his children," Cohee continues. "But if you're so caught up in your career that you can't make time for him, or if you view wealth as being all about money, not lifestyle, then it can be a problem for him." Well, ladies, there you have it. One successful black man's opinion. Here's another: New York psychologist and radio host Jeffrey Gardere, PhD, author of *Love Prescription: Ending the War Be-tween Black Men and Women*, suggests that the animosity that arises between black men and women is rooted in fear. "One of Black men's biggest secrets is that they truly fear Black women's intelligence and strength," he says. "Black men are terrified by the prospect of being dominated."

Some black men are uncomfortable about having a breadwinning woman at home, but the majority of men are sure-footed and confident in their man-hood. Relationship experts say the secret to happiness, regardless of your unique financial circumstances, is viewing your union as a partnership, not competing entities. It doesn't matter who brings home the most bacon, it only matters that you fry it together.

CHAPTER TEN

Relationship Rescue

How to Keep Your Marriage and Friendships Strong

After talking to hundreds of military spouses, one thing was clear: finding and maintaining relationships is a real challenge. With so much moving around and prolonged periods of single parenthood, finding time to stay connected is difficult. Other times you may feel that others don't understand what you're going through. Ironically, those are the same exact reasons why relationships are so important to your military life. Just because you move around a lot doesn't mean you can't grow deep roots in meaningful friendships old and new. In fact, psychiatrists contend that having a sense of connectedness is crucial for our emotional well-being. Quite frankly, you need this.

Sure, staying connected to your friends and your husband takes more effort with your military lifestyle. Meanwhile, your old friends may not understand your new life and its stressors. But that's no reason to give up. Pamela will tell you she didn't even realize that she had unknowingly given up on developing real friendships. "I subconsciously reasoned, why get connected when I know I'm leaving?" she says. "And I wasn't even aware of what I was doing until my sister pointed it out to me." Others would later tell her how much they felt their efforts to connect with her as friends were rebuffed.

Don't miss out on great relationships because of your military lifestyle. On the contrary, you have the bonus of meeting more exciting people, with whom you have a lot in common. That's all the more reason to keep those relationships. And don't forget that most important relationship—your husband. These days marriages seem to be struggling to survive. With all the increased pressures on military unions, now, more than ever, you need a strong foundation, the right perspective, and the right moves to keep your union strong. This chapter will share some insights on all these relationship fronts.

But first, I want to tell you about Melissa James. When I was traveling around the country meeting military spouses, I met Melissa through a mutual friend. The mocha-complected spunky fireplug from Chicago was about to leave for Fort Dix. Like many other spouses, she knew nothing about military life before she started her long-distance relationship with her now-husband.

"When my husband and I began dating, I didn't know much about what he did. I even Googled to see what these mysterious BDUs he always talked about were (FYI, BDU stands for 'battle dress uniform'—those dark green camo uniforms that are being replaced by ACUs, 'army combat uniform').

"This of course also means I didn't know anything about military spouses. My knowledge was pretty much limited to movies, where all the military wives wear gloves, pearls, and heels, or a couple girls I'd gone to high school with who married right after graduation and had kids right away. I didn't fit into either of those groups, so I had no idea where I'd fit in. I don't think I even owned a pair of heels at the time, I'd gone to college, and I had no kids.

"I wanted to know how on earth I was going to maintain friendships when faced with frequent moves, and how I was going to build a strong marriage with lengthy separations from my husband. I didn't know if other military wives would like me, or if I would like them, or if we'd have anything at all in common."

When Melissa and I met, she didn't think she had much to add to the conversation about maintaining relationships because she was a relatively new spouse of three years. Turns out, with a little initiative, she had created a great prescription for keeping old friends, making new ones, and keeping her marriage intact during long separations. Her primary advice was to get involved. Take the first step.

You'll never meet anybody inside your living room. You gotta get out there, girl! "Shortly after I joined my husband at Fort Bragg, we hosted a small barbecue for the guys he worked with so I could meet them and their families and get a feel for the community here. I met another vegetarian, another runner, and a mom of four beautiful children—and got along with all of them, because, as I soon realized, the military is its own little subculture. Without even having to say a word, we all knew we had something in common: our amazing husbands, who were crazy enough to take this job—and like it.

"I was also amazingly lucky to meet the woman who would become my best friend while walking my dog one afternoon. As a former military wife, she was active duty herself, and helped me so much through my first deployment with my husband. I quickly learned that in the military community, you always have a shoulder to cry on, or someone happy to celebrate when something goes right. There's always someone who has been through something similar and can offer their perspective, insight, and a warm hug when you need it," says one military wife.

Other Military Spouses

Military wives come in all shapes and sizes, from all walks of life, all backgrounds, all nationalities, and all financial situations. That means, with a little searching, you're bound to find someone like you. But first, a few tips:

1. *Take it for what it is.* The world of military wives is a forced group of comrades brought together because of men who are just guys who chose a certain career—and any woman can fall in love with any man. Understanding this will help you make friends.

2. *Work the Web.* If you can't connect with women on your base or you're living off post, there's a large virtual community waiting for you online. The Internet is loaded with great sites like www.cinchouse .com where you can find chat rooms, message boards, and online communities of military spouses just like you. Women who are facing deployments or separations can turn to the Dealing With Deployments board, where women in all stages of deployments are there offering hugs, support, and helpful advice. This particular board is indispensable in times of separation.

    Sometimes military wives just need to talk to women who have been through something similar and can reassure us we're normal, especially when dealing with deployments. The regional boards are great for meeting other wives face-to-face and learning about the area you're now (or soon to be) living in. This is a fantastic resource, especially for military spouses who are PCSing to a new area because you can "meet" women already at the base you're going to be stationed at, find out about neighborhoods in the area, and maybe even find a job.

You can also use social networking sites like Myspace and Facebook. Searching the groups for military wife support groups, you'll find worldwide support groups, and post-specific groups.

3. *Create your own group.* Melissa found herself in a quandary. Her husband's unit had an FRG, but she hadn't attended any of the events. "Many of them are geared toward women with children, and as we don't have any yet, I haven't gone," she says. However, she found that the spouses of the guys in his particular shop get together fairly regularly, and together they've built somewhat of their own mini-FRG. "I think that works for us, because our husbands are in a specific, close-knit shop, and we're all dealing with the same emotions, separations, and stress. The women are all very different—some have been married over ten or fifteen years, while others, myself included, started out in the group as fiancées. Some have children, some work, some volunteer. What we have in common is our husbands' career, and we are able to support one another building on only that one bond," she says.

4. *Avoid being cliquish.* Even in her brief three years, Melissa says she's seen all types. Yes, some military wives are cliquish—but that's usually a personality trait they had long before their husbands came along, she says. You may experience this, too. In fact, there seems to always be a debate over cliques when it comes to enlisted versus officer wives. This is an issue that comes up all the time in online and offline chats among spouses. When it comes down to it, your husband's rank has nothing to do with what kind of person you are, and it's up to you how you want to treat others. True, in some in-

stances, an officer and an enlisted military member shouldn't be spending a lot of time together if the officer is in the chain of command, but that doesn't mean the spouses can't be friends. Here's what we've found: women who base their friendships on their husband's rank don't seem to be well received in the military community. Judging a military spouse on her appearance or her husband's rank before getting to know her may cause you to miss out on a dear friend, but luckily this doesn't seem to be the norm.

5. *Don't be afraid to get close.* Great girlfriends are such an asset to any woman, military or not. Even though you know you'll be moving eventually, there's no reason not to become close with female friends. They'll be there for you to cry to when you're PMSing and your husband is deployed and you just want to hear his voice. They'll listen when you vent about your husband and know that you don't mean it (to quote a friend, "He's a good man, I'm just in a bad mood"). When your husband is gone and you need help picking a homecoming outfit, they're there to help you shop. The bond between women friends goes deeper than that, too—even when you've moved away and haven't seen each other's faces in years, a phone call can bring you right back to "the good old days" and put you in a good mood if you've been feeling down. During deployments, a lot of wives visit old friends and reconnect with those who've helped and shared in their lives. Knowing you're going to move isn't an expiration date for a friendship—it's a reason to build one, and come back to visit.

Old Friends and Family

Keeping close ties with your old friends can be a challenge. Whether you married your husband at eighteen and right out of high school or later on in life, you're still starting a new life that those who haven't actually done it may never understand. When Melissa first married, she had plenty of friends and family repeatedly ask, "Is this *really* what you want? Deployments, moves, separations? There was no way for them to fully understand why on earth I would willingly put myself in this position, whereas my military-spouse friends asked, 'When's the wedding?' They couldn't wait for me to 'join their club' so to speak, and be a full-fledged member of the military spouse subculture."

Your true friends will always be there to support you and be a part of your life. Thankfully, e-mail, instant messaging, and cell phones are great ways to keep tabs on old friends. Your job is to stay connected to them.

"It's also on me to maintain old friendships even though I'm in this 'new club' of military wives. I can't just ignore my single friends who are dealing with breakups now that I'm married. I was there for them before, and it's up to me to continue to be a support system for them, too."

The Internet is fantastic in helping maintain old friendships. Social networking sites like MySpace and Facebook also let you share photos and stories with old friends, and to check out their lives at the moment.

Other creative ways of staying in touch with family and friends include the following:

- E-mail is another great tool because in the military you're going to be moving a lot—so even if friends and family don't have your physical address, they'll still have your e-mail address. Send photos and stories to keep them connected with your new life.
- Keep an address book—in pencil!—to send out holiday cards and moving announcements.
- Be sure you have current cell phone numbers for everyone (because you never know when you might need to talk to someone just like your old college roommate who was the only one who really got your sense of humor).

It's also important to build new friendships with people you meet in your daily life, whether they're military related or not. If you work outside the home, your job is probably where you'll meet the most new friends. You may meet individuals who have lived in your new city their whole life, so they can clue you in to the best unknown restaurants, good hiking trails, or areas to avoid. You may also encounter people with interests similar to yours. Even if the only thing you have in common at first is the fact you both have kids, you might soon have an invitation to a kiddie party, where you can make more mommy friends, and eventually someone to swap babysitting favors with when your spouse is away.

Making friends is so important, even though it's often difficult to be the "new kid in town" knowing you're going to leave in a couple years anyway. It's much easier to just rely on your husband for companionship, but there will come a time when your husband will have to deploy, or go TDY, or even just into the field, and you will have to entertain yourself. "I ended up moving into an empty house when I first moved in with my husband, because he was sent to Airborne school thirty-six hours before we'd planned for me to arrive at our house. At first I was a little nervous because it was the biggest move I'd ever done alone, but in the end it was the best thing that could have happened. I relied heavily on GoogleMaps and some friends of my husband's to show me around in the first few days, but by the end of my first week, I had a job and new friends, and I was settled into a routine. By the time he got back, I had a pretty good handle on what I was going to be doing in North Carolina," says Melissa. We like her style!

Other Places to Connect

We know that you are more than an MS; you had an identity before marrying a soldier and that's important. So whether it's your sorority, professional trade association (even if you are no longer actively working), a local black church, or other civic organization, you can always find a local chapter and try to stay connected. Here are some black organizations that may have chapters, volunteer opportunities, events, and like-minded folks in your area.

National Urban League Inc.
120 Wall Street
New York, NY 10005
212-558-5300 | Fax 212-344-5332
www.nul.org

National Coalition of 100 Black Women
Diane Lloyd, Program Associate
38 West 32nd St.
New York, NY 10001
212-947-2196 | Fax 212-947-2477

National Black Nurses Association
Millicent Gorham, Executive Director
8630 Fenton St., Suite 330
Silver Spring, MD 20910
301-589-3200 | Fax 301-589-3223

National Assn. of Black Women Entrepreneurs Inc.
Marilyn French-Hubbard, Founder and Meeting Planner
P.O. Box 311299
Detroit, MI 48231
313-203-3379 | Fax 248-354-3793

NAACP
Ana Aponte, Director, Events Planning
4805 Mt. Hope Drive
Baltimore, MD 21215
410-358-8900 | Fax 410-764-7746

Black Women's Network
Marva Smith Battle-Bey, Chairperson
P.O. Box 56106
Los Angeles, CA 90056
323-964-4003

Rainbow/PUSH Coalition
www.rainbowpush.org
313-963-9005

Jack and Jill of America
jack-and-jill.org
1930 17th St., NW
Washington, DC 20009
202-667-7010 | Fax 202-667-6133
E-mail: info@jack-and-jill.org

The National Council of Negro Women, Inc.
633 Pennsylvania Ave. NW
Washington, DC 20004
202-737-0120 | Fax 202-737-0476
E-mail: ncnwinfo@ncnw.org

Mocha Moms, a national organization of black stay-at-home moms
www.mochamoms.org

Your Marriage

One of the first things that comes to mind for those unfamiliar with military marriages is infidelity. With military marriage comes the added stress of lengthy separations, sparse communication, and often adjusting to life in a new area. TV shows like *Army Wives* and movies like *Jarhead* perpetuate the idea that military marriages are constantly plagued by infidelity.

We're here to tell you that's not true. You can have a strong successful marriage.

We don't think there's any more adultery in the military world than in the civilian world—you just hear about it more with military marriages. When two people are wholly committed, no separation, no lack of communication, no new "friend" is going to drive them to cheat. The important thing is to be sure your marriage is getting everything it needs to thrive, and this often means getting creative, especially across the miles. If you're dealing with a fifteen-month deployment, you're not having sex for the next fifteen months of your life. That sucks. But if you accept and understand this early on, and are open with your spouse about your needs and desires, this too can even become a game. Many couples send racy photos back and forth, write steamy love letters, or send sex coupons to be redeemed upon the military member's return. Naughty e-mails should be avoided since most e-mails are checked, but some couples have developed their own "code language" to let each other know how they are feeling. Explicit phone conversations aren't for everyone, but they are a way to connect sexually with your spouse (see Chapter 3 on separation and deployment for more tips for managing these times).

When your spouse is training or deployed, you will meet new people, and it's important to surround yourself with positive influences and friends who support you and your marriage. Unfortunately, it's easy for some people to start leaning on someone else for support, especially when dealing with limited contact with their spouse. This is where having supportive friends comes in, because they can be sure you are still respecting your marriage.

Cheating is not only physical, but emotional, and either way is devastating. One spouse we interviewed was, unfortunately, going through a divorce at that time because her husband was emotionally cheating on her while he was deployed. She found out through MySpace about the messages he was sending to another woman, how explicit they were, and how he was saying he didn't love his wife any longer. Being apart from your spouse may cause you to start thinking about someone else, but it should never lead you down this path. Supportive friends and family are very important in keeping your marriage strong.

There will always be temptation, that's just the way life is. The important thing is not acting on it, and putting your marriage first. Living in a military town, you will probably be surrounded by singles of the opposite sex. This can be quite uncomfortable for some, and I know a lot of women who just didn't go out at all while their husbands were gone. For others, this isn't even an issue, because they know where they stand on their marriage, and no amount of pickup lines from some guy in a bar is going to change that. And for still others, these single guys can become friends—so when the spouse does choose to go out, she has someone with her and doesn't have to go out alone. These "stand-ins" can keep the creeps at bay and allow the spouse to have a fun night out—as long as she remembers to go home alone.

SOME FRIENDSHIP CAUTIONS

The biggest precautionary measure to take when making new friends is to be sure not to form too close of a bond with single male friends. First of all, the military is a close-knit community and people do talk! And there are too many stressors on a military marriage before adding temptation into the mix, and there is no need to put yourself in that position. Your husband should be your first priority, the person you go to for better or for worse, before you lean on anyone else. Another piece of advice is that while your husband is away, if you "can't take a kindergartner with you" somewhere, then you probably don't belong there either. Your friends should respect your wishes if you choose not to attend a certain event or go to a certain bar.

"We're Just Friends!"—Five Signs of an Emotional Affair

"But we're just friends" can be four of the most dangerous words for your relationship and marriage. Affairs, including emotional affairs, are typically unplanned events. An innocent friendship turns into something more, but we continue to convince ourselves that everything is okay. In fact, if you find yourself thinking or saying "but we are just friends," you are probably already in trouble.

Experts say there are typically at least nineteen steps that a person goes through before physically consummating an extramarital affair. Each of those phases give you a choice to stop and change your course and avoid going further down the road.

The late Shirly Glass was a pioneer in the area of emotional affairs. In her 2003 book *NOT Just Friends: Protect Your Relationship from Infidelity and Heal the Trauma of Betrayal,* Glass identifies three red flags that indicate that you have progressed from a safe friendship to a romantic emotional affair.

1. *You feel closer to your friend than you do your spouse.* You find yourself thinking of this person more and more often and looking forward to the next time you are together. When something happens during the day, the first person you think of telling is this friend, not your spouse.

2. *Keeping secrets.* You no longer feel comfortable telling your spouse about this person. You begin to cover up so as not to be found out.

3. *An increasing sexual tension.* You admit your attraction for each other, but promise or lament that you can never act on it. You fantasize what it would be like to be with this person. This helps to create a pretend world where everything would be wonderful if the two of you could just be together.

One of the most overlooked and dangerous facts about emotional affairs is that everyone is vulnerable. If you believe that this fact does not apply to you, then you are even more vulnerable than everyone else.

∽ HOW TO PROTECT YOURSELF AND YOUR RELATIONSHIP ∽

1. *Keep clear boundaries.* A boundary is simply what folks mean when we say "don't go there." Avoid being alone with and/or emotionally close to someone to whom you are attracted.

2. *Talk often about your spouse.* "Spouse bashing" does not count. Talk about what you have done lately and what you are looking forward to with your spouse. If you are going to talk about emotional issues in your marriage, make sure you are talking to your spouse, a trusted friend who is on the side of you and your marriage, or a professional who is on the side of your marriage.

3. *Be especially careful at work.* More and more emotional affairs are occurring in the workplace. You spend time together, you go through crises together, and you solve problems together. People even joke about having "work husbands" and "work wives." In the military, "TDY wives" are becoming more common. Do not make a habit of taking private lunches or breaks with the same person over and over.

4. *Set up a review committee in your mind.* Ask yourself, "Would my husband, my mom, my dad, my mother-in-law, or my sister approve of what I am doing right now?" If the answer is no, then I offer you what I call my RLH prescription. RLH stands for Run Like Hell!

Wondering if your spouse has cheated or is facing temptation can eat you up inside and this is a big reason to make sure you know who you're marrying. With the military, you're never going to always know where your husband is and who he's with. You have to be able to trust and believe in what he tells you. If you're unsure about him, or constantly worrying about his faithfulness to your relationship, he may not be the guy for you. You can't spend your entire marriage worrying that on his last TDY, since he couldn't call for a couple days, he was out with another woman. You want to be sure you're building your marriage on trust and faith.

If you do suspect your husband has been unfaithful, the best thing you can do is to ask him about it—in a nonaccusatory way. Let him know you feel like something's missing in your marriage, and you're wondering if he feels it, too. Ask him if there's something going on you should know about. Try to talk to him about it first. If you can't get a straight answer out of him, ask if he's willing to attend marriage counseling with you. You can arrange marriage counseling on post through the chaplain's office, or by calling Military OneSource. Military OneSource will offer up to six sessions free of charge, with the option to be referred to another counselor after the six sessions.

Moving on in a marriage that has been shaken by infidelity is not impossible, but certainly not easy. When my husband and I got married, we decided infidelity, by either partner, would be devastating to the marriage, something neither of us would want to work through. But there are couples, civilian and military, who have been able to work past cheating and build a stronger marriage after they realized what the underlying issue is. If a partner is looking for something elsewhere, it's a sign they're missing something in the marriage, and either not communicating their needs, or the partner doesn't understand them. If a couple can learn from the infidelity and move on to build a healthy marriage, that's great—but it's not the norm.

Many chaplains' offices offer marriage retreats for military couples. Different branches and units offer them at certain times and places and on certain topics. Several couples we met had attended such retreats as newlyweds. Mostly everyone had rave reviews! Although run by the chaplain, the retreats aren't focused on religion. They are focused on each person bringing his or her individuality to the marriage. Melissa and her husband, Anthony, attended a retreat a few months after tying the knot. "The first night we took a personality test—and no surprise, my husband and I scored completely opposite high scores. As the weekend went on, we learned that the opposite things we bring to the relationship are part of why we work. The chaplain very eloquently pointed out that 'Your partner isn't lying awake at night thinking up ways to drive you nuts. That's just their personality. It's no excuse for them to continue to behave a certain way, but now you know where they're coming from.'

"Although my husband and I knew we were polar opposites, I don't think we fully understood just how much our personalities impacted our marriage. I am spontaneous and fun-loving, whereas he likes to look at everything logically. So understanding that he's not trying to push my buttons when he has to sit down and make a spreadsheet about something was a major eye-opener for us. It helped us to see why we do what we do, and how to find some common ground," says Melissa.

The great thing about these marriage retreats is they're held in beautiful vacation destinations. Melissa's was at a resort in Myrtle Beach—plus they're free, child care is available, and you get the evenings off to actually go on dates together. Pamela and I are strong supporters for both marriage retreats and marriage counseling, because anything that can help you strengthen your marriage is an asset for sure.

The other thing we can tell you is to remember this mantra, "Lack of communication does not mean lack of love." There are so many times, especially in a new relationship, where spouses may think "He's not calling . . . is he mad at me? Does he love me anymore? What did I do?" when in reality, his phone lines are down, or someone messed up and their e-mail privileges were taken away, or he's just not in an area he can contact you. The need for human contact is important, so even if you are dealing with a time when your spouse can't call, write, or e-mail, you need to know that your spouse is still thinking about you all the time.

Creative ways of staying in touch with your husband during separations include the following:

- Write him a handwritten letter every night—these mean more than anything else you can do.
- If you can, send care packages with homemade snacks, photos, and letters.
- Send him a cottonball (or a pair of lacy panties!) sprayed with your perfume in a Ziploc bag.
- E-mail as often as you can; even if he doesn't have a chance to respond, he'll appreciate you keeping him "in the loop."
- Let him know if you need something from him (to hear he misses you, an e-mail once in a while, to help boost you if you're feeling down) so you can keep your marriage strong and temptation at bay.
- Stick little notes in his bags before he leaves.
- Send him a box or jar full of reasons why you love him.

Pamela's Pick: Internet Connected

Sergeant First Class Gary Gunn stood by his wife, Regan, as she gave birth to their daughter at Alta Bates hospital in Berkeley, California. He was in Iraq at the time, watching via webcam. Too quickly, he returned to his unit in Iraq, dodging IED explosions as his unit transported supplies in the war zone. Thanks to the power of technology, especially VoIP (voice over Internet protocol) services, you can speak and see in real time through the Internet using both voice and video. Skype is a popular free service. With Skype you can call over the Internet to other Skype users for free or to landlines and cell phones for less than typical phone company rates. All you need is a computer with Internet access, a microphone, and a webcam. Then go to www.skype.com to download the application onto your computer. Your honey needs to do the same on his computer. With good use of technology, your man doesn't have to miss out on as much.

The bottom line is a successful military marriage is not impossible. Every relationship ebbs and flows, and although the military does place a lot of strain on marriages, as long as both parties are committed to each other and their marriage, they can reap the benefits of a military union. These benefits include an extended "honeymoon" phase due to frequent separations, living in foreign countries, building friendships with other wives from all over the world, and the knowledge the couple's marriage is strong enough to weather anything life throws at them.

Staying Connected, Staying Strong

Maintaining communication helps me feel connected to the family and lets the family know I'm there for them the best way I can. If you can't be there, call. Listen to the birthdays over the phone. Ensure you are on the phone directly after key events. Don't wait two or three days to make contact.

Also, remember to tell your family you love them as much as you can. It's tough to show compassion and sensitivity toward your family when you are in an environment that requires you to be so brutal. But make the effort.

—Terry Phillips, Army, based in Kansas

The Mocha Mix
Real Talk on Staying Connected When Apart

★ ★

I don't have any children yet, so when my husband is deployed for a long time, I plan a long weekend to visit my old college friend. It's a great girlfriend getaway and they're very supportive of my marriage so I always return rejuvenated to continue on.

—TASHA SMALLS, FORT DIX, SPOUSE OF SEVEN YEARS

All I can say is webcam, webcam, webcam. I know one friend who even leaves hers on while she sleeps so her husband can watch her when he wakes up! We use it to talk, show off what new stuff the kids are doing, and have some private time!

—GINA, AIR FORCE SPOUSE, ELEVEN YEARS

I got into the habit of having only superficial friendships. By the time I realized it, I had missed out on some great people. I had a chip on my shoulder that these spouses were nothing like me and I just put on a good face for the social stuff. I really regret that.

—KARINNE, ARMY WIFE, EIGHT YEARS

The spouses are all around you, I worked hard to stay connected to my old neighborhood and college friends because I need some non-MS contact. I want to be well rounded and an individual and not just an MS. And my other friends help me keep my other sides alive and kickin'.

—SABRINA HAYES, ARMY WIFE, SEVENTEEN YEARS

During my first few deployments I went to the FRG meetings. But I never went back. My experience is that in certain circles FRG is more of a gossip fest than being helpful. It's a lot of who's sleeping with whom, and who did this to that while their husband was deployed. I found one close friend and that was it.

—LAUREN, ARMY WIFE, FORT BRAGG

Mrs. Teresa Rice

It didn't take long for Teresa Rice, wife of Air Force Lieutenant General Edward A. Rice Jr., to realize that the military is a twenty-four-hour-a-day job, seven days a week. And it's a family life, not just a military life. After twenty-nine years of military marriage, and eighteen moves, she has experienced plenty of time without her husband and still insists that it has to be a family affair and that family is not only your husband and children, but also your military family. She shares these thoughts for others.

I am a strong believer in the family life, not just the military as a job. And whether you are stateside, on an isolated base, or overseas, it's people who make the difference.

We spent our first four years at Loring Air Force Base in Maine and it was very isolated. There were only a handful of businesses there. We had a Zayre's (a chain department store that closed down in 1990), Pizza Hut, and McDonald's and that was about it. The air force community was very close-knit. The guys got alerted every three weeks so you had to get to know your neighbors because they were really your network.

The first winter we were there we had 220 inches of snow. Our first Christmas was −85 degrees with the wind chill factor. My husband was on alert and I was new at the base and couldn't get my car to start. I called the gas station and they told me there were thirty people ahead of me, so I went knocking on doors to find a man who could help me get my car started so I could move it to the other side of the street for the road to be plowed. I met someone who became one of my closest friends. And I discovered that everyone just kind of looked out for each other there, and I became active in the community. I knew I needed to find an outlet for me because he was going to be away from home a whole lot.

As military wives there are a lot of times when neither you nor your husband will have control over your time and schedules. There are going to be times when he will miss some very important occasions—holidays, graduations, weddings—and if you are not able to adapt to that, you will have a rough time with military lifestyle. I don't believe that my husband's job takes precedence over me because it doesn't. But realistically he cannot control where he is and where he is going all the time and so I have to be able to make the best of it.

For me, making the best of it will mean meeting other people and getting involved. The more you get involved, the more you will understand his job, the dynamics of it, the importance of it, and the more you will understand that he does not have the control over it you might think he does. It was very apparent to me as he moved up in rank and responsibility.

I always tell people to take a look around you at other spouses. The ones who are most involved always seem to fare better with managing military life. But you also have to realize that when you are out of the house being involved, it can take a toll on the rest of the family, so bring them into the involvement so that you understand it all together.

Nowadays we have a lot of spouses who are working, going to school, and involved in church. I feel like we are missing a lot of the networking because they have other outlets. My fear is that we are going to lose that military family life that we have always had. I have always tried to reach out to other families by welcoming them when they arrive on base, telling them what events are going on and find out how I can help them transition to their new home. I strongly encourage all of us to take the extra steps to make new spouses feel a part of the military. And to new spouses, don't be afraid to talk to those wives who are senior to you. When they offer help, know that they realize we are all in this together.

Once when my husband was a commander, I volunteered in the thrift shop. Toward the end of our assignment we were having a farewell luncheon of the ladies who volunteered. One lady told me she had purposely stayed away from me because she had a bad experience with a senior spouse before. She told me that as she continued to watch me she realized that she really missed out on getting to know me as a person and as a friend because of what happened to her elsewhere. The fact that she told me I was different and very approachable really meant a lot to me. Because she saw that I was Teresa—I was a person and not wearing my husband's position—she will give other senior spouses a chance. Yes, you too might have an experience at one base where something didn't happen the way you wanted it to or it was a negative experience in general, but it's the learning experience that you need to take with you. What happens in one place, doesn't necessarily happen in every place. People are different. Whatever happened with that other senior spouse may have been something she had no control over or maybe something serious had happened to her or she was just having a bad day. No matter what, don't carry negative experiences with you on to the next place. Give people a chance and try new opportunities.

This military family life is such a special thing to have that I hate to see anyone miss out on it. We are in need of sponsorship and taking care of each other every chance there is to do so. You have to be strong within yourself and develop your own interests and friends. If you are not involved and just sitting at home waiting for your spouse to come home from work, it's a very long day, a very long week. I can't impress how important it is for you to have a life. In most cases, it's not like you can run down the street and see your mom and dad or best friend. You have to make friends on the base where you are.

CHAPTER ELEVEN

Dealing with the Unthinkable

Domestic Violence, Injury, and Loss

Nobody wants to think of the unthinkable. This isn't a military thing; this is a human nature thing. How many people can't bring themselves to write a will? How many relatives have you had who passed away with no life insurance and then the proverbial collection plate has to be passed between relatives to cover funeral expenses? And even though many military spouses live in fear and hope every day, they never really expect the worst will happen to *their* man. *Their* love. Nobody wants to think of the worst, so we tend to not plan for it. The military, on the other hand, has a host of procedures and resources in place to support you in case your service member is injured or killed.

Besides the most traumatic of losses, military families are also prone to suffer from combat stress, suicide, depression, injury, abuse, neglect, and divorce. Living with these issues can be as traumatic as death. And all of these are hitting the home front at an all-time high. Deployments are longer and more frequent. For some, it has spanned fifteen months during the surge of forces into Iraq. The impact is hard to ignore:

- According to the Pentagon, 20 percent more soldiers committed suicide in 2007 than 2006.
- Divorce rates have risen from 2.9 percent before the war to about 3.3 percent now.
- The female service member divorce rate is an astounding 9 percent.
- An estimated one in five service members who are in or were

deployed to Iraq or Afghanistan are displaying symptoms of post-traumatic stress disorder or major depression.

There are also correlations between deployments and domestic violence, sexual assaults, and alcohol offenses. All of this is very real. War is ugly, and so are many of its side effects.

Combat Stress

So what does this mean to service members and their families? We need to be able to recognize the normal reactions to stress and when loved ones might be leaning toward something more serious. When your husband gets home, you may notice that he is less sociable and less energetic than usual. He may also seem sad, paranoid, and angry; feel worthless; and use drugs or drink too much. He may be forgetful, unable to concentrate, relive bad experiences, and have thoughts of death or suicide. To some degree, these reactions are said to be normal given the fact that service members have been exposed to extremely traumatic events in a combat zone for a very long time. To help your hubby adjust to postdeployment life, make sure he does the following:

- Spends time interacting with his immediate family as a unit
- Spends special time alone with each family member
- Eats balanced meals
- Exercises regularly
- Gets enough sleep and rest, to include naps if needed
- Spends time engaged in his favorite activities
- Slowly and moderately moves back into the social realm
- Doesn't take on too much day-to-day responsibility or too many special projects too soon
- Talks about his feelings
- Attends church

However, if after a reasonable time, things don't seem to be improving, those aforementioned reactions might also be signs that something else is very wrong.

Posttraumatic Stress Disorder (PTSD)

PTSD occurs as a result of experiencing a horrible, scary, or life-threatening event. When fear, confusion, and anger don't go away, seem to worsen, or disrupt your life, your honey may be developing PTSD. These reactions can happen soon after the event, develop much later, or come and go over time. Some people who develop the condition eventually get better. Others will not and will have to get treatment to cope with the following symptoms:

- Reliving the event: They have nightmares or flashbacks, often triggered by a sight or sound. For example, a car that backfires or a car accident.
- Avoiding reminders of the event: They don't want to talk about or think about the event and avoid any situations that might trigger memories of it. For example, they keep very busy just to avoid seeking help because seeking help would mean having to talk about it.
- Feeling numb: They don't want to express their feelings and have little interest in relationships and activities.
- Feeling on edge: They may be easily angered or irritated, be unable to sleep, and overreact when startled or surprised.
- Experiencing problems related to these reactions: This includes abuse of drugs or alcohol, hopelessness, problems at work, domestic violence, and physical symptoms.

If any of these symptoms persist, gently encourage your spouse to check in with a doctor. There is no need for him or your family to suffer through this trying time. Treatment can be as straightforward as counseling and/or medication.

Traumatic Brain Injury (TBI)

TBI occurs when something hits a person's head very hard, when something goes through the skull and enters the brain, or when the head is shaken violently. TBI may not be noticed right away because for the most part, the person looks and acts normally; they just don't feel or think normally. Also, the symptoms may be delayed or subtle. Some of the symptoms include fatigue, headaches, dizziness, loss of balance, difficulty remembering or concentrating, nausea or vomiting, slurred speech, and problems with sight and hearing. TBI can be diagnosed as moderate or severe. Treatments include medication, surgery, and rehabilitation.

Depression

Depression is a disorder that affects a person's mood. It can be described as a general state of prolonged sadness. People who are depressed may feel hopeless, lose interest in activities, feel tired, have a negative attitude, sleep a lot more or a lot less than usual, eat a lot more or less than usual, or think about death, dying, or suicide. Understand that depression doesn't mean that one is weak or a failure, so make sure your man is not constantly down on himself. Whenever it seems like he is having more bad days than good days, encourage him to go talk to someone. Hopefully it won't take long for you to convince him because the symptoms can begin to decrease in a few weeks with counseling and/or medication.

There is a strong taboo in the black community about depression and other mental health issues that needs to be addressed. It is particularly destructive to our black men, who often don't get help unless there are extreme circumstances. Some researchers say our neglect of emotional disorders is slowly leading to racial suicide. Other historians say the problem can be traced back to the time of slavery when it was believed that blacks were incapable of feeling inner pain because we had no psyche. Over the years, this has been damaging to black men and black women.

Depression is a serious illness. Sometime we can call someone "in a funk" or "battling the blues," but when it continues for a prolonged period of time, this is serious business. We often think that God can help you through anything. And he absolutely, sure enough can, but that doesn't mean you don't need medical assistance. If your spouse is depressed, it does not mean his faith is weak, he is "crazy," or that you and the family are not enough to make him happy. If you feel your man is unwell beyond just a funk, please help him get help. There is no shame in depression or seeking medical assistance. Please read *Black Men and Depression: Saving Our Lives, Healing Our Families and Friends* (Harlem Moon Publishers) by John Head. Head, a successful journalist who spent twenty years battling undiagnosed depression before seeking help, shares his story, his journey, and his thoughts on the implications for all black men.

Substance Abuse

Be on the lookout for unhealthy ways your husband might be attempting to cope with any symptoms he is having as a result of any of the preceding conditions. Risky behaviors, such as substance abuse, are not only unhealthy for him, but they can lead to other problems such as domestic violence, poor work performance, and driving under the influence. Risks like this can cost your family a lot, literally and figuratively. Remind your husband that he can lose his job for using drugs and ask him to stop immediately or seek treatment if he is unable to do so on his own. Get help when you and your relatives or friends begin to notice excessive use of alcohol, guilt about using or abusing, and when it is causing him not to be able to handle his business at work or at home.

Domestic Violence

There's a dirty little secret in the military related to domestic violence and it's important that we talk to you about it. Evidence shows the violence against women is a pervasive problem in the military. This problem came into the blaring light in the summer of 2002 when four military wives were murdered, allegedly by their husbands or exes, within a six-week period at Fort Bragg, the nation's largest military base. In that summer, it was statistically more dangerous to be an army wife than a Fort Bragg soldier. What's more, the rate of domestic violence in the military is two to five times higher than in the civilian population. According to a report by the Family Violence Prevention Fund, the highest rates of domestic violence are in the army, followed by the marines, navy, and air force. Yet wives are less likely to report the abuse for fear of retribution or that the military will not properly punish the service member.

The military has coined the euphemistic phrase, the "spousal aggression issue." I call it ugly and unacceptable. What's usually behind it? Some misguided attempt to gain or regain some degree of control or power over the person, whether it is a spouse, child, or elder. However, it may also be a reaction to extremely stressful situations in one's life, relationship problems, alcohol and drug use, poor coping skills, or inappropriate expectations of family members. It is also linked with a history of abuse in one's own past. Domestic abuse can be in the form of physical, emotional, verbal, and sexual abuse or neglectful acts. The abuser may use fear, intimidation, guilt, shame, isolation, control of finances, and threats in an effort to dominate the person. He may hit, punch, slap, grab, or use weapons such as knives, guns, or household items to hit the victim. Forcing someone to engage in any form of sexual activity using any of these means is considered sexual abuse. Whatever the root cause of it, you don't have to tolerate it. And you shouldn't.

It is also helpful to be aware of what abuse looks like. For one, abuse incidents are typically cyclical in occurrence.

> *Every day he came home from work, he was agitated about something but he never said what it was. He complained about the meals, the house not being clean enough, my clothes not fitting well, the kids being too noisy. It just went on and on and on. He called me names, yelled in my face, and constantly put me down. Finally, one day when the dinner was not warm enough, he accused me of wasting so much time doing nothing that I couldn't take care of him. He threw the entire meal onto the floor and told me I had better clean it up and start again and that the meal had better be done right. And he wanted to eat in exactly one hour . . .*
>
> *His favorite line was: Who is getting all your attention while I am working my butt off every day? Maybe he should take of this house for you 'cause you ain't getting it right. He would grab the keys and storm off to go drinking with the boys. When I pretended to be asleep for fear of his finding an excuse to start again, he'd roll me over and do whatever he wanted, and fall asleep. By the time he woke up, he'd tell me he was sorry and hug and kiss me all morning as if nothing happened. He would promise to have a quiet evening at home together that night. That usually lasts a few days, but then we go right back down the same road again. I am scared because with each incident, the violence gets worse and worse. —Anonymous*

Even if the details of this incident don't sound familiar, the cyclical nature of the event is probably very similar to your experiences if you are abused. You may be uncertain of whether it really is abuse. Maybe you want to "get it right" so he will be the loving man you met. Maybe you really believe it really will get better once the bills get paid or when you move to the next duty station or once his new boss finally moves on. The reality is, whatever is the underlying "reason," his acting that way is not going away unless it gets addressed.

These days, the military is taking domestic violence a lot more seriously. The Department of Defense has established the Family Advocacy Program (FAP) specifically to address violence in military families. You can access it through the Family Readiness Center or Family Support Center (FSC). FAPs are available on post to help prevent child and spouse abuse through education, prompt reporting, investigation, intervention, and treatment. They have dozens of counselors on hand to help you deal with critical issues and also provide services that enhance relationship skills and improve the military family life. The services are available to victims of violence, the abuser, and the persons who are impacted by the violence, such as children who live in the household. Service members are required to attend annual two-hour Family Violence Awareness training in the unit. However, many courses are also available for families, couples, and individuals.

It needs to be said that family advocates aren't perfect (we've heard some horror stories), but all in all they can do a good job to go to bat for you as an abused spouse especially when your service member is backed by a command full of men. Ladies, you must remember that the military is in the business of protecting and representing their service members, not their families. We've heard of some military supervisors who, when they first begin to see a family breaking up, they figure the spouse should be immediately cut off from important services, like access to legal and financial support in order to protect the interests of the service member. Know your rights! The family advocates know and understand the process and can help you work the system.

DEPARTMENT OF DEFENSE DEFINITIONS

Child abuse and neglect includes physical injury, sexual maltreatment, emotional maltreatment, deprivation of necessities, or combinations for a child by an individual responsible for the child's welfare under circumstances indicating that the child's welfare is harmed or threatened. The term encompasses both acts and omissions on the part of a responsible person. A "child" is a person under eighteen years of age for whom a parent, guardian, foster parent, caretaker, employee of a residential facility, or any staff person providing out-of-home care is legally responsible. The term "child" means a natural child, adopted child, stepchild, foster child, or ward. The term also includes an individual of any age who is incapable for self-support because of a mental or physical incapacity and for whom treatment in a medical treatment facility is authorized.

Domestic abuse includes domestic violence or a pattern of behavior resulting in emotional/psychological abuse, economic control, and/or interference with personal liberty when such violence or abuse is directed toward a person of the opposite sex who is a current or former spouse, a person with whom the abuser shares a child in common, or a current or former intimate partner with whom the abuser shares or has shared a common domicile.

Are you being abused?

The U.S Department of Health and Human Services, Office of Women's Health provides a checklist of signs of abuse on its website, www.4women.gov/violence/signs/.

Sometimes it is hard and confusing to admit that you are in an abusive relationship, or to find a way out. There are clear signs to help you know if you are being abused. If the person you love or live with does any of these things to you, it's time to get help:

- Monitors what you're doing all the time
- Criticizes you for little things
- Constantly accuses you of being unfaithful
- Prevents or discourages you from seeing friends or family, or going to work or school
- Gets angry when drinking alcohol or using drugs
- Controls how you spend your money
- Controls your use of needed medicines
- Humiliates you in front of others

- Destroys your property or things that you care about
- Threatens to hurt you, the children, or pets, or does hurt you (by hitting, beating, pushing, shoving, punching, slapping, kicking, or biting)
- Uses or threatens to use a weapon against you
- Forces you to have sex against your will
- Blames you for his or her violent outbursts

STOP THE VIOLENCE!

If you are afraid for your immediate safety or that of another, call 911.

If you are in an abusive relationship, but not in immediate danger contact Military OneSource at 1-800-342-9647 to locate a victim advocate in your area.

If you suspect child abuse in a DoD-sponsored out-of-home care facility, including child development centers, family child care, youth programs, or DoDDS/DDESS schools, report it to FAP or the DoD Child Abuse Safety and Violation Hotline at 1-800-336-4592. (OCONUS service members should access the AT&T operator first.)

You may also contact the National Domestic Violence Hotline at 1-800-799-7233 or 1-800-787-3224 (TTY).

The National Sexual Assault Hotline can be reached through www.rainn.org (Rape, Abuse & Incest National Network) or at 1-800-656-4673.

WHERE TO GET MORE ASSISTANCE

Confidential help for personal or emotional problems:

- Military One Source, 800-342-9647, www.militaryonesource.com
- Veteran's Center, 800-905-4675 (Eastern), www.vetcenter.va.gov
- Veteran's Center, 866-496-8838 (Pacific), www.vetcenter.va.gov
- VA Medical Treatment Center, 877-222-8387, www.va.gov/directory
- National Military Family Association, 800-260-0218, www.nmfa.org and follow the health-care link
- Department of Defense (DoD) PTSD and TBI Quick Facts, www.pdhealth.mil/downloads/TBI_PTSD_Final04232007.pdf
- National Alliance on Mental Illness (NAMI), 800-950-NAMI, www.nami.org/veterans

- The Veterans Affairs (VA) National Center for PTSD, www.ncptsd
.va.gov/ncmain/ncdocs/manuals/GuideforMilitary.pdf; www.ncptsd
.va.gov/ncmain/ncdocs/videos/emv_newwarr_vets.html
- American Psychiatric Association information on PTSD, www
.healthyminds.org/multimedia/ptsd.pdf
- Defense and Veterans Brain Injury Center, 800-870-9244, www
.dvbic.org/
- Department of Veterans Affairs, www.va.gov/environagents/docs/
TBI-handout-patients.pdf

Your Physically Wounded Loved One

The Notification Process

Notification that a loved one has been wounded is just the beginning of ongoing stress for the duration of the treatment and recovery. Not only will you be concerned about the injury, but expect to be completely frustrated that no one will be able to give you enough information to satisfy your need to know. The initial details may be sketchy, and subsequent ones may seem inconsistent. Add to this mix the fact that you can't get there fast enough to see for yourself and you are likely to feel as though you are going insane. But for your sake and the sake of other family members, understand that the military will make your service member's care a priority, even if you are not aware of every step along the way as it occurs.

The Enemy Within: When Fellow Soldiers Attack

Some service women found that their attackers were on the same side. Increasing numbers of women veterans have sought treatment for "military sexual trauma," a pseudonym for rape by a fellow American soldier or officer. "I see a lot of women who have been raped in the service," says Barry Campbell, a New York City benefits counselor with the Veteran's Administration Hospital. "They get attacked by superior officers or guys in the ranks."

Kymber Lea Durant, thirty-eight, says that's what happened to her while she was one of the ten women among 300 men stationed in Egypt with the 101st Airborne in support of the first Desert Storm. "I went to the guy's tent to borrow a tape because he had a big collection of CDs and movies," she says. "He attacked me." Afterward, nobody believed her. "I told my sergeant, and he took it to the first sergeant."

Durant says she was labeled as a troublemaker, a reputation that followed her when she was deployed at King Faud Airport in Iraq in 1991. "When I got to Iraq, there was a lot of what I called 'mental ass whipping,'" she says. "They called me Dead Beat Durant. Nothing I did was good enough."

A supply clerk, Durant suffered back injuries on the job that left her infertile when an Army surgeon removed one of her fallopian tubes during an ectopic pregnancy. "I went into the Army to get money for college," says Durant, who now lives in Brooklyn, New York. "If I could go back, I would never have joined."

Durant's mental trauma was such that she was homeless for a time. She now lives in her late mother's house, survives on 50 percent disability pay of $728 a month, and takes care of her ten-year-old adopted sister. She takes four different drugs daily to deal with migraines, depression, panic attacks, and gynecological issues. "I can't hold a job," she says, "because some days I can't get out of bed."

Permission has been granted by Heart and Soul Enterprises LLC to use excerpts from "The Aftermath of War" by Clem Richardson, originally published in the April/May 2008 issue of *Heart and Soul* magazine.

But they will keep you informed. Every service branch has a process of notification. If you are reading this and do not have a wounded service member, you should immediately seek to find out what the notification and transition process entails for your service branch. For the most part, they are all similar, and variations will occur based on the degree of injury.

When you hear about your loved one or someone you know being referred to as a casualty, don't panic. Although we associate the term with death, it actually refers to any person who is unavailable to his organization due to injury, illness, hospitalization, missing in action, or death, just to name a few examples.

Within twenty-four to forty-eight hours of an injury or illness, the notification begins with telephonic notification to the primary next of kin (PNOK) and occurs between the hours of 0600 (6:00 A.M.) and 2200 hours (10:00 P.M.), your time. As additional information becomes available you will know more. In the case that the service member has died or is missing, notification will be made in person to the PNOK, the secondary next of kin (SNOK), and anyone else he has listed on his Record of Emergency Data (DD Form 93). The notifier will hold the same grade as or higher than your loved one or the same or higher grade as you if you are also a service member. Regardless of what other duties the notifier has, your notification is his or her highest priority over any of them.

The PNOK is determined by the following order of precedence: spouse, children, parents, persons who were charged with parental duties for at least five years prior to the casualty's eighteenth birthday, person with legal custody, siblings, grandparents, other relatives in order of relationship according to the civil laws. If no other persons are available, the secretary of the military department may act on his behalf. The SNOK can be any other NOK.

Pamela's Pick:

The Family Medical and Leave Act has been expanded to allow up to twenty-six weeks (up from twelve weeks) of job-protected, unpaid leave to care for injured service members.

If you have heard stories about spouses not getting the information about their loved one fast enough, here are two common reasons why delays in notification happen. Either the contact information on the emergency information card was incorrect, or the family member left the local area without telling or providing a contact number to the rear detachment commander (the person who is left behind and is in charge of the unit/family interaction when the commander is deployed) or the family readiness point of contact person. Don't let that be you.

If a doctor determines that the PNOK and immediate family members are critical to the recovery of a very seriously injured or ill service member, and the hospital commander verifies that, the military can pay for the family to travel to the hospital as well as lodging. This funding will apply to up to three family members in two-week increments. Immediate family members are spouse, children, mother, father, siblings, and those acting in parental stead. The situation is evaluated every two weeks and authorization of additional time may be given. Discuss with your notifier the availability of child care, but count on having to foot the bill for this expense.

Your family may stay at a local hotel, military installation, or, where available, the Fisher House, which is temporary housing for those visiting service members receiving medical care. The $10 per night fee is waived if the service member is wounded. The homes are usually very close to the medical facility or transportation will be provided. Visit www.fisherhouse.org for more information about this home away from home.

OTHER THINGS TO KNOW

A case manager will be assigned to your family during the recovery period.

Additional resources may be available depending upon the location of the medical facility.

If the patient is medically retired, referred on to the Department of Veterans Affairs, or separated from the military, he or she will be considered to be in transition. Such patients can attend the Department of Defense mandated Transition Assistance Program (TAP) to receive relevant information prior to the departure from service.

Military OneSource has a section called "Entering the Work Force When Your Spouse is Severely Injured" in the Special Needs section of www.militaryonesource.com.

All service members who are covered by the Servicemember's Group Life Insurance (SGLI) are automatically covered for TSGLI, coverage for traumatic injury protection that pays out a lump sum of up to $100,000 depending upon the extent of the injury. For more in-depth information and help, contact:

- Air Force Casualty Assistance Representative, 888-774-1361, www.severelyinjured@militaryonesource.com
- Army AW2 (Wounded Warrior Program), 800-237-1336, www.aw2portal.com

- Marine M4L (Marine for Life), 866-645-8762, www.m4l.usmc.mil
- Navy Safe Harbor, 877-746-8563, www.militaryhomefront.dod.mil
- MSIC (Military Severely Injured Center), 888-774-1361, www .militaryhomefront.dod.mil, click on Troops and Families link
- Deployment Health Support Directorate, 800-497-6261

THINGS TO CONSIDER WHEN VISITING YOUR LOVED ONE

Your life and that of your children will be thrown completely out of whack. Give careful consideration for the best approach, rather than making a rash decision to pick up and go. Will taking the children be possible or should you leave them with a caregiver? Plan out your child care whether they are left at home or taken with you. Will they be able to visit with the family member while there? Will you miss work? If so, how can you lessen the financial setback? Be familiar with the Family Medical Leave Act (FMLA) and how it impacts you. Make sure you are in the know about any recent advances for military spouses with respect to taking time off from work to care for a wounded spouse. This information can be found on the National Military Family Association website (www.nmfa.org) in various forms, such as publications, e-newsletters, and more. Plan for your children to miss school, and contact the teachers to obtain their schoolwork if possible.

Things to consider when dealing with the injury itself: learn as much as you can about the injury, the treatment, and the recovery. Become a part of the treatment team so you can help your loved one through uncertain times. Ask questions when you don't understand, and make sure you take breaks that allow you to eat, sleep, and exercise throughout the day so you can function a lot better.

Pamela's Pick: Tips for Dealing with an Injured Spouse

- Learn everything you can about the medical condition.
- Be compassionate.
- Listen to what your honey is willing to share.
- Let them do what they can for themselves.
- Seek spiritual guidance for you and for your loved one.
- Connect with other families who are going through the same thing.

- Take care of yourself (eat, sleep, take a break).
- Seek help when you become overwhelmed.
- Research medical assistance for at-home care.
- Trust your instinct. If something appears to be wrong, seek help.
- Take the slow road to reestablishing intimacy.
- Don't forget to be friends.
- Find new ways to have fun if the old ways are no longer possible.
- Make your loved one the focus, not his injury or disability.
- If a disability changes the logistics of sex, talk about how to make it happen.

Dealing with the Ultimate Unthinkable: Death

CAROL'S STORY

"John and I had decided to move out of the apartment when he arrived home for an emergency leave from Iraq. He wanted to have his two daughters come live with us and my two sons. We went house hunting, started the paperwork, and worked to get the children ready for school before he returned to Iraq.

"Every day after school the kids and I loaded up the car, took our things to the new house and unpacked them and put them away. Within a couple weeks I could finally have the utilities and cable transferred to the new house. Of course, the cable company promised to be here to turn on the service in our new house sometime between eight and five. So I was sitting there waiting and waiting all morning. I put some of our things away and watched the clock. I didn't even want to leave to get the kids from school because I thought they would come while I was gone. I waited and waited some more, saying, "Please come, please come." And then the doorbell rang and I said, "Yes! Cable! Finally." I was so excited I didn't even bother to look out the window I just flung the door open because I was so happy.

"And there stood the guys. And it just takes your breath away because you're not expecting that. All you can think of is: he promised me he was going to come home and he didn't! And you want them to be at the wrong house. I prayed and prayed they were at the wrong house because we just moved in! This isn't for me because they don't even know our new address. It's for whoever lived here last. Maybe they were military because this is a military town, people come and go. It's just the wrong address.

"Then they asked for me by name and I knew that John wasn't coming home anymore. They asked to come in and I just closed the door and went to my room and cried. And they rang the doorbell again. And they rang it again. I knew they were not going to leave. When I opened the door, they asked to come inside again and I said no. Because I knew that once they say it, it's final. But then, they asked to come in again and I let them in. They told me and I just cried. I didn't even talk to the guys. They were in the kitchen getting ready to fill out paperwork and I got on the phone and started calling my family and friends. I called my dad first and told him, 'John died, he's not coming home.'"

Carol Rivera lost her husband on September 26, 2006, during his second deployment to Iraq. They never had the chance to live in the house together as a family.

Like many wives, Carol had been very nervous about the deployment and his safety. Although her dad had been deployed to Saudi Arabia and Kuwait, she grew up in a military town, and she had friends with deployed husbands, so she was very stressed about the whole thing. Carol had heard too much on the news. And she hadn't been married to Jay during the first deployment so she kept asking him, "What if . . ."

"He kept telling me it was his job and he knew what to do. He always tried to make me feel okay and told me not to worry about anything because nothing was going to happen," she recalled. But something did happen and in an instant, her life was changed forever.

The ensuing months will be a blur for new military widows. And unfortunately, they may not be well prepared enough to make sense of the fast cash and slow recovery. There has been numerous accounts of young widows, and maybe some not-so-young widows, who attempt to drown their sorrows in shopping sprees to buy things they couldn't previously afford but now, with a $100,000 payment upon death and $400,000 maximum in insurance money, they believe they can afford to live the glamorous life. Well, at least for the time being. And after all, with everything they are going through, they deserve it, right?

Well, not exactly. What military spouses who lose loved ones deserve is an understanding of the grieving process, the benefits available to them, sound financial advice, and close friends and family who will look out for their best interests.

Did you know that the military provides casualty assistance? They will assign a military person who is well trained to provide you help in navigating through filling out all the paperwork, making funeral arrangements, accessing your benefits, and answering any questions you may have. The services are consistent throughout the different branches, but the job titles are different. The army has a casualty assistance officer (CAO). The marine corps and navy call it a casualty assistance calls officer (CACO). Casualty assistance representative is the name used by the air force.

Even though you will have the help of a casualty assistance person, you still need to have certain things in order ahead of time. None of us like to think about it, but even when you are not talking about the war, any of us can go at any time. Without planning ahead and putting things in order now, you could wind up having problems on your hands that you never would have imagined. Recall Chapter 2, where we discussed making sure the DEERS was always up-to-date. Pamela can share plenty of stories where loved ones who were supposed to receive benefits did not, simply because the records had never been updated by the service member. This happens mostly in times of marriage, divorce, remarriage, and, of course, death. Once the service member has passed on, there will be nothing to prove that what was in his record wasn't what he meant to be there.

So, not only is it a good idea to have things in order, but review it with your honey every year to make sure no changes are missed. This includes wills, powers of attorney, life insurance paperwork, and the like. And there will be some things that don't necessarily get automatically documented that you might want to discuss.

Ask "what if," before something happens, so you can avoid having to say "if only."

Two years after she lost her soldier, Carol still can't decide what to do with some of John's things. And although some of those things are not major, they are causing her major grief because she just wants to do what he would want her to do.

"I don't know who he would want to have his car. Should I give it to one of his best friends? Which one? One from the military or one from high school? I don't know if he'd want me to give his clothes to charity or to family and if to family, who gets what? I don't know if he would want me to continue to pay the mortgage on our brand-new house or move back home or move into something less expensive. I just don't know what he would want me to do.

"I suggest that everyone talk about the 'What if.' There is nothing wrong with talking about what he wants you to do if something goes wrong," she said. "'Ask, What do you want for the kids' futures?, what do you want me to do with the money we have in savings?' Jay and I talked about the big things, but you should review the will together to make sure he left out nothing that was important; even the smallest things matter, because now I can't ask him. Write down more than just who should be in charge of his remains and funeral as required, but also make note of some of the things he would want and didn't want."

What benefits and privileges continue?

You will still have TRICARE coverage. Your access to the commissary and Exchange are indefinite unless you remarry. Children can use them until they are eighteen years old or twenty-three if they are in college. Some Morale, Welfare, and Recreation (MWR) programs will also be available to you.

You can continue to live in government housing for 365 days without being charged. If you leave before then, you will receive a basic allowance for housing (BAH) for the remaining period. If you live off post, you will continue to receive BAH for 365 days after the death.

VA BENEFITS

Surviving family members may receive the VA Home Loan Guaranty for Surviving Spouses, work-study employment benefits, educational assistance, bereavement counseling, vocational rehabilitation, and financial counseling for beneficiaries. Find out more at www.va.gov or by calling 1-800-827-1000 or by visiting a regional VA office.

WHAT TO EXPECT AFTER THE DEATH OF YOUR HUSBAND

A few months after the death, your husband's belongings will arrive in footlockers and boxes. And you won't want to go through everything, especially not in front of somebody, because you'll most likely just want to sit there and cry. But you can't put it off indefinitely. The military won't let you. They have to go through everything and mark it off the inventory list. They need to know it was sent from there, and now it's in your hands.

But truth be told, sometimes not everything makes it back to you. Some things may be missing. Maybe it is something small like a movie missing from a movie case. Or maybe something is irreplaceable like memory of the camera, mp3 player, and computer. For the safety of all the soldiers over there, the military gets rid of anything they deem inappropriate, but how do you ever know if something that was meant for you was accidentally erased?

Sometimes the missing are big-ticket items. There are stories that some wives didn't get a lot of important things back, like laptops, video cameras, digital cameras, and jewelry. You never know who packed it up and who touched it at all the places it went through before you got them. Not everyone is trustworthy. You would hope the ones who packed up your spouse's possessions would be respectful, but you just never know. Nor do you know where they may have been misplaced. At that point, though, there is almost nothing that can be done about it.

Pamela's Pick: Honoring Your Spouse's Memory

Throughout history, military widows have honored the memory of their fallen soldiers in ways big and small. One widow, Melissa, started a camp scholarship for Boy Scouts in her husband's name. In Ohio, a widow named Jayme created a "Field of Honor" with two hundred flags flying outside an elementary school.

Here are some other ways spouses have honored the memory of the loved ones they have lost:

- Make a T-shirt quilt or photo bangle.
- Have a bag or quilt made from his uniforms (www .campfollowerbags.com).
- Have a free, custom, hand-drawn family portrait made from a favorite family photo (www.fallenheroesproject.org).
- Get a free sterling silver, 3-D memorial photo pendant on an eighteen-inch chain in a custom "folded flag" box with a personal note from Project Never Forget (www .projectneverforget.com).
- Mount and display his cap, medals, flag, and other military effects with the help of the on-post trophy shop. Don't

forget to ask the Casualty Assistance Office to obtain a list of all the medals and then order them at www.usamilitary medals.com if you don't live on or near post.

- Create a cabinet or bookshelf to house things as big as the flag case and urn with his ashes and as small as his keys, cell phone, love letters, dog tags, favorite book, hobby-related items, favorite souvenir, favorite CD and movie, and so on.

A Widow's Might: The American Widow Project

"When you lose your husband, you don't care about the money; the checks are just a reminder of the tragedy. Instead, what you need is people who reach out to you and not pull back from you on the days when you tell them you are not doing well," said Taryn Davis, the founder of the American Widow Project. "Here, you are surrounded by widows who will cherish whatever memories of your loved ones you share with them.

"And we are focused on the legacy part of it because our loved ones are not just a name or some engraved headstone on a wall. Mike is a person and I am making memories in the rest of my life that I will share with him when I join him."

Taryn started this project after exhausting every resource for military spouse widows and was not being fulfilled. "When other people lost loved ones, Michael, my husband, would contact them and offer his support. No one did that for me." Having experienced firsthand the fact that other widows are the only ones who will really listen even on the bad days, Taryn started a nonprofit organization to help all widows. The American Widow Project (www .americanwidowproject.org) is an organization dedicated to helping military widows heal through sharing stories, tears, and laughter with other widows. By dialing the 24/7 hotline number at 877-AWP-WIDOW, you can be connected with another military widow who is ready to listen and help.

The project connects military widows all over the world with the single greatest resource they could have: someone who will listen and help, just like Michael did. And when they get to the point where they are ready to continue the legacy of their lost husbands, there are ideas for that, too.

In addition to helping others honor the memory of their lost spouses,

Taryn did not forget to tend to her own spiritual needs. "I walked two hundred miles across Spain with only a backpack and my thoughts. Being a widow who, for eighteen days, was completely disconnected from everything except her thoughts of her late husband was more challenging than the walking. I rehashed the last seven years of my life with Michael while walking with another widow and we didn't talk at all."

But she wanted something more. And whenever she wanted something, Mike always told her, "Look for it, babe, and if you can't find it, make it happen." And so she did. The AWP connects widows with others in like situations or who live in your area, facilitating the opportunity to network.

The American Widow Project has also completed a DVD documentary on the lives of widows from the Iraq and Afghanistan wars. They hope to distribute these healing stories free of charge to widows (others will be asked for a donation) along with a card from a fellow military widow. "When I look back at myself right after his death, I remember that I was a vegetable for a while. What I wanted was for someone to come over and talk to me," she said. The DVD is her way of providing that link to other military widows.

TAPS (Tragedy Assistance Program for Survivors)

Hundreds of survivors volunteer their time to help their newly bereaved peers by becoming their mentors in a time where love and support is priceless. By calling 800-959-TAPS, survivors can receive case management, crisis intervention, and resources and information 24/7. And this help is available to anyone who has lost a loved one in the military "regardless of relationship, circumstance, or geographic location."

TAPS delivers Military Survivor Seminars for adults and Good Grief Camps for young survivors. At a time when the remaining parent is being educated on benefits, what to expect, the grief process, and more, the children of the deceased are also being equipped to cope more effectively with what has happened. With trained staff and loads of fun the children have an opportunity to interact with other children who understand. There were thirty-four nationwide events listed on the website from January 2008 through July 2008!

The online community at www.taps.org contains weekly chat-room discussions and forums, plus special chat sessions that focus on specific topics as well as an extensive list of links of interest to survivors. TAPS is currently developing a new outreach initiative for Latina/Latino survivors.

Colin Powell has been quoted as saying, "When an untimely and tragic event occurs and a service member is lost . . . members of the military family are ready to step forward to help shoulder a burden and to help the grieving cope and heal. In its countless contributions, TAPS helps to deliver the triumph of tenderness and kindness over pain and loss."

National Military Family Association

In 2004, the National Military Family Association (NMFA) created Operation Purple, a summer camp experience for children impacted by the deployment of a parent. The twelve locations across the country offer fun, friendships, and coping skills to military children. NMFA's dedication, the success of the program, and a growth in corporate sponsors will fund camps in sixty-two locations in thirty-seven states and territories in 2008.

Also in 2008, NMFA piloted a new camp called Operation Purple Healing Adventures, a weeklong retreat for wounded service members and their families. There are traditional camp activities for families in addition to various seminars for individuals and couples.

NMFA is dedicated to providing information directly to and representing the interests of military families. Known as "The Voice for Military Families," it also provides scholarships, awards, programs, advocacy, and other initiatives and services that enhance the quality of life. Find out more at www.nmfa.org.

> **Pamela's Pick:** **Honoring Those Who Gave the Ultimate Sacrifice**
> The structure, the discipline, the rigidity, the hierarchy—it's how the military controls its environment. But the one thing it can't completely control is death. Death is a reality of military life that is not taken lightly. Service members train every day of their careers to avoid it. And they take very seriously honoring their comrades who have made the ultimate sacrifice. Here are some of the ways service members pay respect to their fallen comrades, all of which

are extremely touching no matter how many times I experience them.

Fallen Soldier Ceremony: At one point I worked in the Army Reserve Command Headquarters at Fort McPherson, Georgia, from 2003 to 2008, at a time when deployment was not only a fact of life, but repeated deployments were the norm. There were regular Fallen Soldiers ceremonies held right outside the building, and all were expected to attend. As an army wife, it was my personal duty, not a mandated duty, to attend. But at some point, I had to give myself a break. My husband was deployed in Iraq and being in the midst of that event on some days was just too much to bear.

Final Roll Call: During memorial services there stands a symbol of the fallen soldier. It is a Kevlar helmet atop an inverted rifle with identification tags hanging on it. At the bottom of the rifle are a pair of boots and a framed photo of the deceased. One of these displays stands for each service member who is being memorialized. The roll call symbolizes the last formation of the deceased with his unit. The leader begins by calling the name of the deceased as the whole group stands in deafening silence:

"Sergeant Jones!"

There is no response.

"Sergeant John Jones!"

Silence.

"Sergeant John Robert Jones!"

Only sobs can be heard. The deceased is no longer present in the unit.

Taps: A twenty-four-note musical arrangement played on a bugle or trumpet during a memorial service or funeral. Service members in uniform salute during the song, while others place the right hand over the heart. The eloquent, very slowly played twenty-four notes elicit unimaginable depths of overwhelming sadness.

The POW/MIA (Prisoner of War/Missing in Action) Table: During the very traditional program of formal military balls, tribute is paid to fallen soldiers in the form of a table set for one that remains empty except for the items placed at it in remembrance. The following is read from the podium:

You may notice this small table here in a place of honor. It is set for one. This table is our way of symbolizing the act that members of our profession of arms are missing from our midst. They are commonly called P.O.W.s or M.I.A.s; we call them brothers.

They are unable to be with us this evening and so we remember them.

This table set for one is small . . . it symbolizes the frailty of one prisoner against his oppressors.

The table cloth is white . . . it symbolizes the purity of their intentions to respond to their country's call to arms.

The single rose displayed in a vase reminds us of the families and loved ones of our comrades in arms who keep faith awaiting their return.

The red ribbon tied so prominently on the vase is reminiscent of the red ribbon worn on the lapel and breasts of thousands who bear witness to their unyielding determination to demand a proper accounting for our missing.

A slice of lemon is on the bread plate . . . to remind us of their bitter fate.

There is salt upon the bread plate . . . symbolic of the family's tears as they wait.

The glass is inverted . . . they cannot toast with us tonight.

The chair is empty . . . they are not here.

Remember . . . all of you who served with them and called them comrades, who depended on their might and aid, and relied on them . . . for surely . . . they have not forsaken you.

Dealing with Loss

Loss can occur at many different times and to varying degrees. Common lesser degree losses are being passed over for a promotion, moving to a new duty station, deployment, loss of home, and child leaving for college. Losing a loved one is obviously a much stronger degree of loss. On both ends of the spectrum, you will experience a series of predictable feelings known as the stages of grief. They are:

- Shock/denial/isolation: We deny the loss happened and withdraw from our friends and family.
- Anger/guilt: We feel anger toward the deceased or ourselves, or the whole world.
- Bargaining: We make promises to God—if He would bring back our loved one, we will . . .
- Depression: We feel extreme sadness.
- Acceptance: Most of the deep negative feelings begin to subside and we accept the reality of the situation.

However long these stages last, how deeply you experience them and the other reactions you might have, your experience will be unique to you. There really is no typical loss experience. Therefore, you should allow yourself time to pass through all the stages; surround yourself with your closest family and friends; and take care of yourself with healthy eating, exercise, and plenty of rest. Most of all, give yourself time to heal.

by Mrs. Nicole Hart,
American Widow Project Member

We talked on the phone for eight hours straight when we were only fifteen years old. After that one night the number 8 became an inside joke only we would understand. As time passed the number 8 meant "David and Nicole" or "I love you." We used the number 8 for everything! At the end of our e-mails, passwords, and love letters. If you asked David "How many," he'd answer "Eight." It didn't matter what it was. When he was away, the number 8 comforted me; seeing it was like getting a kiss from him . . . it'd make me close my eyes and say, sometimes out loud, "I love you, David." Yes, 8 was our special number.

"On behalf of the Secretary of Defense. . . . On January 8 of 2008 . . . Sgt. David Joseph Hart died in Balad, Iraq, from wounds sustained while on a combat mission. . . ." Those words were spoken the moment the number 8 was branded on my heart forever. I couldn't believe those words just came out of a soldier's mouth. I couldn't believe they knew my husband's name! Twenty minutes and a couple signatures later, they were gone. My husband, my best friend, and love of my life, died the morning of the eighth. He was killed while I was sleeping and I had no idea.

It's been a blur since then, but especially the few weeks that followed January 8. It seemed like everyone and their mother needed my signature on a piece of paper. No one bothered me with the details, which I appreciated; they just told me to "sign here." One morning, I was sitting at the kitchen table and papers were brought to me. I was signing where told when I saw it. A checked box next to the word *widow*. I lost it! Literally, I began to scream. My husband had only been dead for a few days and at twenty-two years old I had to check a "widow" box.

From that moment on I hated the word *widow*. I hated hearing it, reading it, or checking the box. In fact, I never checked the box. The thought made me sick. Until recently, I hadn't even called myself a widow. The word never came out of my mouth. I wanted nothing to do with it. Yes, I'm proud of my husband! David was a warrior not a victim. He knowingly gave his life on January

8. His instincts kicked in and he fought. I don't regret my husband's actions. I am proud of them. David has always believed in something bigger than himself. As a result, love was the context of all his missions on Earth. He placed everyone's needs before his own. He was an amazing son, brother, mentor, and above all, the most wonderful, loving, and not to mention gorgeous husband. I was always in awe of the man he became. I still am. How can I not be proud? . . . But a widow?

What I didn't understand then, that I do now, is that being a military widow is actually something I can be proud of. It's no longer a curse word for me. I've turned a corner in my journey through grief, saying it no longer makes me mad or want to cry for hours. A "military widow" is a title I can bear proudly because my husband earned it for me. I'm not just a widow though; I'm a military widow—an American widow. More than that, I have the honor of being the military widow of Sergeant David Hart. For me, it means David loved me well, on Earth, and loves me still. It means I am his ambassador. As his ambassador, I hold his legacy and am commissioned to keep it alive.

If someone were to have told me that my husband was going to die and I was going to survive life without him, I wouldn't have believed them. The hardest part for me has been the mere fact that I can do it. That I can still feel hungry, thirsty, or tired. I still fall asleep at night and wake up in the morning. Even though my high school sweetheart is gone, my heart is still pumping. I am still breathing. The truth is, you never know how much you can truly handle until the worst becomes your reality. David has left Earth but left me with a lifetime's worth of memories! I hold on tight to who we were together, to what we believed, and to who I am now. I hold on tight to David. I feel his love when the wind blows on my face, when I hear a song he loved, when I see a picture of us, when I read a letter he wrote, or when I see the number 8. I survive because our love for each other is stronger than death. I can soldier on because I am David Hart's wife. His military widow.

by Natasha Garrigus

I am Natasha Garrigus and I became the widow of Sergeant Mickel Garrigus on January 27, 2007. Mickel was killed by an IED in Taji, Iraq.

I met my husband in June 2003. I was working at Taco Bell right outside of Fort Lewis. It was a night I'll never forget and a story I love telling. I was closing that night with two other girls and about half an hour to locking the doors three guys came in. They were all cute and very flirty but we didn't really pay them any attention. They ordered their food and then left. About five minutes before closing, my manager noticed the same three guys sitting in a car in the parking lot. So she sent me out on a fake trash pickup of the parking lot. In less than a minute, one of them approached me.

After talking to him, I walked over and met the rest of the guys at his car (a pinkish Tracker). The two in the front seat introduced themselves with no problem, but the guy sitting in the back somehow forgot his own name and age. I thought it was the cutest thing. But I ended up giving the driver of the car my number. After a few days of not hearing anything, I moved on.

About two weeks later I was working and there was this guy sitting at a table for hours. He would leave and then come back. He brought a different friend with him every time (thinking we didn't notice). After a while he came up to the counter and asked for me. He asked if I remembered him. I didn't. He said, I'm the one that forgot my name. I remembered then. I gave him my number and from that day forward we were inseparable. I think it's kind of funny that he stalked me for a day. And even funnier that I married my stalker. We were married January 3, 2004, about two weeks before his first deployment to Iraq.

That first year was a very long and lonely year, but I think it made our marriage strong. Mickel came back January 19, 2005, and shortly after that I became pregnant with our first child. About five months into the pregnancy we got stationed at Fort Drum, New York. Then on January 22, 2006, our son, Ethan, was born. Mickel was the best father I could have ever asked or hoped for. There wasn't a night he didn't want to hold our son all night (which is why he still has trouble sleeping alone in his own bed). From the moment

Mickel walked in the house until the moment he left, he was either holding Ethan or playing with Ethan. Mickel only had ten months with Ethan before he deployed for a second time to Iraq in November of 2006. Less than two months later he was killed.

Mickel was killed January 27, 2007. Ethan had turned one year old, five days before that and I turned twenty-two years old four days after. At the time I thought that our birthdays would be ruined forever because the start of what should have been our birthday celebrations is followed by the worst day of both of our lives. But now I can't help but think that Mickel planned it that way. I know that sounds crazy, but any time I think about our son's birthday or my own, I automatically think about the twenty-seventh and Mickel. And if you knew Mickel, it just seems like something he would have done; that way we wouldn't just be celebrating our own birthdays and not thinking about him for once (which isn't likely to ever happen), but it would also be a week of celebrating his life.

Perhaps it is a blessing in disguise that Ethan was so young when his dad died. He hasn't seemed too affected by Mike's death yet. He knows who his daddy is and I talk about Mickel every day. But I know that one day he is going to ask me where his daddy is and I honestly don't know what I am going to say to him other than, his daddy loved him more than life itself. I'm going to make sure Ethan knows his daddy is a hero and died taking care of his guys. It's because of Mike that no one else died that day.

I'm also thankful that we had Ethan. So many people said that we were stupid for having a child so young. But if it wasn't for our son I don't think I would have been able to hold it together when Mike was killed. My son, Ethan, literally saved my life. The night Mike was killed all I could think about was taking my own life. But then I heard Ethan's voice and thought to myself, Mickel would be very angry if I left him without both of his parents. All Mike ever trusted me or asked me to do was to take care of our son.

About a week before Mickel deployed for the second time, he broke his right hand. He slammed the arms room door on it. He was put on profile and was told he wouldn't be deploying for another four to six weeks. But Mike, being the type of man he was, didn't want to be left behind. He went to his commander and got the okay to go anyway. When he told me, I was so mad because he would have been safe at home for another month or two. But I knew that he wanted to go and I knew why. He wanted to go and make sure his guys were okay. Mike was one of very few in the whole company who had ever been deployed before. He knew what to expect and he had made promises to bring his guys home. And sometimes I can't help but think, if he had only stayed back those four to six weeks, he might still be alive.

I was really mad at the time because I thought he cared more about his men than he did about his son and me. But that's just who Mike was. He loved the army, his friends, and he knew by being over there he was not only helping a country in need but making sure his son would never have to live in fear.

Like many others, my husband joked about being killed all the time. He would say, well, if I die, then my son and wife will be set. And he even told me how long he expected me to wait before dating and all that. I was told that the day he died he was joking about it. Somehow I think he knew, because his first deployment he never ever joked about it. And it just seemed like this deployment is all he could talk about. If there's one thing I've learned since Mickel's death, it's that you can't live your life based on the life you had or would have had with your spouse. The fact of the matter is, they aren't coming back. I know Mickel wouldn't want me to spend the rest of my life crying about what should have been. He would want me to live my life to the fullest. And that's what I'm doing. Not only for myself and our son, but for Mickel as well. You can't let other people tell you how to live. You'll do what's best for you and your children. And only you know what your husband would have wanted.

Your Final Move
Making the Transition:
✒ Easing Back into Civilian Life ✒

The military life can be exhilarating and fulfilling, but at some point it may be time to check out. After several years in the structure and support of the military community, whether you are retiring or opting to change careers, stepping into the civvy life can be a little daunting or even downright scary. It can also be one of the most difficult and stressful times in a marriage. Don't fret. Together a couple can move through this transition successfully. By creating a plan and taking full advantage of military resources you can step out with confidence.

Husband and wife dynamic duo Angela and Terry Smith were both career Air Force service members before they returned to civilian life. They met at basic training and became more than comrades, both climbing the military ladder in the career field of finance technicians all the way to the rank of master sergeant.

Terry joined the Air Force with a plan to only serve twenty years and then retire as his father did. Angela had less of an "out" date. But when the time came, Terry set his transition plan into play about six months before retirement with Angela deciding to stay on an additional three years.

When it was time to consider retirement, Terry was focused on finding a civilian job that mirrored what he was already doing. Angela had something else in mind. "I needed some time for a military detox. I wanted my next move to be something that I love doing not just something I was taught to do," she said. "I needed to reconnect with who I was pre-military and find myself again. I didn't want to step into my next career as Master Sergeant Smith, I wanted to come as Angela."

Part of that journey meant coming to grips with the many sacrifices she made over the years as a mother of two and a service member. "Being a woman in the military takes a lot out of you. We are asked to leave our children for a year. And although I understand men are asked to do the same, there's something about a mother leaving her children that is just not right. For me I needed to come back into my home, reassess my children and my life, and just be here and figure out what to do next," she said.

To do so, advance planning is required. And some early discussions. Decide what your goals are as a family. If there are educational opportunities to take advantage of before retirement that can increase your or your spouse's income or career options after the military, then do it! "I wish I had spent more time looking out for myself. You can't focus everything on the mission and not think about your family and their future," said Terry. Discuss what is most important to both you and your spouse. Even if you don't completely agree with your spouse, there will be no surprises if you openly discuss your feelings. A couple can't address any issues that are not out in the open.

1. Take advantage of military resources

Spouses and service members should take the time to learn about the process of military transition. Each branch of the service may handle the steps differently, but service members and their families are given opportunities to learn about services and benefits they are eligible to receive. If spouses understand these steps, families can maximize the benefits and services they receive. And start as early as possible—some programs may allow you to begin as much as one year prior to retirement.

One critical military resource is the Transition Assistance Program (TAP), each branch offers one, and it is specifically designed to help service members during their period of transition into civilian life by offering job search assistance and related services.

The law creating TAP established a partnership among the Departments of Defense, Veterans Affairs, Transportation, and the Department of Labor's Veterans' Employment and Training Service (VETS) to give employment and training information to armed forces members within 180 days of separation or retirement.

TAP helps service members and their spouses ease their initial transition from military service to the civilian workplace with a comprehensive series of three-day workshops. The workshops are presented by trained staff members from the State Employment Services, military family support services, Department of Labor contractors, or VETS.

You will learn about job searches, career decision-making, current occupational and labor market conditions, and résumé and cover letter preparation, and interviewing techniques. Participants also get an evaluation of their employability relative to the job market and receive information on the most current veterans' benefits.

2. Check your disability status

This is very important, say the Smiths. Even if you as a service member or your spouse don't appear to have an injury or they tell you don't, you don't know how twenty years of heavy lifting, for example, may have affected you or will affect you in the future. Your best bet is to go through the process anyway and see if you have any eligible disabilities and document your medical condition in case anything arises in the future. (Note: Be sure to keep a hard copy of your complete medical records.) Depending on the level of injury and disability, you accrue points that can actually improve your attractiveness to some potential employers who are incentivized to hire disabled former service members.

If your military spouse is classified with some sort of disability, it also opens the door to other benefits like free health care and education incentives. For example, Angela says with a disability ranking of 30 percent or higher, the children of service members may be entitled to attend a state university for free.

The Disabled Transition Plan (DTAP) is an important part of transition assistance that helps service members who may be released because of a disability or who believe they have a disability qualifying them for VA's Vocational Rehabilitation and Employment Program. DTAP helps potentially eligible service members learn about VA's Vocational Rehabilitation and Employment Program and helps them to complete the application for vocational rehabilitation benefits. The entire process could take several months so starting the process early is key.

Check out these helpful online resources:

www.acap.army.mil

www.dawnbreaker.com/navytap

www.Usmc-mccs.org/tamp

3. Release the fear

There is a lot of uncertainty related to returning to the civilian world after so many years in the military family and community. Will it work? Can I survive? How will we do this? You can help reduce some of the fear by starting early, creating a plan and using the military resources to the fullest extent. At the end of it all, you and your spouse have to step out on faith and belief in yourself that his military career (and your MS degree) has provided you with the character and professional skills to create a fulfilling civilian life.

If your service member is going through a transition, be a listening ear. Many associate the military with stability and the thought of leaving the military raises all sorts of concerns about finances, insurance, and housing. Listening costs nothing and allows your spouse to voice anxiety of which you may not be aware.

The military transition will affect you, too, as a spouse, especially if you're used to the close-knit community and accessible resources of the military community.

If the transition becomes too stressful for you or your spouse, get help. If you, your mate, or children seem overwhelmed, overly anxious, or downright depressed, seek out professional assistance.

4. Consider working for the government as a federal contractor or employee

These days many military jobs are handled by government contractors. Many soldiers work right alongside civilians who are paid to do the same job. That could be you. There may be several civil service jobs that are very close to your current work or match your skill set. The TAP program can really assist you here.

The positions are on military installations and typically are right alongside soldiers, sailors, marines, and airmen, but don't require the uniform. The best source of federal jobs is: www.usajobs.opm.gov. For contractor positions, start networking with the staff of the installation transition office and spouse employment office to find out what contractor companies are on base. Service members, don't forget to obtain a copy of your transcript of military training and experience (www.aarts.mil and https://smart.navy.mil). Whatever you do, don't use it in lieu of a résumé or application, but instead, use it to help you prepare them. Finally, both service members and spouses may need to translate your military terminology to civilian descriptions. For example, many employers may have no idea what battalion means and they won't have a glossary of acronyms to decipher your résumé.

5. Expect the culture shock

"I only know one culture—the military culture," Angela said. The civilian world doesn't operate like the military world. "The management and communication are different. One of the biggest issues is probably accountability and teamwork. In the Air Force you have a concept that everyone contributes and everything is in its place," said Angela. For example, soldiers are used to letting everyone, including lower ranking coworkers know of their whereabouts. In the civilian world, there's often less of that. Terry recalls constantly checking in with his supervisor, until his supervisor let him know that it wasn't really necessary. Another concept is teamwork. Depending on where you work, there may be less camaraderie and teamwork than you are used to in the military community. "Some workplaces are more 'every man for himself,' something is missing when you lose that team," said Angela.

6. Plan financially

This is one area many military families can get tripped up. Start planning your finances long before leaving the military.

Make a written budget of what your family spends now while in the military. Figure out how much you owe on debts such as car loans and credit cards. Be realistic about how much money you have in savings.

Consider how much money you receive in housing and living entitlements. Then, create an estimated budget for life outside the military. Note that you will most likely now be paying more for housing, health insurance, car insurance, and personal taxes. Factor in any military discounts you can continue to receive.

7. Don't forget your military hustle!

The military life is all about getting it done. Mission accomplished! The same energy and commitment you brought to your mission as a service member or to your support role as a military spouse can be put to good use mastering a transition. "Use those resources, get that résumé together then get out there and pound the pavement," Angela says.

8. Stay connected post-transition

Retirement or separation doesn't necessarily mean the end of your military life or your membership to the MS club. Stay connected with old friends by joining online forums like www.homefrontonline.com or the discussion boards at www.military.com. You might also check out mainstream social networking sites like Facebook or MySpace which have groups for military spouses.

You can also stay connected by volunteering with groups that serve military families such as Operation Military Kids (www.operation militarykids.org), United Service Organizations (www.uso.org), the Boys and Girls Clubs of America (www.bgca.org/partners/military/) or the U.S. Department of Veterans Affairs (www.volunteer.va.gov/).

Note from the Authors

We are thoroughly and unequivocally convinced that with the right tools and the right attitude, any woman of color can thrive in the military life. Sure, there's frustration and resentment, but what civilian doesn't face that in their lives, too. Regardless of what the journey brings, we know your ride as a military wife will be a heart-racing adventure. Where will it take you? How will you be inspired, changed, and challenged? Let us know at www.mochamanual.com/military.

Digging Into the Alphabet Soup

Your Guide to Military Terms and Acronyms

AAFES: Army Air Force Exchange Service.

AC: Active Component.

ACS: Army Community Services.

AD: Active Duty.

AFB: Air Force Base.

AKO: Army Knowledge Online; secure Web access to websites, tools, and services for soldiers, army employees, retirees, and family members.

Alert: Call to be ready to depart on short notice.

Allotment: Money automatically deducted from the paycheck to pay an organization or individual.

APO: Army Post Office.

AFN: Armed Forces Network; makes it possible for service members living overseas and on navy ships to watch broadcast and cable network shows they are used to watching back at home (in the states) through the AFRTS (see below).

AFRTS: Armed Forces Radio and Television Service; provides stateside radio and television programming to those who live overseas and on navy ships. One such service is through AFN (see above).

AR: Army Reserve or Army Regulation.

Article 15: Punishment for minor disciplinary offenses.

ASYMCA: Armed Services YMCA.

AT: Annual Training; minimal training army reserve soldiers must perform each year.

AWOL: Absent Without Leave; being away from a military job or post without permission.

BAS: Basic Allowance for Subsistence; money to offset (not completely cover) the cost of meals of service members (not their family members). The 2008 rates were about $200 for officers and almost $300 for enlisted. For those who are required to eat in dining halls, most of it is deducted from their paycheck.

BAH: Basic Allowance for Housing; pay to help cover the cost of housing in the local market when you do not live on post. It is determined by location, rank, and number of dependents.

Barracks: Buildings where unmarried members live or those who are temporarily assigned to a place for training.

Basic Pay: The biggest chunk of your paycheck (before the extras are added). It is determined by rank and numbers of years in the military.

Billets: Where service members are assigned to sleep.

BX: Base Exchange; air force department store where prices are lower than civilian stores and a portion of the money spent goes back into on-post activities and services.

CDC: Child Development Center; on-post day-care center.

CG: Commanding General; the boss.

Chain of command: The boss, the boss's boss, the boss's boss's boss with respect to the unit . . . formal progression of raising issues and getting assistance through military channels.

Chain of concern: Informal communication and assistance channels used by family members and Family Readiness Groups.

Chaplain: Military pastor.

Chow hall: Where service members eat meals on post.

CINC: Commander in Chief; the President of the United States.

CPO: Civilian Personnel Office; where employees, supervisors, and job seekers can get help and information on federal employment.

CO: Commanding Officer; the boss at each unit level.

COLA: Cost of Living Allowance; amount of money paid to make up for the high cost of living.

Command sponsored: When it is approved for family to travel at the military's expense, usually overseas, with their active-duty sponsor.

Commissary: On-post grocery store where prices are only 5 percent above cost, is about 30 percent less expensive than "regular" stores *and* the profit goes back into modernizing stores and building new ones.

CONUS: Continental United States; does not include Alaska and Hawaii.

CY: Calendar Year; January 1 to December 31.

CYS: Child, Youth and School Services; child care, school-age care, teen programs, sports, recreation, teen centers, school liaison services, summer camps, day camps, and anything else the post can think of to offer military kids.

DFAS: Defense Finance and Accounting Service; agency responsible for military pay.

DeCA: Defense Commissary Agency; operates the commissaries worldwide.

DEERS: Defense Enrollment Eligibility Reporting System; database that contains everyone who is eligible for military benefits.

Dependent: A person for whom a service member is legally and financially responsible and who is therefore qualified to receive military bennies.

Deployment: All-expenses-paid trip for a military unit overseas, usually for months on end.

Dining-in: Social gathering to which only military personnel are invited.

Dining-out: Social gathering where significant others can attend.

DFAC: Dining facility; where service members eat on post.

DIY move: Do-It-Yourself move; you pack, ship, unpack, pay for the move, and get paid 95 percent of what it would have cost the government to move you.

DOD: Department of Defense; oversees all government agencies that deal with national security and the military.

Dorms: Where unmarried service members live.

EFMP: Exceptional Family Member Program; program for family members with special needs.

ETS: Estimated Time of Separation; the date when service member can get out of the military.

Exchange: Military department store where prices are lower than civilian stores and a portion of the money spent goes back into on-post activities and services.

FAC: Family Assistance Center; provides assistance to Army Reserve and

National Guard members and families. Typically includes help with ID cards, DEERS enrollment, financial and legal referrals, and more.

FAP: Family Advocacy Program; addresses violence in military families with prevention, identifying, reporting, and treatment.

FCP: Family Care Plan; mandatory designation in writing of who will care for the children during training, mobilization, deployment, whether there is one impending or not.

FGLI: Family Service Members' Group Life Insurance; life insurance extended to the spouses and dependent children of service members who are covered under SGLI.

FPO: Fleet Post Office.

FLOTUS: First Lady of the United States.

FM: Family Member; family members who are eligible for military bennies.

FOUO: For Official Use Only; keep it to yourself or others who are "authorized" to know.

FPC: Family Program Coordinator (Guard and Reserve); works to increase family readiness through support and information.

FRG: Family Readiness Group; support network of military families but is the responsibility of the commander. Facilitates communication between family members, the command, and the community.

FSA: Family Separation Allowance; amount of money received when not living at home with your family.

FSC: Family Support Center.

FY: Fiscal Year; October 1 to September 30.

Garrison: Post or community.

GO: General Officer.

Guidon: Unit flag.

HOR: Home of Record.

HS: Home Station.

KIA: Killed in Action.

ITT: Information, Tours, and Travel/Information Tickets, and Travel; any combination of words that refers to the agency on post with leisure travel, recreation tickets, sporting events, usually at discounted rates.

Last four: A request for you to provide the last four digits of your service member's social security number when conducting business on post.

Latrine: Restroom.

LES: Leave and Earnings Statement; military paycheck.

MCEC: Military Child Education Coalition; information, training, and resources for parents, educators, and professionals who provide support to military children.

MIA: Missing in Action.

MP: Military Police.

MRE: Meal Ready to Eat; meal that is packaged to last through almost anything, even a parachute drop. Is eaten when no dining facilities are available, most often "in the field."

MOS: Military Occupational Specialty; job title, area of expertise.

MTF: Military Treatment Facility; military hospital or clinic.

MWR: Morale, Welfare, and Recreation.

NEX: Navy Exchange; navy department store where prices are lower than civilian stores and a portion of the money spent goes back into on-post activities and services.

OCONUS: Outside the Continental United States; Alaska, Hawaii, and other places overseas.

OPSEC: Operations Security; protecting information about the military for the sake of security.

Ombudsman: The person appointed by a navy commanding officer to act as the official contact between command and families.

Orders: Written or spoken directives; can refer specifically to the paperwork that tells the service member his or her next assignment.

PAO: Public Affairs Office/Officer; deals with the newspapers and other local media for covering military events and topics.

PCS: Permanent Change of Station; relocation, service member reassignment, move to the next post.

POA: Power of Attorney; designates a person, usually spouse or parent as someone who can legally act on behalf of the service member. Can be specific (banking) or general (almost anything).

POC: Point of Contact.

POTUS: President of the United States.

POV: Privately Owned Vehicle; your car.

PT: Physical Training; jogging or other exercise performed at the crack of dawn with the entire unit and usually includes cadence, a spoken song where each line is yelled by the leader and repeated by the unit.

PX: Post Exchange; army department store where prices are lower than civilian stores and a portion of the money spent goes back into on-post activities and services.

R&R: Rest & Recuperation/Rest & Relaxation; usually refers to the two weeks of time off that is allowed during a deployment.

RC: Reserve Component; U.S. Army Reserve and National Guard members.

RD: Rear Detachment; military personnel who remain as liaisons between deployed units and family members as well as POC for providing assistance to family members.

Re-up: Re-enlist; commit to another specified time frame for staying in the military; is sometimes done as a ceremony.

Reveille: Bugle call at beginning of the day that can be heard on the entire post.

Retreat: Bugle call at end of the day that can be heard on the entire post.

RFO: Request for Orders.

ROTC: Reserve Officer Training Corps; officer training program in colleges. JROTC is offered in high schools.

RSVP: French for *Respondez s'il vous plait;* means please reply to an invitation as to whether you will or will not attend.

SBP: Survivor Benefit Plan; an insurance plan that provides a monthly income to your spouse (or possibly a parent or business partner under certain circumstances) upon your death to replace your retirement income.

SGLI: Servicemember's Group Life Insurance; low-cost life insurance for service members; may be converted to VGLI (Veterans Group Life Insurance) upon release form active duty.

Short tour: Overseas assignment without family members, generally lasts for a year.

Sponsor: Your service member or someone who assigned to assist you when you move to another installation.

SSN: Social Security Number; when requested, it usually refers to that of the service member, not yours.

Staff duty: 24-hour security watch performed by an assigned service member/unit over unit area and barracks.

TAP: Transition Assistance Program; DoD program that provides information and assistance to service members leaving the military and their spouses.

May include job search assistance and workshops, benefits and financial counseling, and relocation information.

TAPS: Tragedy Assistance Program for Survivors; program that offers support, crisis response, intervention, grief care, counseling services, community outreach, and more to those impacted by the death of a military service member.

TDY/TAD: Temporary Duty; business trip, school attendance.

TLA: Temporary Living Allowance; pay received for temporary lodging expenses when you move overseas.

TLE: Temporary Living Expense; pay received for temporary lodging expenses when you move within the states and to the District of Columbia.

TRICARE: Military medical insurance.

Unaccompanied tour: When an active-duty member goes to an installation without his/her family, usually in a foreign country.

United Concordia: Dental insurance for family members.

USAR: U.S. Army Reserve; previously known as weekend warriors because they had nonmilitary jobs but would do military training one weekend a month and two weeks each year. Have become a much more active part of the military in recent years due to mobilizations and deployments.

USARC: U.S. Army Reserve Command.

USO: United Service Organization; provides morale, welfare, and recreation activities to service members and families.

VA: Department of Veterans Affairs; provides patient care and federal benefits to veterans and their dependents.

vFRG: Virtual Family Readiness Group; mirrors the "regular" FRG concept and functionalities but is online, making it possible for people to receive information without commuting to installation-based meetings.

VGLI: Veterans Group Life Insurance; allows service members to convert the SGLI to term insurance when they leave the military.

VHA: Variable Housing Allowance; monthly payment to offset the cost of living in high-cost housing areas. Amount depends upon rank, number of dependents, and location.

VTC: Video Teleconference; conversation of people in different locations using audio and visual equipment.

WIA: Wounded in Action.

MILITARY ALPHABET

Instead of saying P as in Peter, A as in Apple, and M as in Mary, the military uses a uniformed list as shown below. Pam would be papa, alpha, mike. Also refers to letters of the units, as in B Company or Bravo Company.

A   Alpha
B   Bravo
C   Charlie
D   Delta
E   Echo
F   Foxtrot
G   Golf
H   Hotel
I   India
J   Juliet
K   Kilo
L   Lima
M   Mike
N   November
O   Oscar
P   Papa
Q   Quebec
R   Romeo
S   Sierra
T   Tango
U   Uniform
V   Victor
W   Whiskey
X   X-ray
Y   Yankee
Z   Zulu

Resources

General Information
Joint Family Support Assistance Programs (JFSAP) for Guard and Reserve
www.GuardFamily.org
www.defenselink/ra
800-342-9647

MilitaryHOMEFRONT (Department of Defense)
www.MilitaryHOMEFRONT.dod.mil
www.MilitaryINSTALLATIONS.dod.mil

Military OneSource
24/7 call center.
www.MilitaryOneSource.com
800-342-9647

National Military Family Association (NMFA)
Scholarships, rights and benefits education, deployment and family support, camps, retreats.
www.nmfa.org
800-260-0218
National Military Family Association, Inc.
2500 North Van Dorn St., Suite 102
Alexandria, VA 22302-1601

Career and Employment Planning
Association for Financial Counseling and Planning Education (AFCPE)
Offers fellowships for military spouses to attain the accredited financial counselor

(AFC) certification.
www.afcpe.org
614-485-9650
National Office
1500 W. Third Avenue, Suite 223
Columbus, OH 43212

Black Women's Network
www.blackwomensnetwork.net
323-964-4003
P.O. Box 56106
Los Angeles, CA 90056

Career One-Stop Centers
Career and employment support for military service and family members at state
employment offices.
www.careeronestop.org
877-348-0502

Federal Employment
www.usajobs.gov

Military Spouse Career Advancement Accounts (CAA)
(Departments of Defense and Labor)
Provides funding for licensing and credentialing training programs that provide
portable careers for military spouses.
www.CAA.MILSpouse.org

Military Spouse Career Center
www.military.com/spouse

Military Spouse Corporate Career Network
www.msccn.org
877-MYMSCCN
MSCCN Headquarters
Attn: Deborah Kloeppel, President and CEO

10 Stone Falcon Court
Lake St. Louis, MO 63367

Military Spouse Job Search
www.msjs.org

Military Spouse Virtual Assistant (MSVA)
www.msvas.com/entry.htm

MILSpouse (Departments of Defense and Labor)
Support, information, and referrals for military spouses seeking portable careers
and employment opportunities.
www.MILSpouse.org

Office of Personnel Management
Federal jobs and information
www.opm.gov
202-606-2532
1900 E St. NW
Washington, DC 20415

REALifelines (Department of Labor)
Offers support for wounded, ill, injured, and disabled service members; search
engine for civilian careers; an online résumé writer; and a military-to-civilian
skills translator.
www.hirevetsfirst.gov/REALifelines
202-693-4700
877-US2-JOBS

U.S. Department of Labor Veterans' Employment & Training Service
200 Constitution Ave., N.W.
Rm. S-1325
Washington, D.C. 20210

The President's National Hire Veterans Committee
U.S. Department of Labor
Veterans' Employment and Training Service

200 Constitution Ave., NW, Rm. S-1325
Washington, DC 20210

TurboTAP.org (Department of Defense)
Employment hub, military-friendly employers, transition assistance
guides, checklists, decision support planning tools and benefit e-mail
alerts.
www.TurboTAP.org

Educational Online
www.edonline.com/cq/hbcu
Listing of HBCUs, career information, scholarships, financial aid,
standardized testing tips, and more.

Charitable Organizations
American Legion
www.legion.org/homepage.php
www.legion.org/national/contact to find type of assistance

American Red Cross
www.redcross.org
202-303-5000
2025 E Street NW
Washington, DC 20006

Angels of Mercy Program
Clothing and supplies for wounded service members.
www.supportourwounded.org
703-938-8930
P.O. Box 5447
McLean, VA 22102

Children of Fallen Heroes
Housing, college grants, and scholarships for survivor children and
spouses as well as disabled service members.
www.cfsrf.org

304-274-3538
866-96-CFSRF
P.O. Box 3968
Gaithersburg, MD 20885-3968

United Services Organizations (USO)
USO centers, recreational activities, regional veterans, and family
services.
www.uso.org
703-908-6400

Wounded Warrior Resource Center
Specialized support for wounded, ill, and injured service members and their
families.
www.MilitaryOneSource.com
800-342-9647

Yellow Ribbon Program
Food, clothing, shelter, medical assistance, and education for veterans.
www.yellowribbonfoundation.com
888-99-4VETS
The Yellow Ribbon Foundation
2433 La Granada Dr.
Thousand Oaks, CA 91362

Children, Youth, and Teens
Armed Services YMCA (ASYMCA)
Child care, after-school programs, hospital assistance, military spouse support,
wellness support and recreation, and more.
www.asymca.org
1-800-597-1260
703-313-9600

Boys and Girls Clubs of America
Youth centers provide educational, recreational, cultural, and social
activities for military youth.

www.bgca.org
404-487-5700
National Headquarters
1275 Peachtree St. NE
Atlanta, GA 30309-3506

Department of Education
www.ed.gov/parents
800-USA-LEARN
U.S. Department of Education
400 Maryland Ave. SW
Washington, DC 20202

Home School Internet Resource Center
www.rsts.net
334 Second St.
Catasauqua, PA 18032

Home School Legal Defense Association
www.hslda.org
540-338-5600
P.O. Box 3000
Purcellville, VA 20134-9000

Jack and Jill of America
www.jack-and-jill.org
202-667-7010
1930 17th St. NW
Washington, DC 20009

Military Child Education Coalition
www.militarychild.org
254-953-1923

The Military Child Education Coalition
108 East FM 2410, Suite D
P. O. Box 2519
Harker Heights, TX 76548-2519

Military Impacted Schools Association (MISA)
www.militaryimpactedschoolsassociation.org
800-291-6472

Military K-12 Partners
http://militaryk12partners.dodea.edu/
703-588-3272
Educational Partnerships Branch
Department of Defense Education Activity
4040 N. Fairfax Dr.
Arlington, VA 22203-1635

**National Association of Child Care Resource and Referral
Agencies**
www.naccrra.org/militaryprograms
703-341-4100
3101 Wilson Blvd., Suite 350
Arlington, VA 22201

National Home Education Network
www.nhen.org
NHEN
P.O. Box 1652
Hobe Sound, FL 33475-1652

National Home Education Research Institute
www.nheri.org
503-364-1490
National Home Education Research Institute (NHERI)
P.O. Box 13939
Salem, OR 97309

National Institute for Trauma and Loss in Children
www.tlcinst.org/tlc.html
www.tlcinst.org/PTRC.html
877-306-5256
900 Cook Road
Grosse Pointe Woods, MI 48236

National Military Family Association (NMFA)
Scholarships, rights and benefits education, deployment and family support, camps, retreats.
www.nmfa.org
800-260-0218
National Military Family Association, Inc.
2500 North Van Dorn St., Suite 102
Alexandria, VA 22302-1601

Operation Military Kids
www.operationmilitarykids.org
U.S. Army Family & Morale, Welfare and Recreation Command
ATTN: Operation: Military Kids
4700 King St., 4th Floor
Alexandria, VA 22302-4418

Our Military Kids
Grants, enrichment activities, and tutoring.
www.ourmilitarykids.org
866-691-6654
Our Military Kids, Inc.
6861 Elm St., Suite 2-A
McLean, VA 22101

Scholarships for Military Children
Scholarships for military children regardless of service member's status.
www.militaryscholar.org

Specialized Training of Military Parents (STOMP)
Special education and health needs.
www.stompproject.org

800-5-PARENT
6316 S. 12th St.
Tacoma, WA 98465

Student Online Achievement Resource (SOAR)
An Internet-based tutoring program for students grades 3–12.
www.soarathome.org

Yellow Pages for Kids with Disabilities
www.yellowpagesforkids.com

Compensation and Benefits
Compensation and Benefits Handbook
www.TurboTAP.org

Defense Finance and Accounting Service (DFAS)
www.dfas.mil/
DFAS Headquarters
1851 S. Bell St.
Arlington, VA 22240

Department of Veterans Affairs (VA)
800-827-1000
www.va.gov
810 Vermont Ave. NW
Washington, DC 20420

Manpower Data Center (DMDC)
Benefits enrollment.
www.dmdc.osd.mil/rsl
800-538-9552

MyArmyBenefits Calculators
http://MyArmyBenefits.army.mil

Office of the Secretary of Defense
www.defenselink.mil/militarypay/pay/calc/index.html

Thrift Savings Plan (TSP)
Retirement savings plan for military personnel offers tax-free investments prior to withdrawal of funds.
www.tsp.gov
1-TSP-YOU-FRST

Deployment and Separation
My Mommy Wears Combat Boots, Sharon G. McBride
The 6 Most Important Decisions You'll Ever Make, Sean Covey
Daddy Got His Orders, Kathy Mitchell
To Keep Me SAFE! Sarah R. Jones, M.S.

Domestic Violence and Abuse
American Healthy Marriage Initiative (AAHMI)
www.aahmi.net

Domestic Abuse
DoD Child Abuse Safety and Violation Hotline
800-336-4592

Federal Substance Abuse National Referral Services
www.health.org
800-662-4357(HELP)

National Alliance on Mental Illness (NAMI)
www.nami.org/veterans
800-950-NAMI

National Domestic Violence Hotline
800-799-7233

National Sexual Assault Hotline
through www.rainn.org (Rape, Abuse, and Incest National Network)
800-656-4673

National Suicide Prevention Lifeline
Support and assistance for military personnel, veterans, and their families.

www.suicidepreventionlifeline.org
800-273-TALK (8255)

U.S. Department of Health and Human Services, Office of Women's Health
www.4women.gov
800-994-9662
8270 Willow Oaks
Corporate Drive
Fairfax, VA 22031

Emergency Assistance
Army Emergency Relief (AER)
www.aerhq.org
866-878-6378
200 Stovall St.
Alexandria, VA 22332

Air Force Aide Society (AFSC)
www.afas.org
800-769-8951
Air Force Aid Society, Inc.
National Headquarters
18th St., Suite 202
Arlington, VA 22202

Coast Guard Mutual Assistance
www.cgmahq.org
800-881-2462

Military OneSource
Personal and family financial counseling, emergency loans, consumer advice, and
basic assistance. For your local office, www.MilitaryINSTALLATION.dod.mil or
call Military OneSource:
800-342-9647

Navy/Marine Corps Relief Society (NMCRS)
www.nmcrs.org
703-696-1481

Family Service Center Organizations and Locations

Airman and Family Readiness Services
www.AFCrossroads.com
info@afcrossroads.com

Army Community Services (ACS)
www.MyArmyLifeToo.org

Army Reserve Family Programs
www.arfp.org

Coast Guard Work Life Program
www.uscg.mil/worklife
202-475-3654

Marine Corps Community Service (MCCS)
www.usmc-mccs.org/installation

National Guard Family Programs
www.GuardFamily.org

Navy Fleet and Family Services (FFSC)
www.nffsp.org
www.LIFELines.navy.mil

Reserve Components
www.Defenselink/ra
1-888-777-7731

Injury and Death

Air Force Casualty Assistance Representative
www.severelyinjured@militaryonesource.com
888-774-1361

Army AW2 (Wounded Warrior Program)
www.aw2portal.com
800-237-1336

BlackandChristian.com, online community for information and inspiration for people of African descent

Marine M4L (Marine for Life)
www.m4l.usmc.mil
866-645-8762

Military Severely Injured Center (MSIC)
www.militaryhomefront.dod.mil, click on Troops and Families link
888-774-1361

National Institute for Trauma and Loss in Children
877-306-5256
900 Cook Road
Grosse Pointe Woods, Michigan 48236

Marine Corps League
Help for wounded marines, scholarships, health and comfort items, youth programs, and veterans medical center activities.
www.mcleague.org
703-207-9588
800-625-1775
Marine Corps League
P.O. Box 3070
Merrifield, VA 22116

Navy Safe Harbor
www.militaryhomefront.dod.mil
877-746-8563

Warriors to Work Program
Job search assistance for wounded warriors transitioning to civilian jobs.
https://wtow.woundedwarriorproject.org
1-877-TEAM-WWP
Warriors to Work Program Director
7020 AC Skinner Pkwy, Suite 100
Jacksonville, FL 32256

Service Member Organizations
Association of the U.S. Army (AUSA)
www.ausa.org
800-336-4570
2425 Wilson Blvd.
Arlington, VA 22201

Marine Corps League
Help for wounded marines, scholarships, health and comfort items, youth programs, and veterans medical center activities.
www.mcleague.org
703-207-9588
800-625-1775
Marine Corps League
P.O. Box 3070
Merrifield, VA 22116

Navy League of the United States
Scholarships, youth mentoring programs, employment opportunities, educational programs, and outreach.
www.navyleague.org
703-528-1775
800-356-1560
2300 Wilson Blvd., Suite 200
Arlington, VA 22201-5424

Marriage and Relationships
Jumping the Broom: The African-American Wedding Planner, 2nd ed., Harriette Cole, Owl Books, 2004.
10 Great Dates for Black Couples, DVD and curriculum, www.marriagealive.com/10Dates/programs/blackcouples.cfm
The Treasure of Staying Connected for Military Couples, Janel Lange
Deployed Fathers & Families: Deployment Guide for Enlisted Personnel, National Fatherhood Initiative

American Healthy Marriage Initiative (AAHMI)
www.aahmi.net

Medical and Healthcare
Fisher House Foundation
Donates "comfort homes" on the grounds of major military and VA medical
centers
www.fisherhouse.org
888-294-8560
Fisher House Foundation, Inc.
1401 Rockville Pike, Suite 600
Rockville, MD 20852

Caring Bridge
Free online service that allows military families to remain updated on their service
member's medical condition while in a military hospital or major medical center.
www.fisherhouse.org/caring/aboutCaring.shtml
888-294-8560
Fisher House Foundation, Inc.
1401 Rockville Pike, Suite 600
Rockville, MD 20852

Operation Hero Miles
Allows family members and spouses to visit their wounded service members in
military hospitals across the country at no cost.
www.heromiles.org

TRICARE
www.tricare.mil
North Region 877-TRICARE, www.healthnetfederalservices.com
South Region 800-444-5445, www.humana-military.com
West Region 888-TRIWEST, www.triwest.com
TRICARE Management Activity
Skyline 5, Suite 810
5111 Leesburg Pike
Falls Church, VA 22041-3206

Mental Health, Trauma, and Stress
American Psychiatric Association information on PTSD
www.healthyminds.org/multimedia/ptsd.pdf

National Alliance on Mental Illness (NAMI)
www.nami.org/veterans
800-950-NAMI

Veterans Affairs (VA) National Center for PTSD
www.ncptsd.va.gov/ncmain/ncdocs/manuals/GuideforMilitary.pdf
www.ncptsd.va.gov/ncmain/ncdocs/videos/emv_newwarr_vets.html

Defense and Veterans Brain Injury Center
www.dvbic.org
800-870-9244
Finding My Way: A Teen's Guide to Living with a Parent Who Has Experienced Trauma, Michelle D.
Sherman, PhD, and DeAnne M. Sherman

**Department of Defense (DoD) Posttraumatic Stress Disorder (PTSD) and
Traumatic Brain Injury (TBI) Quick Facts**
www.pdhealth.mil/downloads/TBI_PTSD_Final04232007.pdf

Department of Veterans Affairs (VA)
www.va.gov
800-827-1000
810 Vermont Ave. NW
Washington, DC 20420

Deployment Health and Family Readiness Library
Online, easy-to-understand family readiness resources, articles, and mental health
fact sheets.
http://deploymenthealthlibrary.fhp.osd.mil

Personal Finance
Association of Military Banks of America (AMBA)
www.ambahq.org/resources.htm
540-347-3305
P.O. Box 3335
Warrenton, VA 20188

Defense Credit Union Council
www.dcuc.org
202-638-3950
601 Pennsylvania Ave. NW
South Building, Suite 600
Washington, DC 20004

Military Money Magazine, InCharge Institute of America
No-cost/reduced-fee debt elimination programs and "Military Money Minute"
radio broadcasts.
www.inchargefoundation.org
www.militarymoney.com

Military Pay Calculator
www.MyPay.gov

Military Saves and America Saves
Campaign aimed at persuading, motivating, and encouraging military families to
save money every month, and to convince leaders and organizations to promote
automatic savings.
www.militarysaves.org
www.americasaves.org
Military Saves
Consumer Federation of America
1620 Eye St. NW, Suite 200
Washington, DC 20006

**National Endowment for Financial Education (NEFE) Military Family, Money
and Mobility**
Pamphlet, Web-based training, to promote financial independence for mobilized
members of the National Guard and reserve and enlisted members of active duty
forces, and free financial counseling from certified professionals.
www.nefe.org
www.smartaboutmoney.org
303-741-NEFE
5299 DTC Blvd., Suite 1300
Greenwood Village, CO 80111

Women's Institute of Financial Education (WIFE)
www.wife.org
760-736-1660
P.O. Box 910014
San Diego, CA 92191

Military Sentinel (FTC)
Identifies and targets consumer protection issues that affect members of the U.S.
Armed Forces and their families.
www.consumer.gov/military/

Relocation Assistance
Transition Assistance Advisors (TAAs)
www.TurboTAP.org

Relocation Information
http://benefits.military.com/misc/relocation/relocation.jsp

WarriorCare/National Resource Directory
www.WarriorCare.mil
www.nationalresourcedirectory.org
800-565-8953
2101 Park Center Dr., Suite 310
Orlando, FL 32835

Shopping and Leisure
Armed Forces Recreation Center Resorts
www.armymwr.com/portal/travel/recreationcenters/default.asp

Army and Air Force Exchange Service
www.aafes.com
214-967-2011
HQ AAFES
3911 S. Walton Walker Blvd.
Dallas, TX 75236-1598

Navy Exchange

www.navy-nex.com

800-NAV-EXCH

Navy Exchange Service Command

3280 Virginia Beach Blvd.

Virginia Beach, VA 23452

Defense Commissary Agency

www.commissaries.com

ATTN: OC

1300 E Ave.

Fort Lee, VA 23801-1800

Operation Homefront

Support and assistance to military and their families.

www.operationhomefront.net

Online community of wives and military women (articles, forums, blogs and more)

www.homefrontonline.com

Survivor/ Widow Assistance

American Widow Project

www.americanwidowproject.org

24/7 Hotline: 877-AWP-WIDOW

Military Widow: A Survival Guide, Joanne M. Steen and Regina Asaro

Tragedy Assistance Program for Survivors

www.taps.org

800-959-TAPS

Support and Networking

Chicken Soup for the Military Wife's Soul: Stories to Touch the Heart and Rekindle the Spirit, Jack Canfield, Mark Victor Hansen, Charles Preston, Cindy Pedersen

Mocha Moms

A national organization of black stay-at-home moms.

www.mochamoms.org

National Office
Mocha Moms, Inc.
P.O. Box 1995
Upper Marlboro, MD 20773

NAACP
www.naacp.org
410-358-8900
4805 Mt. Hope Dr.
Baltimore, MD 21215

National Association of Black Women Entrepreneurs, Inc.
313-203-3379
Marilyn French-Hubbard, Founder
P.O. Box 311299
Detroit, MI 48231

National Black Nurses Association
www.nbna.org
301-589-3200
Millicent Gorham, Executive Director
8630 Fenton St., Suite 330
Silver Spring, MD 20910

National Coalition of 100 Black Women
www.ncbw.org/
212-947-2196
Diane Lloyd, Program Associate
38 West 32nd St.
New York, NY 10001

National Council of Negro Women, Inc.
www.ncnw.org
202-737-0120
633 Pennsylvania Ave. NW
Washington, DC 20004

National Urban League Inc.
www.nul.org
212-558-5300
120 Wall St.
New York, NY 10005